WOMEN IN RUSSIAN LITERATURE, 1780–1863

By the same author

WRITERS AND SOCIETY DURING THE RISE OF RUSSIAN
REALISM
RUSSIAN WRITERS AND SOCIETY IN THE SECOND HALF
OF THE NINETEENTH CENTURY
THE STRUCTURAL ANALYSIS OF RUSSIAN NARRATIVE
FICTION (*editor*)
THE FUTURISTS, THE FORMALISTS AND THE MARXIST
CRITIQUE
(*translated with Christopher Pike*)

Women in Russian Literature, 1780–1863

Joe Andrew
Lecturer in Russian Studies
University of Keele

St. Martin's Press   New York

First published in the United States of America in 1988

Printed in Hong Kong

ISBN 0-312-01626-3

Library of Congress Cataloging-in-Publication Data
Andrew, Joe.
Women in Russian literature, 1780-1863.
Bibliography: p.
Includes index.
1. Russian literature—19th century—History and
criticism. 2. Russian literature—18th century—
History and criticism. 3. Women in literature.
I. Title.
PG3015.5.W6A53   1988   891.7'09'352042   87-28502
ISBN 0-312-01626-3

For Susan

Contents

Contents

1
Introduction

Since its re-emergence as an important cultural and political force in the late 1960s, feminism has presented 'incontestably the most important challenge'[1] in recent years to accepted academic approaches to literary studies. In the course of the last two decades several 'feminisms' have emerged, but each in its own way may be said to have the aim of radically reinterpreting established literary practices, strategies and analyses. As Carolyn Heilbrunn said of *Sexual Politics*: 'for the first time we have been asked to look at literature as women; we, men, women, Ph.D's have always read it as men.'[2] Underlying this view are a number of assumptions, well summarised by Greene and Kahn:

> Feminist literary criticism is one branch of interdisciplinary enquiry which takes gender as a fundamental organizing category of experience. This enquiry holds two related premises about gender. One is that inequality of the sexes is neither a biological given nor a divine mandate, but a cultural construct, and therefore a proper study for any humanistic discipline. The second is that a male perspective, assumed to be 'universal', has dominated fields of knowledge, shaping their paradigms and methods. Feminist scholarship, then, . . . revises concepts previously thought universal but now seen as originating in particular cultures and serving particular purposes.[3]

The present volume has as its aim a reading, from a feminist perspective, of a number of major works of Russian literature of the last century, with a view to understanding the 'particular purposes' of the way women were represented in this culture. Central to this enterprise will be the notion that literary texts have an impact on contemporary and later audiences' perceptions of the world, including such matters as the roles of women in society. This impact occurs irrespective of the authors' intentions. By rereading works, by reproducing meanings in this way, we achieve two things: we see the images of women in a particular culture (and we can assess the

1

purposes of these images); and we derive a new perspective on the world of the work concerned.

It is important to re-evaluate works in this way, especially those which have been 'canonised' as having 'universal' significance. This 'universality' is something of a myth as de Beauvoir maintains: 'Representation of the world, like the world itself, is the work of men; they describe it from their own point of view which they confuse with absolute truth.'[4] We may be trained to read the works of our cultural history as if they were of universal significance, whereas they are usually partial, if not distorted, representations of humanity.

However, this approach to literature begs other, underlying questions; in particular, the relationship between an artistic product and the society for which it is produced. Assuming that art does have some effect on its consumers, we may see it as having one of two relationships with society. Art either challenges existing patterns and models, it acts as 'an alternative government',[5] or even undermines accepted notions of reality itself and creates other worlds, 'anti-worlds'; or else it operates as part of the process of social control. My present argument will run along these latter lines. For these purposes, I will consider literature as an element of the ideological processes in society by which a group or class maintains its power over other groups. In the present instance, the dominant group is the patriarchy.

This term has had a variety of definitions and different applications throughout history. For our purposes it can be described as 'a set of social relations between men, which have a material base, and which, though hierarchical, establish or create interdependence and solidarity among men that enable them to dominate women'.[6] Patriarchy, which would seem to have existed, and to exist, in all human societies,[7] has also been described as 'the oldest, most rigid class/caste system . . . the class system based on sex – a system consolidated over thousands of years, lending the archetypal male and female roles an undeserved legitimacy and seeming permanence'.[8] In Engels, and in Marx, this system was also considered as the prototype of all subsequent power systems.[9] Patriarchy, given its longevity and ubiquitousness, must therefore be seen not as accidental phenomenon, but as one that is *systematic*. Consequently, it permeates all aspects of culture, including, of course, literature. Women, perennially the subordinate if not actively dominated group, are seen as, and are represented as, the

Other, from primitive times, to the present day.[10] Accordingly, as de Beauvoir again argues: 'Men have always held the lot of woman in their hands; they have determined what it should be, not according to her interest, but rather with regard to their own projects, their fears, and their needs.'[11]

Although Fetterley may argue that 'The history of civilization is the drama of male robbery of female power',[12] the transactions between men and women have not always been marked by the use of crude force which her metaphor suggests. In ways similar to other ruling groups, the patriarchy has established and maintained its supremacy by much more subtle means. Central to these means of control is the concept of *hegemony* most fully developed by Gramsci:

> By hegemony Gramsci meant the permeation throughout civil society – including a whole range of structures and activities like trade unions, schools, the churches and the family – of an entire system of values, attitudes, beliefs, morality etc. that is in one way or another supportive of the established order and the class interests that dominate it.[13]

As Boggs here suggests, these values permeate *all* aspects of society, including culture and, subsumed within this, literature. Rule is not by force, but by consent, so that the oppressed willingly accept their oppression. This is because the institutions of society work 'to shape, directly or indirectly, the cognitive and affective structures, whereby men [sic!] perceive and evaluate problematic social reality'.[14] Increasingly, Gramsci came to see hegemony as the important face of power, with actual force only resorted to in extremes. Deriving this point from Marx and Engels, he further argued that control of the means of material production has important consequences for the overall ideology of society. Marx and Engels had stated: 'The class having the means of material production has also control over the means of intellectual production, so that it also controls, generally speaking, the ideas of those who lack the means of intellectual production.'[15] Women, along with other groups who experience this lack, are thereby persuaded to accept the legitimacy of their subordination. Indeed, they *actively* consent to it.

In almost all known societies, therefore, there exist two basic discourses, that of the 'dominant' group and that of the 'muted' group,[16] in this instance, male and female. Usually only the dominant code will be heard or listened to and, what is worse, the muted/female group, in order to gain a hearing, must express itself in the dominant code rather than in one it might develop itself. Its own occupations and concerns are trivialised, and the restrictions placed on this group play a vital role in ensuring its submission to the dominant, hegemonistic culture.

As has already been argued, this dominance permeates *all* manifestations of societies and their cultures. Philosophy is another case in point. Okin argues that 'the great tradition of political philosophy consists, generally speaking, of writings by men, for men and about men'.[17] Language, and sign systems more generally, can also be said to play an hegemonic function. Tanner puts this view succinctly: 'we can say that men owned the signs that defined women and determined their role and position in society'.[18] In a patriarchal society, the Word of the Father is absolute.

It would seem to be incontestable that in all literate societies literature plays a central part, either explicitly or implicitly, by intention or effect, in expressing the dominant code. The novel, particularly in the eighteenth and nineteenth centuries, functioned – amongst other things – as an instrument of education and socialisation and, thereby, helped in the general process of policing women, of persuading them to consent to their subordination. Literature, that is, acted (and still acts) as a reinforcing mechanism of established social roles long after primary myths had lost their power and relevance: 'fiction not only reflects and expresses values but transmits them to future generations'.[19] This had many implications for the writers and consumers of the fiction of the period which concerns us, whether we look at Russia, Western Europe or America. As Gorsky puts it: 'To protect and enhance the social tradition – the goal of marriage, the ideal of home – seems part of the purpose of these novels.'[20] Popular writers, such as Trollope in England, were deemed to have 'played a commanding role in reinforcing prevailing literary stereotypes,'[21] while, at times, it seemed almost impossible to write a novel which completely defied the sex-role system, 'for society everywhere upholds this system and social realities are staples of the realistic novel'.[22] The hegemony of patriarchal culture did, indeed, reach everywhere – the basic level of language, as we have already seen – but other primary ingredients of fiction as well. Lieberman notes: 'The most subtle, pervasive level at which sexism affects literature, however, is that of literary convention.'[23] In other words, a writer (whether male or female) does not create a work *ex nihilo*, but has to use the codes, the sign systems and linguistic materials available in the culture. All of these are expressions of the dominant/male code.

As feminism has developed as a body of critical theory and practice, the effect of this on consumers of literature (especially the muted/female group) has been well documented. Adrienne Rich has encapsulated the problems of the feminist reader admirably:

> Until we can understand the assumptions in which we are drenched we cannot know ourselves . . . . A radical critique of literature, feminist in its impulse, would take the work first of all as a clue to how we live . . . how we have *been led to imagine ourselves, how our language has trapped as well as liberated us.* [my italics][24]

It is the aim, then, of this book to look at key works of Russian literature, to see how they have 'led [us] to imagine ourselves', to see to what extent they were an expression of hegemonistic, patriarchal culture in its nineteenth-century Russian variation. In order to assess the extent to which this culture reflects the central themes of patriarchy, or whether it displays more radical variations, it is important to offer a brief overview of the images of women in recorded cultures. How have women been represented?

Perhaps the first and most obvious point to be made is to repeat that women have generally been represented either by men, or within the context of the dominant male code. Rarely are they seen from a female point of view, and male writers, on the whole, have not understood women.[25] Paradoxically, women have been one of the central themes of art, precisely because of their problematic place in culture. Consequently, one of the central myths surrounding women is their enigmatic, mysterious nature: 'the beliefs that women are emotional, irrational, and closer to nature are near cultural universals', as Stewart argues.[26] In more particular terms, *coherence* of female characterisation is relatively rare, because women are perceived and represented within an alien culture, that of patriarchy, as 'Mirrors for men, they serve to indicate the involutions of the male psyche with which literature is primarily concerned, and their characters and identities shift accordingly. They are projections, not people.'[27]

Given that women tend to exist in art – as in culture more generally – in relation to men, they are all too often represented if not as subordinate, then as 'The Other – she is passivity confronting activity, diversity that destroys unity, matter as opposed to form, disorder against order'.[28] And so, woman is viewed with profound ambivalence, and therefore has a double and deceptive image, all that man desires and all he does not attain. She is both the prize the questing hero seeks, and also the obstacle in the path of his quest. She is the archetypal outsider, on the edge of culture, allied to nature, the irrational and evil; 'Her condition is isolation . . . that is the consequence of the patriarchal predication that to be human is to be male.'[29]

Central to these paradoxes and dilemmas is female sexuality. Ancient myths from Eve, Delilah and Pandora onwards (and so too in other cultures), tend to see female sexuality as desirable but *therefore* dangerous. The female (sexual) principle is a curse, disruptive, destructive. Indeed, both the mirror images – the *alter egos*, the sisters of Virgin and Whore, Mother and Seductress – are defined by their sexuality, which produces 'romantic idealisation and embittered, accusatory disgust'.[30] Woman is both (sometimes simultaneously) angel and demon. This may be considered by some to be a reflection of reality. In fact, it is once more a product of the overriding tendency of a male view of women. In this instance man has projected onto these opposites 'all that is worst in man's own inner view of himself, all that is primitive, immature, degrading'.[31]

All in all, then, women have tended to be represented by men as partial creations, as projections of their own fears and fantasies, as stereotypes – the temptress, the virgin, the goddess – associated with the natural, the passive, the irrational or the insane. She is a shrew, a witch, the Muse, 'The Angel in the House'. This last phrase is particularly associated with the image of the rather sickly Victorian heroine, and it is the case that many of the stereotypes have persisted into the period with which we are concerned, if in a modified form.

In the eighteenth and nineteenth centuries, the common view was that women were mentally inferior, and so were morally superior.[32] The principal types could be said to be the angels, the saints and the martyrs. Alongside these positive images remained their polar opposite, the demon destroyer (who was rarely allowed a full measure of happiness[33]). More complex *characters* did, of course, emerge, such as Dorothea Brooke or Anna Karenina, who were able to combine several conflicting stereotypes. But sexuality remained the cornerstone of women's being:[34] women were seen as chaste and pure, or potentially polluting and destructive. The nineteenth century continued the ancient tendency of the dangerously sexual woman, in the *femme fatale*, the Dark Lady, whose beauty was narcissistic and, therefore, not under male control.

For both this type and her sister, the fair maiden, love and marriage, seduction and adultery, were the principal plot paradigms. In each case, the typical situation represented women as objects within a male discourse, either waiting for their lives to be filled by love and marriage, or experiencing the destruction of their sanity or their very being by seduction and betrayal. Women remained intimately allied to the world of feeling and of love. Even in the nineteenth century 'experience for women characters is still primarily tied to the erotic and the familial. The sexual *faux pas* is still a fatal step.'[35] Rarely, in whatever literature one looks, do women escape these discourses: 'Marriage, in fiction . . . has been the woman's adventure, the object of her quest, her journey's end.'[36]

As a result, the *Bildungsroman* for a woman is a rarity for many reasons. They are partial creations, stereotypes, projections, static rather than dynamic images. When they are the central protagonists, and are perceived and represented as *characters* rather than as mere images, their development remains severely circumscribed. When heroines do fight for a better life it is usually *within* the patriarchal system – a better husband, for example. Only in the later years of the nineteenth and in the present century, have female characters been allowed to aspire to a destiny of their own. Elaine Showalter offers an excellent typology of why this could not have happened before:

> To waken from the drugged pleasant sleep of Victorian womanhood was agonising; in fiction it is much more likely to end in drowning than in discovery . . . [heroines] wake to worlds which offer no places for the women they wish to become; and rather than struggling they die. Female suffering thus becomes a kind of literary commodity which both men and women consume.[37]

However, the weight of over two thousand years of literary production and consumption need not be entirely oppressive. Meaning within a text is not static, for each new reading can produce new meanings, and the primary role of feminist criticism is to produce a meaning which would not have been possible before it came into existence. As Okin has put it: 'when women who have always been minor characters in the social and political theory of a patriarchal world are transformed into major ones, the entire cast and the play in which it is acting look very different.'[38] So too with literature. Feminist criticism has as its aim a transformation of our understanding of existing literature, the achievement of an awareness that the 'great tradition' is not a reflection of a universalist, humanistic culture, but of a predominantly male discourse. Within this, women are marginalised, subordinated and oppressed. As Fetterley has argued about American literature: 'Our literature neither leaves women alone nor allows them to participate. It insists on its universality at the same time that it defines that universality in specifically male terms.'[39]

But one can overcome these tendencies and become, to use Fetterley's apt term, 'a resisting reader': 'The first act of the feminist critic must be to become a resisting rather than an assenting reader and, by this refusal to assent, to begin the process of exorcizing the male mind that has been implanted in us.'[40] Once we achieve this consciousness, we not only perceive a work and its world profoundly differently, but the work, and literature more generally, have a new effect on us. For Fetterley, such a feminist critical procedure has very far-reaching implications:

> To expose and question that complex of ideas and mythologies about women and men which exist in our society and are confirmed in our literature is to make the system of power embodied in the literature open not only to discussion but even to change . . ... In making available to women this power of naming reality, feminist criticism is revolutionary.[41]

It is the purpose, in the end, of the present collection of readings to offer new meanings and interpretations of the major works of Russian literature, in the hope that this enterprise will not merely shed new light on the works of fiction concerned, but will also alter our perception of the tradition which produced these works.

Most of the works considered here were first published, roughly speaking, in the second quarter of the nineteenth century, that is, between the Decembrist Revolt in 1825 and the Emancipation of the Serfs in 1861. This period was the formative period of the 'great tradition' of Russian realism.[42] It is the period in which there was a high level of literary and aesthetic debate, experimentation with form, plot and character type. Consequently, it is a fascinating proving ground for the applicability of any theory of literary criticism, including the feminist.[43] The texts considered are major works of the period – *Yevgeny Onegin*, *A Hero of Our Time*, Gogol's stories, Turgenev's second and third novels, as well as shorter works by the same writers. Preceding the major chapters is a brief survey of three earlier works (from the last two decades of the eighteenth century), while the final chapter concerns itself with the first novel of the century in Russian literature (or perhaps *any* literature) which addressed centrally the issues raised by my analysis, namely the images and roles of women in Russian literature. This is, of course, Chernyshevsky's *What Is To Be Done?*

One contradiction may immediately present itself to the 'assenting' or 'resisting' reader, feminist or otherwise. All twenty-four works discussed in the following pages were written by men. However, this merely reinforces the paradoxes already alluded to: in a patriarchal culture, the means of intellectual production were owned by men and, consequently, almost all works considered of major importance in this period were produced by men, often explicitly *for* men. And so it is highly appropriate that a feminist reading of Russian literature should commence with the dominant male code quite explicitly.[44]

The present work deliberately eschews any biography. The image of women in the writings of Gogol may or may not be a product of his alleged latent homosexuality; Pushkin's representation of women may mix romantic idealisation and accusatory disgust because of his youthful Don Juanism; Turgenev's view of women may have been coloured by his tyrannical mother – and so on. All these and other claims may or may not be valid. What the present work attempts is a reading of the *texts* produced by these men from a feminist point of view. The reason the chapters (with one exception) are author-based is partly for convenience, but also because it seemed likely that other works by the same man would illuminate the longer work. For the same reasons as the lack of biography, there is no real attempt to trace the sociology of women in the nineteenth century: the reader must look elsewhere for that.[45] I did not want to draw the banal conclusion that women are subordinate in Russian literature because they were in Russian society. Again, I wanted almost exclusively to look at the *texts* to see what they could tell us.

Finally, the academic reader may be surprised to find only a general bibliography and precious little secondary material in the

notes. In this respect I am following the 'procedure' of Tony Tanner
in his *Adultery in the Novel*: 'the book is deliberately written "blind"
because I wanted to try having my say in my own way'.[46] Of course,
what follows is far from being entirely 'my own way': rather it is an
attempt to read these works through feminist eyes. Where secondary works have already covered similar ground (as with Karlinsky's book on Gogol, to take just one example), I do refer to them,
but on the whole not. As Tanner says, such a 'procedure' can hardly
be termed a 'methodology'. What methodology there is in the
ensuing pages (apart from the feminist underpinning) is a modified
version of that compiled by Michael O'Toole (and previously used
by myself and others), which in turn goes back to the Russian
Formalists.[47] Each of the works considered is approached in terms of
different levels of analysis, such as plot, narrative structure, point of
view, theme, characterisation, setting and symbol. I have been
eclectic within this methodology, dropping certain categories on
occasion, and adding others where appropriate, in particular
relations between male and female characters, and images of
women, which subsumes 'character'. I do not claim to add anything
to literary theory in these areas. Rather, I have used these categories
as useful tools of analysis, to help me to unpack the feminist
approach which has been my overall purpose.

It might be argued that feminist literary criticism is merely a
passing fashion which will go the way of all those that have
preceded it. However, it has been the contention of many recent
feminist critics (and those of earlier incarnation) that they are
rediscovering rather than inventing their approaches. Indeed, over a
century ago Chernyshevsky was advocating feminist solutions to
social and literary problems and, before him, Charles Fourier
(amongst many others) argued most eloquently for the necessity of
such principles in human society:

> The change in an historical epoch can always be determined by
> the progress of women towards freedom, because in the relation
> of woman to man, of the weak to the strong, the victory of human
> nature over brutality is most evident. The degree of emancipation
> of women is the natural measure of general emancipation.[48]

To some it may seem that 'emancipation', female, general or
otherwise, is not the business of literary criticism. Equally, however, if literary criticism has no bearing on the power structures

implicit (or explicit) within the literature it analyses, then it perhaps has no purpose at all. On a more limited front, the aim of the present volume is to offer new readings of nineteenth-century Russian literature so that we can appreciate the 'particular purposes' of this 'particular culture' more deeply and more fully.

One last personal point. Some feminist critics would argue that for a man to attempt to write a 'feminist' analysis of literature is merely yet another example of male colonisation of the female sphere, although Toril Moi for one allows 'that men *in principle* can be feminist critics', while arguing that feminists do not have 'to hire male liberals . . . on their behalf'.[49] There is, of course, a venerable tradition of male feminists (not an oxymoron in my view!) going back at least to Fourier, Mill and Engels, while Chernyshevsky was among the leading exponents of early Russian feminism.[50] While in no way wishing to place myself in such august company, I would argue that the contribution of these four men (as well as many others) to feminist theory and practice can hardly be ignored and does establish a worthy precedent. Moreover, and very regrettably, there is a marked dearth of feminist analysis of Russian literature, for political reasons perhaps in the Soviet Union, and for slightly less apparent reasons in the West. Apart from the excellent contributions of Barbara Heldt Monter and a few others, there is precious little extant work in this field. It seemed to me, therefore, that the present work simply needed to be done, and that my own gender was not a necessary impediment.

2
Prelude: Radical Sentimentalism or Sentimental Radicalism?

For most of the second half of the eighteenth century Russia was ruled by a woman, Catherine II. Her reign opened with liberal hopes, but, particularly after the shocks of Pugachev and 1789, ended in reaction. It also saw the flourishing of the arts and sciences conventionally known as the Russian Enlightenment.[1] In literature cautious criticism became emboldened as, on the one hand, the reading public increased rapidly, and, on the other, political repression precluded most other forms of civic expression. Loyal Classicism shifted gradually into a kind of proto-Realism (Fonvizin, Novikov, Derzhavin) and a more fully formed Pre-Romanticism, or, to use the more traditional term, Sentimentalism (Radishchev, Karamzin).[2]

1. FONVIZIN

1.1. Theme

Denis Fonvizin's second major play, *The Minor*,[3] was written in 1781, six years after the *Pugachevshchina* and at a time of growing reaction. Fonvizin himself has been termed 'the bold lord of satire . . . the friend of freedom',[4] and his play is conventionally seen as the first original Russian comedy[5] and the first *political* Russian comedy, especially in terms of its exposure of corruption and serf-abuse amongst the provincial nobility, as represented by the vicious Prostakov family. However, another reading seems as plausible. Even taking into account the possibility of self-censorship, much more emphasis is laid elsewhere. The play's opening situation may be seen, in the Prostakov family relationships, as an inversion of the natural patriarchal order, which is restored through the interven-

12

tion of the Wise Father, Starodum.[6] In the opening situation power lies in the hands of Prostakova (who abuses it) and by the end she has it taken away: she can be seen as an archetypal figure, the demon woman, the shrew, whose 'own men' are unable to tame her, and so the Law of the Father must be reinstated from outside. (By inference, this may also be seen as an allegorical discussion of the 'unnatural' order within Russia whereby a woman has usurped a rightfully male crown.) One important sub-theme within this is that of language and knowledge: Prostakova abuses the correct patriarchal discourse, as expounded by Starodum, and again she is defeated, and the power that knowledge confers is restored to its rightful male hands. (I shall return to this in more detail in the discussion of point of view.)

1.2. Narrative Structure

Although partially original in content the play follows the conventional Neo-Classical pattern of the three unities and five acts. Moreover, its structure charts the ancient five-part schema of prologue/exposition – complication/peripeteia – denouement . – epilogue, the last being extremely brief.[7] This schema is parabolic in both senses of the term.

The prologue and exposition provide the setting of the play: Act One mainly concerns itself with delineating the foolishness and stupidity of the Prostakov men and the violence of Prostakova. Sofya, the demure heroine, is clearly set apart from this – by her silence, and her relatively late appearance, in Scene Six. Her quiet virtue is set in relief at once, but equally one of the variations on the theme of abuse of power and of violence is adumbrated, in that it is precisely Sofya's virtue which makes her vulnerable to the rapacious evil embodied in Prostakova.[8] Act One, particularly in the coarse, violent execrations of Prostakova, gives ample illustration of the 'false discourse' which also will be remedied in the latter parts of the play. Act Two sees the complication, with the gathering of the younger men of virtue, Pravdin and Milon, who guard Sofya as they await the coming of their 'leader' Starodum. His arrival at the opening of Act Three precipitates the peripeteia as the forces of good score an easy and, indeed, predetermined victory. This victory is marked by Starodum's initial anger, and then scornful laughter at the violent, noisy behaviour of his hostess (p. 135). Acts Four and Five provide minor renewed complications in the attempted abduction of Sofya by Prostakova, but essentially, in terms of its narrative structure, the play, which eventually ends with its sententious lines on '[female] vice punished' and 'virtue rewarded', could have ended two acts earlier. The delay is occasioned by the lengthy discourses, primarily between Starodum and Sofya, to which we may return. For the moment it should be noted that they are clearly foregrounded by the way in which they interrupt the otherwise schematic structure.

1.3. Plot[9]

As in many literary works which are still close to relatively primitive, unsophisticated origins, the plot of *The Minor* is predetermined, or even overdetermined,[10] in this case by the device common in eighteenth-century Russian theatre, of 'telling names'.[11] Even before the action opens, the grouping of characters into the good (Starodum, Pravdin, Milon and Sofya) and the bad (Prostakov, Prostakova and Skotinin) implies that it will revolve around the disposition of the virtuous, unindividuated heroine, Sofya. Traditionally, the evil world could be represented by her parents (in this instance, her temporary guardians). Significantly, however, for the play's sexual politics, all the evil emanates from the female, Prostakova: she is the main motive force behind the scheme to cheat Sofya, and it is she who later plots her abduction, while her husband is merely stupid. In these terms, Prostakova is a curse to *all*, including her beloved son Mitrofan. Once more, *she* is the organiser of his appalling education, a significant factor given the centrality of enlightenment and knowledge in general in this play as well as Fonvizin's other works. Prostakova it is who is the one to be punished – not simply for malfeasance on her estate, but for attempting to gain power over men.

   She may be the source of all evil, but otherwise it is only the male characters who could be termed *actants*. All the active destinies are theirs, and it is they who organise and control the destinies of the women, including Prostakova in the end. The plot is, indeed, remarkably simple: as the military metaphors suggest, it is a battle between Absolute Evil, represented by the traditional shrew/witch figure of Prostakova, and Absolute Good, whose chief champion is, predictably, male, namely Starodum. The sub-plot concerns the surface action of the struggle for the bride's hand. Significantly, both plots reveal another typical motif of patriarchal literature: the disposability of the virtuous heroine. Unlike much of the literature of the period, there is no seduction theme as such, but virtue is shown to be vulnerable. Although the extended disquisitions of Act Four may suggest that Sofya is free to act as she pleases, the plot shows the opposite to be true: her destiny is fought over, with the forces of Good and Evil each rivalling the other to control and dispose of her destiny. Sofya herself, despite, or perhaps more accurately, *because of* her virtue, is powerless. She may be given (by Starodum) or taken (by Skotinin, or Prostakova for her son), but that is all.

On another level, the plot is even more primitive, in that its basic subject matter is closely linked with the world of the fairy-tale. Sofya is Sleeping Beauty who must be rescued from the Evil Step-Mother. Interestingly, it is the *Father*-figure, rather than the younger men of virtue, who plays the part – comically enough – of St George against Prostakova the Dragon. In the end, of course, Evil is conquered, and the Law of the Father is restored.[12]

1.3.1 Male/Female Relationships

An important sub-section of the plot is the picture given of male/female relationships, and, to a lesser extent, that of male/male relationships. As in other aspects of the play, the Prostakovs offer a picture of all that is evil in family relationships, while those relationships revolving around Starodum both implicitly and explicitily provide a model to be emulated.

Prostakova's relationship with her husband is a travesty of the marriage of mutual trust which Starodum outlines in Act Four (pp. 153ff). Her very first words denote an 'unnatural' domination of her husband, whom she nags and berates on every occasion, while he is reduced to a nervous stammerer. Arguably, her greatest crime is her inversion of patriarchal Law, particularly as the most positive character is depicted as a true, superhumanly virtuous patriarch, and much of the 'foregrounded' discussion in the second half of the play is devoted to marital relationships of the 'correct' kind.[13] Equally, her maternal love is a grotesque parody of this traditional virtue: Mitrofan is crushed and he too is reduced to a will-less male by this 'castrating' female.

Even before he appears, Starodum stands for the Law, the honourable, genuinely patriotic Father (at least a surrogate one) to whom all the junior males pay their respects. The 'sons' in this instance are profoundly deferential and never once dare to contradict the fount of all wisdom. In turn, Sofya, the obvious embodiment of female virtue and wisdom (as her name suggests) is dependent and an utterly dutiful daughter. Initially she is under the protection of *two* men, Pravdin and Milon, and once Starodum has arrived to rescue her she asks for nothing but to be told what to do. Indeed, she explicitly asks him to speak his Law, to give her 'instructions': 'Give me rules, which I must follow. Guide my heart' (p. 150). She wished only 'to obey' and the message is clear: the woman of virtue is one who will be subordinate to the wishes of the Father, in either the literal or, as here, the even more powerful, *symbolic* sense. The ideal male/female relationship is that of Master/Pupil.[14] The actual discussion which ensues in Act Four, and which provides the key to the centrality of this theme to the play, may appear rather more egalitarian and even 'feminist' in tone, but these tendencies are profoundly undermined by Sofya's plot situation, her lack of self-determination and her wish for subordination.

1.4. Images of Women

All the above makes it clear that although Fonvizin may appear somewhat liberal in his social thinking, his images of female characters were stereotyped and the overall implications of the play are unmistakably misogynist. A little more elaboration will make this clearer, I think. Both female characters cannot strictly be termed 'characters':[15] both are overdetermined signifiers, symbolising Absolute Evil and Absolute Good. (It is, of course, traditional to use women as mere symbols, rather than as rounded, developing characters.) In the completeness of the stereotyping both verge on caricatures: Sofya symbolises what is most valuable in the female character (and, therefore, what is most to be risked), while Prostakova accrues virtually every recorded negative female characteristic.[16] This level of the play is even more overdetermined than the plot – indeed, to a farcical degree. Prostakova is described as a 'most evil *Fury*, whose *Hellish* character makes the rest of the house unhappy.' (p. 117) Elsewhere we are told she is soulless, mad and like an animal (several instances). In more 'human' terms, she is hypocritical, vicious, a tyrant, ignorant (she cannot read or write and does not know the meaning of the word 'geography'). Most notably, in terms of the play's value system, her language is coarse and violent, a desecration of the linguistically pure patriarchal code.

By contrast, Sofya, when she is not demurely silent, speaks the almost archaic language of Starodum, and by her very speech pattern allies herself with the triumphant and dominant male group. She is virtuous, innocent, 'feminine', sensitive and, as we have seen, a truly dutiful daughter. The symbolic relationship between the two women (and it *is* largely symbolic as they rarely address one another) dramatises the twin poles of the loathsome, disgusting shrew, and the adorable, immaculate virgin. Their relationship, though, has another dramatic imperative, one of the central issues of the play – power, and who wields it. Prostakova seeks power, is shown to be evil by so doing, and is finally stripped of it. Conversely, Sofya's very powerlessness is seen as a weakness, in that it necessitates her being protected, but it is also to be regarded as estimable. In the end, the play pivots on this issue of power, especially that afforded by knowledge, as a discussion of point of view illustrates.

1.5. Point of View

As Foucault has argued: 'power and knowledge directly imply one another . . . there is no power relation without the correlative constitution of a field of knowledge, nor any knowledge that does not presuppose and constitute . . . power relations.'[17] Power, knowledge and their expression in language, or modes of discourse – these can be seen as the central themes of the play and amongst the main criteria by which the characters may be arrayed. It may seem strange to speak of 'point of view' in a play, yet dominating almost every utterance, lurking unseen and expectantly awaited, like Gogol's *Revizor*, implicitly watching all other characters, like Foucault's panopticon,[18] stands the central moral referent, the figure of the true, benevolent, yet punishing Father of the Freudian archetype, namely Starodum.[19] It is he who has the true knowledge of the true Enlightenment, and, consequently, it is he who has the power, whether over his dutiful 'daughter' Sofya, or the parody wife and mother, Prostakova.

This symbolic role of Starodum emerges some time before he appears on stage, significantly in the form of the written word, the letter that heralds his arrival and his intentions to control Sofya's estate and her destiny. It is as if the Father's Word, his Law, is laid down as a harbinger of his avenging justice. Henceforth it is to be *his* utterances which direct the course of the play. His word in a double sense, in that, as we have already seen, the linguistic theme, the theme of correct discourse or linguistic purity, is an important point of reference for assessing the two female polarities. Indeed, all the characters are grouped according to this central signifier. Pravdin, Milon and Sofya all ally themselves with the Father's Word by speaking his language, while Prostakov, Skotinin and, most notably, Prostakova desecrate (the word is not too strong) this lapidary code (pp. 144ff).[20]

Of all the characters Starodum alone speaks with the true authority of the self-determining man. Others listen dutifully to his utterances or ignore them. If control of language leads to control of knowledge, and therefore to power, Starodum should be viewed as the exemplary figure, the true Patriarch. Indeed, one of Prostakova's many crimes is signalled by her misappropriation of the right to label: her husband, son and brother all introduce themselves in terms of her, and not as autonomous self-uttering males (p. 137).[21] Starodum, their antithesis, has been sent to return the patriarchal order to its primary, 'natural' state. Amongst his first remarks, when he arrives at the opening of Act Three, is his reference to Peter I, and to the linguistic corruption that has occurred since those days. Language, knowledge, power, then, are signs of the overall themes of the play. Prostakova, the shrew, the witch, the Fury from Hell, has misappropriated them and reduced her men to timorous stammerers. Starodum, the man of the old ways, arrives to return the knowledge and power to where it properly lies, and in the end the woman of wisdom, Sofya, is elevated to her proper sphere – a happy marriage. Female Evil is punished and the patriarchal order is restored.

2. RADISHCHEV

2.1. Themes and Values

Alexander Radishchev is the most famous, although not the best, writer of eighteenth-century Russia. He was exiled for his subversive book *Journey from St. Petersburg to Moscow* (1790),[22] and has been celebrated ever since as the first inspiration of the Russian radical tradition. Yet his overt espousal of the cause of the Russian peasantry, whether for reform or revolution, does not disguise a misogyny which is both profound and far-reaching. Few of the many encounters in the *Journey* feature women, which is revealing in itself, and those that do do not depict them in a very favourable light.

As Pushkin was perhaps the first to note,[23] Radishchev's thinking has many sources in the different currents of eighteenth-century philosophy. Amongst his chief mentors was Rousseau, whose ambivalence towards women he shares. He also takes from Rousseau the 'religion of the heart': from the first page, Radishchev's appeal is to the feelings. At the same time, he makes frequent reference to so-called 'natural justice' and 'natural law', most notably in the defence of peasant revenge for the masters' rape of one of 'their' women (pp. 275ff). Elsewhere he discusses the nature of freedom and equality: perhaps the corner-stone is the reprinting of his ode *Liberty*. Yet in all these appeals – to the feelings, to nature, to justice, for liberty – a discussion on the rights of women is absent, although there is a long discussion of sexual matters. Clearly the work was intended to be an *Encyclopaedia* in its own way, but this crucial topic is omitted. As for Rousseau, so too for Radishchev, it is *men* who are born free.

2.2. Images of Women

When women do appear in the text, they almost always fit into the familiar, traditional stereotypes, usually reinforced by a prurient sentimentalism that verges on the Sadeian. As already noted, women are not really very important in Radishchev's thinking. They are peripheral to his main concerns, and when they do appear it is as objects for male pleasure, violence or violation: indeed, there is an unnerving and rather distasteful emphasis on this last matter. Not once is a female character depicted as a desiring subject and their image is almost uniformly dystopian. Women are unable to live without men, as in the recruiting scene at Gorodnya (p. 362): the old wonder who will care for them once their men are taken, while the young *devka* is equally hopeless. The very first image of a woman in the text is the wife of the victim of injustice. While he is a mixture of stoicism and bitterness, she is fainting, and later dies after childbirth. Realistic, perhaps, but our first impression of the fair sex is of a frail, suffering, oppressed and, indeed, a weaker species.

The next woman we meet is the raped peasant girl, whose men avenge her. Once more the female is suffering, in the best traditions of Sentimentalism. She fits neatly into the stereotype of 'defiled maiden', and indeed the scene is described in near pornographic detail. Her virtuousness is especially emphasised, and it is a gang rape. Equally noticeable is that it is precisely this action which incenses the male peasantry. 'Their' woman is defiled, so they must seek retribution: males compete over the virtue of women in a tradition going back to *Clarissa*. Later we encounter another favourite *frisson* of the darker side of Sentimentalism as our noble narrator laments the death of his wife, whose 'pure body' had been destroyed by the corruption his debauchery had introduced into it. The Sadeian echoes are only just below the surface.[24] Defiled femininity is everywhere – as in the grotesque instance of the sixty-two-year-old, and recently married, Madame.

Radishchev's ambivalence towards these strange creatures who flicker on the margins of his vision is best exemplified in the depiction of the town of Valdai, which would appear to have been a large-scale brothel (pp. 300–2) (once more women as objects for male gratification). The emphasis now shifts from defiled virtue to unashamed and unadmired sensuality. Valdai is populated by sirens, who deprive the weary traveller (male, of course) of his money, time and – once more the gruesome obsession – his health. Moreover, these shameless harlots are faithless, as in the admonitory tale of the brave monk who dies while striving to reach his beloved: she was probably entertaining another traveller at the time. Women do not die of love in Valdai, or elsewhere in Radishchev's quasi-Sadeian world: they die in painful childbirth, from violent violation or disease. Women are pure, or shameless, but either way they are punished for their loathsome sexuality.

On two occasions more positive stereotypes emerge, but they are stereotypes nonetheless. In the *Spaskaya Polest'* section (pp. 241ff) there is the famous dream in which a visiting female wanderer removes the cataracts from the eyes of the self-deceiving ruler: woman as symbol of spiritual inspiration. Later, our world-weary narrator encounters Anyuta (pp. 304ff), the only woman to be treated in any way as an individual. Certainly she is relatively independent, wishes to organise her own life and even, with her equally staunch mother, refuses the Sentimentalist's charity. Yet profound reservations must remain. Anyuta is completely unindividualised and remains a figment of the Rousseauesque vision of the pure country maiden (at least undefiled!). Indeed, she is explicitly contrasted with the perversions and hypocrisies of urban women, and the narrator sighs that if only he had met Anyuta fifteen years earlier, he would have been rescued from debauchery, corruption of his wife's flesh and so on: Anyuta is simply a variation on the theme of the Pure Angel as Redeemer. In no way should she be seen as an autonomous character, and there is no 'heroine's text'[25] to be found in the *Journey*.

2.3. Male/Female Relationships: A Reformed Rake's Point of View

Our Sentimental Traveller clearly found dealings with 'the sex' somewhat problematic. Women exist in the *Journey* for him and for the other male characters, as indeed was typical for the eighteenth century in general, as objects: objects for male rivalry and competition, as the rape incident illustrates, and as was paradigmatic in the novel of seduction.[26] Even the chaste and independent Anyuta, initially at least, is treated in this way – the target for an amorous *baiser volé*, which the narrator, hypocritically, claims to be a token of his esteem and respect. Anyuta might have been his salvation he continues: implicit in this assertion, and throughout, was another typical male view of the time, namely that women were necessary for the urgent sexual needs of men, and better the innocent country girl than the corrupt (and diseased) city whores. Equally, following the Pauline view, marriage is a 'sacred union' which also may rescue the unfortunate errant male from his baser instincts.

This is the present view of our narrator. However, there are many hints, some more explicit than others, of dark and murky secrets hidden in his 'misspent youth' – although it is not so misspent that he does not justify it now.[27] Sexual self-indulgence is generally viewed as part of the male's normal, 'natural' self-expression when young. There are lamentations for the disease this may bring to 'pure wives', concern for healthy heredity, but *no* anxiety for the whorish recipients of these lusts. Indeed, the loudest plaints are the somewhat distasteful and usually hysterical (a female complaint!) outbursts of self-pity and hypocritical self-lacerations over his sinful past. Apart from the regret he expresses over his wife's untimely death, he usually talks of his erstwhile female associates (anonymous and, indeed, interchangeable, of course) with disgust and loathing: 'You have rouge on your cheeks, rouge on your heart, on your conscience rouge, on your sincerity . . . soot' (p. 303). This openly misogynist view is paralleled by an admiration of the 'pure' country girls, the language of which speaks for itself: 'Look how the limbs of *my* [my italics] beauties are round, developed, undeformed, unspoiled' (p. 303); the language of the horse fair.

So, Alexander Radishchev, celebrated for his passionate defence of the rights of Man, finally reveals himself as a typical defender of the rights of men to use and abuse women. The women are unindividualised, there are no female narrators and women are shown as existing purely for men, and impurely for the destruction of their health and well-being.

3. KARAMZIN

'Perhaps the most famous line ever written by Karamzin [was] – "for even peasant women know how to love".'[28] Nikolay Karamzin's *Poor Liza* (1792)[29] may also seem to champion the cause of the oppressed group of peasant women, but a close reading of his most famous work reveals it to be a naive and admonitory little tale, which does nothing for the rights of women, peasant or otherwise.

3.1. Plot

From its very title onwards, *Poor Liza* can be read as a paradigmatic dysphoric heroine's text.[30] Even before we begin *any* reading we know that the eponymous heroine will come to an unfortunate end which, as it turns out, involves *beda* (disaster) as well as the already doubly signifying *bednost* (poverty/pitiableness): consequently, Liza, like most heroines of this paradigm, has no control over her destiny, which is predetermined by her situation within the patriarchal world in which she is located. Indeed, her character (such as it is beyond the ludicrous degree of stereotyping) becomes largely irrelevant. For the most part she exists merely at the level of a plot function. Mechanically she follows the paradigm of virginal virtue leading to seduction. Unlike her celebrated predecessors, most notably Clarissa Harlowe, Liza offers no resistance. At each stage she complies with Erast's wishes and, indeed, delights naively in her 'love'. The procession is automatic without the slightest variation on the predictable tradition. Once she has given her all she has nothing left to exchange in this rake's economy and the inevitable next stage ensues – betrayal. This, tediously, is rapidly succeeded by abandonment and finally her death.[31] The law of this particular theorem is that lost innocence must be redeemed and the only currency available is her now worthless life. Significantly, death is by suicide: as so often in this version of the story this is the only self-determining action the heroine is allowed.

As in *The Minor*, echoes of even more traditional plots are not far beneath the surface. Liza is simultaneously Cinderella, Sleeping Beauty and Little Red Riding Hood; Erast a comical version of the latter's lupine Grandmother. Prince Charming does not rescue her from the kitchen: the kiss, instead of awakening Liza, sends her to what Raymond Chandler was to call the 'Big Sleep'.

3.2. Narrative Structure

This level of our reading merely reinforces the predictability of the plot and, as in *The Minor*, follows the parabolic five-part curve. The curve rises and then descends to reinforce the already obvious implications. In terms of the narrative structure the title of the story has an even more crushing impact: even before Liza appears we can hazard a very shrewd guess at the denouement of the structure. These predetermining premonitions are exacerbated by the lengthy, gloomy, Gothic prologue/exposition, with its emphasis on morbidity, death and desolation. Doom and foreboding herald the appearance of our poor heroine: like all stages of the narrative structure, the Prologue is heavily marked, to the extent that its function becomes ludicrously overdetermined.

The complication, too, is *announced* with the first change in scene (ominously, from idyllic pastoral to corrupting city – the same naive correlation as in the equally Sentimental Radishchev), and by the introduction of a new character, the duplicitous hero Erast. The peripetaia has several stages, each in turn marked by a new event: each signifies a downward step in the curve to disaster (*beda*). Liza sells her flowers to Erast alone, she ceases coming to Moscow, cannot sleep, and she responds to his first kiss. The encroachment of the denouement is as heavily underscored: the trysts move to the more sombre setting of the evening (the *decline* of the day), and when Liza finally gives the rest of her chaste body (to follow her already doomed heart) the momentous occasion is accompanied by the banality of thunder and lightning. In case any reader should miss the significance of the moment, the narrator tells us as Liza returns home: 'but how everything had changed' (p. 616)!

The extended denouement concludes with a neat framing device of plot rhyme: Liza returns to Moscow for the first time since her story entered its fateful downward journey. This structural parallel merely emphasises the profound change (for the worse) since the starkly worded denouement. Equally, the Epilogue, although much shorter, exactly parallels the Prologue, by a return to the same scene of desolation. Certainly the construction is neat. This craftsmanship has a telling point, in that the parallels, the rhymes and slow inexorable march up and down the traditional parabola, merely emphasise the inevitability of the plot and, therefore, transform it into an immutable law. The paradigm is reproduced in an exemplary form.

3.3. Male/Female Relationships

The male/female relationships of the story also have an air of predetermination from the Prologue's implicit reference to the specific literary tradition of seduction – betrayal – death. Karamzin proceeds, again, to overdetermine what is already predetermined. His first move in announcing the game of seduction which will be played to the death (of the heroine only, of course) is to locate Liza quite explicitly in the patriarchal world. Her father has died before the story begins, and it is this fact which has left Liza in the position the title announces: 'But soon after his death his wife and daughter *became poor'* [my italics] (p. 607). Women without male protection are defenceless: we are told that Liza's only hope for the future is to find 'a good man'. He only appears after Liza's heart has been lost, in the shape of a decent shepherd who wishes to marry her. However, he too acts as a mere plot function. His rivalry in the battle for the virgin's maidenhood is precisely what precipitates Liza's final fall into the state of virtue lost: men compete for women in this world.

The unequal male/female relationship is doubly underscored in this story. Firstly, of course, Liza is a peasant girl (only fifteen, incidentally) while Erast is a *barin*, a master. The class division, while exciting maximum pathos and lyricism, also emphasises the vulnerability of our heroine. Secondly, the couple first meet in a relationship which makes the inequality even more glaring: Liza is the seller (of the virginal lilies of the valley[32]) and Erast the buyer. Female/male, servant/master, seller/buyer – the precise social interface could not be made more obvious. However, for the writer of a Sentimental tale in the late eighteenth century, this triple overdetermination was not yet enough: an added, darker *frisson* was needed. Occasionally this might be incest (as in the same author's *The Island of Bornholm*); here it is prostitution. Liza sells 'her flowers' to Erast way over the odds, and the symbolic motif of prostitution is further transmogrified when she becomes a 'kept woman'. She first sells her flowers to him alone, and then Erast buys her even more completely by paying her to stay at home. Now Liza is bound: she waits passively for her Master to call. At the end of the story, this motif is completed when Erast pays her off with the lordly price of one hundred roubles.

Liza is not alone in her position of powerlessness in the patriarchal world. Her mother, too, had 'become poor'. Regrettably, she shows little maternal care for her naive daughter: instead, she connives at her daughter's seduction and is as foolishly duped by Erast's good looks, masterful graces – and money. This too is a common motif in literature, in that 'the feminine heroine grows up in a world without female solidarity, where women in fact police each other on behalf of patriarchal tyranny'.[33] Even this is not the end of the picture. The third woman in the story is the rich older widow whom Erast marries to pay off his gambling debts. In the patriarchal world of which Karamzin has given such a faithful picture, *all* women, like the lilies of the valley, are commodities to be bought, used up and then thrown away.[34]

3.4. Images of Women

As already indicated, Liza's character is largely irrelevant to the plot, of which she is a mere function. Her portrait, like everything else, is overdetermined and is a bizarre collection of stereotypes, a truly identikit heroine. Liza is passive, virtuous and sensitive, and – as is traditional – closely linked with Nature, with which she communes whenever possible. Moreover, she is incredibly naive – read 'stupid' – trusting Erast implicitly. For all the forebodings she is deliriously happy in her 'love'. Yet, and this is a common trick,[35] she is *simultaneously* a whore. She sells herself to the first bidder, and poutishly throws her flowers into the Moscow river when Erast fails to appear. The clash of stereotypes, common in misogynist literature, is ludicrous, and maintained throughout. Liza is 'timid', but eagerly awaits Erast's every coming. Once she is a 'fallen woman', she is nonetheless described as 'an angel'. Her behaviour is, if anything, even more predictable than the plot. At the first kiss, her response is automatic: she blushes, her heart flutters, her gaze is cast down. When Erast leaves her she swoons, when he finally abandons her she does indeed faint. Her little tragedy is so admonitory precisely because she is so predictable and her behaviour is so ordinary. Her mother, as we have seen, is no less gullible. One's response recalls that of a recent reader of *Little Red Riding Hood*, to which, as I have noted, *Poor Liza* has certain similarities. For 'cakes' read 'flowers', for 'wolf' read 'seducer': '"Little Red Riding Hood" is the story of a girl, bordering on mental deficiency, who is sent out by an irresponsible mother through dark, wolf-infested woods to take a little basket full to the brim with cakes, to her sick grandmother. Given these circumstances her end is hardly surprising.'[36] *Poor Liza* is, in terms of plot and character, little removed from the fairy-tale.

From the first page of *Poor Liza* Death lurks, and later we see that, in the Sentimentalist vogue, Love and Death are inextricably linked, for women at least.[37] The story plays a clever trick on the gullible reader. Peasant women may indeed know how to love, but they are certainly not humanised: every level of the story – the title, the setting, exposition, symbolism – reduces them to mere functions of the generic 'tale of pathos'. Erast escapes with a troubled conscience, while Liza perishes at the bottom of her celebrated pond. The little tragedy of poor, poor Liza conveys a series of grim warnings. Women are 'natural', passive and stunningly stupid. They are defenceless without male protection. They flatter to deceive because they are simultaneously virgins and whores (men beware of the wiles of women!). Women actively seek their own destruction, in which their far from maternal mothers connive. Most generally, and most threateningly, to be awoken sexually is to be condemned to death. This heroine's text could hardly be more dysphoric: 'If you go down to the woods today, you're sure of a big surprise'.

3

Alexander Pushkin and his True Ideal

Pushkin would have done even better had he given his poem the name Tatyana, and not Onegin, as she is unquestionably the main heroine of the poem. She is a positive type, not negative; she is the type of positive beauty, she is the apotheosis of the Russian woman.[1]

Both before and since Dostoevsky uttered these ringing, rhetorical words, the character of Tatyana has taken on quasi-mythical proportions as the exemplar of true Russian womanhood, a symbol, indeed, of the positive feminine. It is equally held as a commonplace in Russian literary criticism that she became the model for later generations of strong Russian women, especially the creations of Ivan Turgenev, to be endlessly contrasted with the weaker masculine types.[2] Pushkin has even been recently acclaimed as the 'first Russian feminist'.[3] The present chapter will mainly concern itself with a re-evaluation of the images of the feminine and masculine in Pushkin's most influential work, *Yevgeny Onegin* (1830), although I will commence with a brief analysis of these issues as they emerge in two earlier works of male/female interaction, namely *The Fountain of Bakhchisaray* (1821–3) and *The Gipsies* (1824).[4]

1. *THE FOUNTAIN OF BAKHCHISARAY*

This relatively early work is often seen as a mere piece of *juvenilia*, in which Pushkin took his youthful Byronic experimentation rather too far; in which he 'was going insane from Byron'[5] and only produced 'a jumble of exotically garish scenes barely connected with each other and seemingly thrown together in an attempt to dazzle and to break free from the laws of classical architectonics'.[6] In the year he completed the poem, Pushkin himself declared, in a letter to Vyazemsky: '*The Fountain of Bakhchisaray*, between ourselves, is

27

garbage.'[7] This does not mean, however, that we can dismiss its depiction of male and female as irrelevant nonsense. On the contrary, many of the (admittedly rather silly) stereotyped situations can be seen as precursors of the more mature version of the interrelationships given in *Yevgeny Onegin*, which was begun, after all, as he was completing *The Fountain of Bakhchisaray*.

1.1. Images of the Male

The first word of this *poema* is the name of Khan Girey, in whose harem the melodramatic action is to unfold, leading to the deaths of both the heroines, the former favourite Zarema, and her replacement, the virginal Christian princess, Mariya. The first lines of the poem offer us a stylised, depersonalised description of this omnipotent man, whose image emerges as an overdetermined icon of the Stern Father.[8] He sits, 'his gaze cast down', smoking his emblematic pipe; 'signs of anger and sorrow' can be read on the 'sombre face' of the 'awesome Khan'. His image is archetypal, punishing and threatening: 'severe Girey' has supreme power over his captive world (of women) and this power is frequently made explicit in such terms as *povelitel'* ('sovereign', line 9) and *vlastitel'* (also 'sovereign', line 106). From these first lines the power relations of the poem's fictional world emerge: the solitary male is depicted as the controlling presence, not only of the 'naked swarm' of women (line 88), but also of the fictional discourse. Implicitly, his is the point of view, and each reference merely increases the menace threatening those, such as Zarema and Mariya, who thwart his Will. The opening lines, then, and the image of Girey delineate the framework in which the sexual relations will be explored.

1.2. Setting

These dynamics are reinforced by the more general exposition, which, because it is rather abstract and deliberately divorced from contemporary social reality, also takes on emblematic, archetypal nuances. The world of the harem is, by definition, one in which many women are the slaves of one man's pleasure. In this protective and protected dungeon (*temnitsa*: literally, 'a dark place') they know no treachery. As we will see, however, treachery is to occur, and vengeance is man's. Significantly for the reader too, there is no real exit from this oppressive locus, and in this instance the destinies of women are determined by their physical setting, as there is to be no abduction from this particular seraglio.

1.3. Point of View and the Discursive World

From the opening lines and the continuing dominating presence of Khan Girey, the point of view of the poem is implicitly male. Within this context the female point of view is almost entirely absent. Collectively the women's talk is referred to as 'babble' (*lepet*, line 95); the virginal Mariya remains determinedly silent, while Zarema's long speech is the desperate plea of a woman trapped within a (literally) foreign discursive system. Indeed, without the all-pervasive male gaze, the women have no reality.[9] Thus, Zarema, once spurned by Girey, must compete on his terms for the return of his affection. When Girey goes back to war after Mariya's death, the harem exists in a death-like calm: once Girey's organising presence is removed, the women languish and, indeed, 'grow old' (line 474). However, Girey's is not the only male gaze which has the power of life and death. The harem of this poem is an almost perfect exemplar of the panopticon.[10] When Girey is absent, or merely loses interest in his wives, the seemingly ubiquitous eunuch ensures that his will and power remain: 'His [the eunuch's] jealous *gaze* and ear/Follow them *all* at *all* times' (lines 61–2; my italics). Even when deprived of their own sexuality, men still control that of the enslaved women. Yet the omnipresent Law of the Stern Father is merely part of the 'eternal order' (line 64), the Law of the Koran. Thus, these wives are watched by the eunuch, the substitute for the Law-Giver Girey, who in turn is located within a seemingly immutable social and religious system. Women who attempt to bypass this system and determine their own destinies pay with their lives. This grim law applies both to Zarema, who had forsaken her childhood Christian faith (the Law of another Stern Father, of course), and to the less pliant Mariya. And, at the end, a fourth level to the discourse emerges when the narrator speaks for the first time and identifies himself as one who shares these objectifying views (in both senses) of women (lines 547–50). In the last lines of the poem he bids farewell to the harem of Khan Girey, but speaks not a word of Mariya or Zarema. Once this male gaze is removed as well, women cease to exist.

1.4. Narrative Structure and Plot

As we have seen, the exposition of the poem locates us in an *explicitly* patriarchal world, detailing an enslaved sex whose sexuality has nonetheless caused a major disturbance within the previously tranquil courtyards. The opening situation presents us with the sorrowful (as well as brooding) Girey. We soon learn that his troubles have arisen not from military defeat (indeed, he has abandoned war), or from any other *public* problem, but rather they are occasioned by a disruptive female (Mariya) who refuses to co-operate with the rules of this exemplary patriarchy. Even when enslaved, women and their sexuality can appear disturbingly threatening to the male order. The Byronic narrative structure,[11] episodic and seemingly chaotic, has the effect in this work of provoking a narrative disturbance to echo that in the semantic and sexual orders, in that the plot and *fabula*[12] are frequently at odds. The causes of Girey's dramatic change (lines 143ff.) only emerge some considerable time after we have seen the effects. This disjunction lends the tale the primary Byronic *cachet* of exotic, dark mystery, but also foregrounds Girey as the guiding centre and controlling presence of the work. Furthermore, it deliberately heightens the pathos of Girey, and that of Zarema, who has been mysteriously (initially, at least) forsaken. A second plot/*fabula* disjunction occurs near the end of the poem (after Mariya's death), and this too lends an almost voyeuristic *interruptus* to the pathetic tragedy that has befallen the two captive princesses.

When the plot proper finally commences (lines 161ff.), the complication, we discover, has been caused by a new captive, another woman. For the rest of the work the plot mechanisms are activated by the two rivals, the old love Zarema and the new, Mariya. Consequently, the plot is constructed entirely in terms of problematic (for men) female sexuality, which is either unwinnable (Mariya) or vengeful (Zarema). The pathos of this situation for the watchful male persona (the reader, an implicit fifth male gaze) is excited by a literal fight to the death for the favours of the Stern Father. The only plot for women, then, in the patriarchal world, is to live, and die, for men. Zarema may be the principal plot agent, but her activity is concentrated exclusively on the vain attempt to regain the love of her lost Master.

Behind this central story we gradually uncover the recapitulated sub-plot of Mariya, which is just as firmly entrenched within inescapable patriarchal structures. She is abducted from her real father into the captive gaze of a symbolic paternal presence. Interestingly, her fate echoes that of poor Liza:[13] 'The Father is in the grave, the daughter in captivity' (line 208). That is, the father's death removes the necessary protection of the virgin Mariya, which leaves her (symbolically, if not in fact) to be raped. Her tears may soften the strict law of the harem (lines 217–20), but they will, in the end, be insufficient to save her life.

The main peripeteia is triggered by the sleepless and jealous Zarema, and is lent added exoticism (and eroticism) by its nocturnal setting. Her actions lead on to the denouement and resolution of the conflicts, but the brutal cathartic action emphasises, once more, that they have both simply been *man*ipulated.[14] The ending reinforces the 'message' of the text outlined earlier. Female sexuality leads to death[15] whether they play the patriarchal game or not. There is a further connection made between *eros* and *thanatos* in Girey's final situation. The peaceful calm which had once reigned in the harem is shattered even more surely by the fact that he has returned to war 'sombre, blood-thirsty' (line 460). The implication of this aspect of the resolution is that the death of the potentially saving Angel in the Harem drives men to kill.

1.5. Themes and Values

In these two female characters we see an early adumbration of what was to become one of the central dualities in Pushkin's thinking, the conflict between rebellion and reconciliation.[16] The latter pole (encapsulated in the concept of *smireniye*) was the one to which Pushkin himself gravitated after the punishments for his own early rebellion and the bitter lessons they taught him. Tatyana, as Dostoevsky most famously argued, was Pushkin's 'true ideal', primarily because she discovered that her (and Russia's) true destiny lay in acceptance and atonement. Those who refuse to accept their destinies and rebel (Aleko, Hermann [in *Queen of Spades*] and Yevgeny [in *The Bronze Horseman*]) end up alienated, insane and/or dead. Zarema here represents the pole of rebellion; she will not accept the changed will of Girey and is punished by death for her refusal. Mariya does not rebel: indeed, in her we see a particularly inert form of *smireniye*. She remains silent throughout, and Pushkin's mature vision of reconciliation is, in this early version, merely the traditional feminine stereotype of complete passivity. And, in the end, acceptance of the 'laws of Fate' on this occasion leads not to spiritual quiet or redemption, but to death.

1.6. Images of Women

If the male presence from the very first word is the given of the text, then women are presented throughout as the unknowable and threatening Other.[17] Girey is named and an individual, while his wives are non-individualised, a mere amorphous collectivity: they play in a 'frisky crowd' (line 114); they are referred to as groups of 'captives', 'prisoners'. Equally, however, they have 'bewitching beauty' and are 'cunning'. All the images are mere stereotypes, and although they are enslaved they still cannot be permitted to go beyond the watchful gazes for a moment. Further, they do not dare 'to think, nor wish', their talk and way of life is that of children and they frequently metamorphose into plants ('Arabian flowers', line 41) or other non-human entities ('a naked swarm'). They live in fear, silence and passivity.

It is against this barely *vivant tableau* that the two heroines are delineated. Zarema appears first, but is immediately reduced to the same dehumanised level: 'Like a *palm*, smashed by the storm/She bowed her young head.' (lines 139–40; my italics). Her introductory depiction is entirely in terms of her physical attributes as a love/sex object. She, we later learn, is as homeless and enslaved as the rest of the women. In her and Mariya we have a ludicrously overdetermined clash of the two traditional archetypes. Zarema is 'born for passion' (line 395), while Mariya's very name announces her as the virgin. She too is plant-like ('She flowered in her native land', line 164) and is the epitome of passivity and virginity. She has a 'quiet nature': 'In the quiet of her soul/She had not yet known love' (lines 189–90). 'The most holy maiden', 'with her resigned faith',[18] is explicitly an 'angel'. Her image becomes increasingly tautologous and overdetermined ('innocent maiden'). These two women, mere projections of male fantasies, eventually collide in the fictional world, and it is revealing that their only possible relationship in this archetypal patriarchy is a metaphorical fight to the death. Even in death the dehumanising process continues, and Mariya's image remains not merely reified as the virginal Other, but petrified, in that the marble fountain of the title is a memorial to 'sorrowful Mariya'. This prefiguration of Tatyana lived and died in silence and remains immortalised as a weeping fountain.

2. *THE GIPSIES*

In this third and final 'Southern poem', Pushkin 'for the first time in a sustained piece of writing showed the direction much of his mature work was to take'.[19] In this first truly problematic piece of Russian literature, Pushkin also provided the first fully fledged version of a 'reconciled' character (the Old Gipsy). But what of his exploration of sexual love, one of the central themes of the poem? Does this investigation also mark a major step towards maturity? The images of women in the poem, it must immediately be said, show little significant change.

2.1. Setting

Although many aspects of *The Gipsies* reveal a marked transition to greater realism,[20] the setting shares with the previous two Southern poems a deliberately rather abstract location. The action takes place in Bessarabia, but we are in a generalised, fictionalised world inhabited by 'noble savages' and a deracine hero, even if one of the central purposes of the work is to explore – if not explode – these typologies. The vague location has the effect, however, of generalising, perhaps even universalising, the themes so that they take on the power of a seemingly immutable Law or *zakon*, one of the key words of this text and Pushkin's work more generally. Whose Law this is will become clearer.

The setting, then, as it unfolds in the early sections, lays before us a vivid natural scene, with its animals (including the famous bear), bright, ragged clothes and the 'nakedness of children and the old' (lines 76–93), which is in sharp juxtaposition to the civilised world from which Aleko is a fugitive, and which he later passionately condemns (lines 150–63). This contrast between 'Nature' and 'civilisation' becomes the key motif for the poem. It provides us with a world which is divorced from the 'real' and the contemporary society, and the theme which emerges of 'nature's children' lends a particular resonance to the themes of love and infidelity. It also explains, if not justifies the 'natural' morality of the principal female character, the young gipsy 'maiden', Zemfira.

2.2. Plot and Narrative Structure

Initially, at least, Zemfira might appear to be the organising plot agent. She it is who introduces the disruptive force to the given world of the gipsies, Aleko, and she also initiates their relationship. Quickly, however, the central focus switches to the male protagonist, and Aleko's adaptation to, and later disaffection from, this wild, free world becomes the central plot line. The main debate concerns the extent to which civilised man can come to terms with a 'primitive' society. Within these parameters, Zemfira fades into the background and acts as interlocutor (lines 146–76) and foil to his socio-psychological dramas. Aleko may be no more individualised as a character than Zemfira, but the power relations within the text are, as in *The Fountain of Bakhchisaray*, weighted towards the male. He does at least have a plot and a destiny to control to some extent. In this sense Zemfira is merely instrumental in his destiny.

Nevertheless, after the passage of two years, Zemfira reappears to initiate the peripeteia with her song of defiance and rejection, 'Old husband, awesome husband' (lines 260ff.). The adjective 'awesome' (*grozny*) is precisely that used of Khan Girey (line 4), and the plot implications of the two works begin to take on a similar dimension. In rejecting Aleko, Zemfira attempts to thwart the wishes of the stern, paternal presence and, in these terms, there is a significant emphasis later in the work on Aleko's apparent agedness. Zemfira, then, asserts her own independence, although this only takes the form, as for Mariya, of moving from one male to another. In each case (and also for Zarema) the rejection of the father-figure leads to death and not to freedom, because, in patriarchy, the Law of the Father is, potentially, omnipresent. In this context, it is interesting to note the number of parallels that are drawn between Aleko and the Old Gipsy. Both are abandoned by (seemingly) younger wives, both have grey hair. Both, indeed, have the mocking song sung to them, and although their reaction to it is profoundly different, they would seem to represent conjointly the two faces of male power which, in this case as so often, when thwarted excites punishing violence against the errant woman.

This grim and admonitory denouement is prepared for by the tale of Mariula, the wife who had abandoned the Old Gipsy and her baby daughter Zemfira.[21] This double crime (which, in rudimentary form, presages that of Anna Karenina) was, wisely perhaps, ignored by the Old Gipsy, but it taught him a salutary lesson:

> . . . since those times
> All the maidens of the world grew cold for me
> My *gaze* [my italics] never amongst them
> Chose for myself a friend! (lines 406–9)

Aleko may go on to kill his treacherous mate; the Old Gipsy implicitly echoes Hamlet's warning to all cuckolds: 'Frailty, thy name is woman!' In the end, the unfaithful Zemfira is murdered (with the phallic knife), while the man who has misled her and thereby challenged the patriarchal ownership of her meets a similar fate. Both deaths occur at a similarly grisly location to the one at which Zemfira had encountered Aleko, a burial mound. Love and death are locked in an eternal, repeated embrace.[22] Aleko is then banished from the gipsy society, but at least he remains alive.

2.3 Images of Women

> But there is no happiness even amongst you
> Poor sons of nature! . . . (lines 564–5)

> And everywhere there are fateful passions
> And there is no protection from the fates. (lines 570–1)

These concluding couplets suggest that life in 'nature' is much the same as in 'civilisation'. In terms of women's destinies the same laws would appear to be similarly universal. Women circulate as currency in a male economy. Zemfira is first referred to in relationship to her father ('His young daughter', line 31[23]), and, as we have seen, her aspiration towards freedom is in reality simply a move to another male. For men, women's sexuality is disruptive and leads either to stoical resignation (or indifference) and fear of further involvement or to vicious revenge.

The images of women in *The Gipsies* are more individualised than in *The Fountain of Bakhchisaray*. We learn a little of Zemfira's psychology, and her attitudes (to men, the city and so on) characterise her. However, much remains the same. She is referred to as a 'maiden' and later on as a 'child' (line 345), despite the fact that she is by now apparently a mother! The first physical reference to her is a banal cliché of Romantic typification: 'black-eyed Zemfira' (line 98). In more general terms, women are perceived as fickle and untrustworthy. They are also dehumanised by at least two nature similes, which are as unoriginal as Zemfira's epithet. The Old Gipsy compares women's love to the 'free moon' (line 350), while he had loved the perfidious Mariula 'like the sun' (line 388). As in the previous work analysed, neither of the two female *dramatis personae* do anything other, from the male point of view, than to bring grief and sorrow and, by more general implication, they are never to be trusted.

2.4. Point of View

And, indeed, the poem's initial, concluding and almost all-pervasive voice is that of men, although other 'voices' can be heard.[24] Zemfira, as we have seen, initiates both the initial and complicating action, and so too she sets in train the first dialogues (lines 42ff. and lines 146ff.). However, her speech, like her character, acts only as a foil to Aleko, and her 'touchingly naive description' of city life[25] is merely the clearest instance of the lack of originality or narrative weight given to her speech. Her song, even though it triggers the fateful denouement, is a quotation. Aleko has much more discursive authority in his ability to command abstract concepts and pseudo-philosophical insights.

However, the real voice of authority is that of the Old Gipsy, who is the first character we encounter and whose words are the last we hear in the narrative proper. He emerges in the course of the text as both literally a father (of Zemfira) and symbolically so. In the latter role it is crucially significant that he remains unnamed, but merely titled *Starik* (literally, 'Old Man'), so that he takes on the resonance of a Law-Giver; his words acquire the abstract, universalised quality of the Father's Law which, given his presence at the opening and close of the text, can be seen to organise the discourse and meaning of the poem. In more traditional terms, his role is that of the Greek chorus, commenting on the action rather than participating in it.

So, when he advises Aleko not to take women seriously and not to trust them, his words are imbued with a resonance reminiscent of Old Testament tablets. His tale becomes increasingly misogynist as he recounts his experiences with Mariula; his advice is to beware these fickle, child-like irresponsible creatures. It is in this sense that Zemfira is a 'primitive, instinctive child of nature'.[26] Moreover, his words take on a generalised significance in that *all* the males in the text come to share this view. As we have seen, Aleko betrays his mistrust through fateful vengeance. Even the unnamed Young Gipsy who is Zemfira's new lover does not trust women: 'She will deceive! She will not come' (line 440) he cries to her promises of an assignation. There emerges, then, a collective male point of view, shared by all, and, indeed, through the examples of Zemfira and Mariula, like mother like daughter, women would seem to have earned this distrust.

The final sections of the poem move to an even more abstract level as Aleko is cast out by the gipsies for his crime and is denounced by the Old Gipsy, who, as we have seen, thereby closes the narrative proper. It is at this juncture that he finally takes on his implicit dimension of the Voice of the Law.[27] Retrospectively, therefore, his words on women's fickleness are elevated to the same rhetorical status. Finally, in the Epilogue itself, we discover that beyond the Old Gipsy and all the other *dramatis personae* stands an even more universal law, that of the Fates, so that the themes of love and death and sexuality embedded in the text are given by the author an even more abstract and, therefore, general significance. The Old Gipsy may say to Aleko 'We have no Laws' (line 513), but the opposite would seem to be the case where women and their sexual behaviour are concerned. 'I will die loving' (line 488) Zemfira declares, and the dangerous nature of women's sexuality underpins the text, threatening, as in the earlier Southern poem, perpetually to disrupt the given patriarchal order.[28]

3. YEVGENY ONEGIN

As indicated at the beginning of this chapter, Pushkin's novel in verse has been amongst the most influential texts produced in Russian. It could be argued, indeed, that it is, for several reasons, the single most important work in the language. It has given rise to a great variety and range of interpretations[29] and many later nineteenth-century novels in Russia, not only those of Turgenev, were re-interpretations of its themes and characters. Its two central figures, the eponymous hero and the 'true ideal' of Tatyana, have since taken on an almost mythological status. The novel covers the central themes of the nineteenth-century Realist tradition – love and marriage (and, implicitly, sexuality), the individual and society, education, the quest for meaning and ideals. It is, for these and other reasons, uniquely important for an understanding of how literary (or even merely literate) Russians perceived themselves then and now, and how the constructs of manhood and womanhood were created in this tradition.[30] The following will concentrate on these problems in particular.

3.1. Setting

In most nineteenth-century novels the setting, particularly the social setting, has a critical function. Character can often emerge as a manifestation of the individual's background, and the *milieu*, particularly in the paradigmatic *Bildungsroman*, plays a decisive, if not determining, role. In *Yevgeny Onegin* it could be said that the social, and more specifically the educational background of the characters almost fatally predisposes the plot. Nearly one quarter of the novel (most of Chapters 1 to 3) concerns itself with the education and more general upbringing of the two couples. We learn here of Onegin's Byronism, Lensky's 'misty Romanticism' (from Germany) and Tatyana's fateful indoctrination in the lessons of English and French Sentimentalism and Romanticism.[31] Chapter 1, in particular, in its detailing of the 'Rake's day',[32] shows the extent to which Onegin is produced by foreign tutors, social etiquette and the 'tender science' of flirtation, coquetry and amorous conquest or seduction. Pushkin deliberately places him in, and makes him a representative product of a conventional high society background, where both male and female play out the roles allotted to them in a social economy and interaction which have their roots in the eighteenth-century novel.[33] At first, however, women are peripheral to the scene-setting, mere instrumental objects of male activities.

When, on his uncle's death, Onegin moves to the country at the end of Chapter 1, the traditional Russian countryside becomes the setting for much of the rest of the novel (until almost the end of Chapter 7). Tatyana, as we shall see in more detail later, is presented to us specifically as a product of the country, and the fact that most of the novel is set there is one of the crucial determining factors in seeing her as the novel's central character. Furthermore, commencing with the punning epigraph to Chapter 2 (*Rus'/rus*), it is a setting in which age-old, specifically *Russian* values are celebrated. This identification between Tatyana and rural traditions is further emphasised by the recurrent near-rhyme on her surname, *Larina* and *starina* ('olden times').

3.2. Plot and Narrative Structure

If the setting is initially foregrounded, it is at the expense of the rather perfunctory plot. Equally, however, the very length of the prologue/exposition, and the specific details of it, control the rest of the action. The sexual interaction as detailed in Chapter 1 is almost entirely within the tradition of Lovelace,[34] a theme that is reinforced by the fact that the first chapter concerns itself with the day not of one rake, but of two, the second being the narrator. Similarly, Onegin is disaffected from the countryside (unlike the narrator on this occasion) almost as soon as he moves there, and this, retrospectively, can be seen to have precluded any possible union between him and Tatyana. The plot patterns of the prologue, the games of seduction, flirtation and marriage are replicated in a different form once the action moves to the countryside. Lensky (who is introduced at the beginning of Chapter 2) is of interest to his rural neighbours primarily because he may be a suitable son-in-law.[35] And so it goes on, each new plot situation emphasising the power of culture and society, the sociolect, to intervene between the individual and her/his aspirations. Tatyana's mother had been married against her wishes, a union which was one of mutual antipathy. Onegin appears in the Larin house in Chapter 3, and it is the social group which designates him, like his friend Lensky, as a *zhenikh* ('fiancé'), before Tatyana has time to fall in love herself. Both Onegin and Tatyana are inscribed in the culture of patriarchy before they are aware of what is being arranged for them.

Once 'in love', Tatyana seeks solace and advice from her *nyanya*, only to be told that the latter had been given in marriage at the age of thirteen, to her Vanya, who was even younger. Traditional Russian culture (as personified by her nurse) may redeem Tatyana in many ways, but it cannot save her from this destiny, as she too is given in marriage in the end.

The traditional aspect of the social connections, which ultimately govern Tatyana's life, is reinforced by the deliberately conventional (if not parodic[36]) nature of the plot mechanism. This is triggered (finally) by the unknown (and, therefore, mysterious) stranger/hero travelling to the countryside where he will meet and (unwittingly) awaken the passive Sleeping Beauty.[37] At the beginning of Chapter 3 the dormant narrative, in a pre-echo of Tatyana's psychology, comes to life as Onegin enters the sleepy world of the old-fashioned Larins to disturb Tatyana's quiescent state.[38] She was, however, prepared, once more by the cultural world she inhabits: 'Elle était fille, elle était amoureuse' reads the epigraph to this chapter, and once more her actions are shown to be predetermined: 'The time had come, she fell in love' (3: VII, line 6). From now until her visit to Onegin's equally parodic 'castle' in Chapter 7, Tatyana behaves almost as if she is sleep-walking, as if bewitched.[39] Unlike her mother and her nanny, she may give herself rather than wait to be given to this 'modish tyrant', but it can hardly be construed as a positive, or even conscious action.

The first peripeteia, Tatyana's letter to Onegin, follows within the same chapter (a sign of how much the pace has accelerated), and it is clearly marked by the narrator in his introduction to it (Stanzas XXI– XXXI) as a product of the seductive power of culture, and not as the act of a self-determining young woman. Once this fateful missive has been sent, the plot becomes, if anything, even more parodic. Tatyana does not notice the dawn, sighs and trembles and can hardly even speak as she awaits a reply from HIM. All efforts are made by the narrator to stress her endangered virginity as Onegin finally speaks to her, the word *nevinny* ('innocent') appearing in both Stanza XI and XII of Chapter 4. Further emphasis is placed on her vulnerability by a reprise of the nature of the 'tender science' of seduction and other amorous games in the early stanzas of this chapter. Onegin, however, refuses both her love and the possibility of a too-easy conquest, and Tatyana now acquires the epithet of the wronged heroine which had already become traditional in Russian literature, *bednaya* ('poor'). Before the narrator and we temporarily part company with her, she lapses into the stereotyped dysphoric heroine's lot:[40] she cannot sleep, grows pale, and so on. Once more, the image may be parodic, but it remains.

To underscore the pathos of the 'wrong'd virgin' (albeit, a maiden still), Pushkin digresses to the bathetic 'true love story' of Lensky and Tatyana's sister, Olga, who is shortly to enter the ranks of the author's perfidious females. Their ridiculous infatuation acts as a counterpoint to the sublimity of Tatyana's sorrow, and the eventual outcome of their 'love' emphasises the rather bleak view of amorous relationships which permeates the novel, as we shall see.

The rest of the story (Chapters 5 to 8) marks the growth of Tatyana to her final state as 'my true ideal', as she changes from the *ditya* ('child') she has been called into a *dama* ('lady'). Whether we can consider these changes as constituting a genuine *Bildungsroman* is a question to which we shall return. For the moment it should be noted that her folkloric dream of Chapter 5, in which she is taken to Onegin, occupies a critical structural position, and can, indeed, be seen as paradigmatic for the novel as a whole because of its narrative location, with the emphasis shifting increasingly to Tatyana.

Before Onegin, 'the proud man' of this story, is banished for his murderous crime, like Aleko, we have the second peripeteia, the duel. Ostensibly between two friends, it follows the pattern which is to be replicated in *A Hero of Our Time*, that is, two bonded and rival males fighting for a woman. The significance of this event is emphasised by the extended discussion of the central themes of the novel which follows it (in Lensky's two possible future lives), and to which also we may return.

Finally, in Chapter 7, Stanza XIII, Tatyana is alone; Onegin has killed Lensky and then departed himself, and Olga has been swiftly and contemptuously dispatched by the narrator into an over-hasty marriage to a passing *uhlan*. The denouement and resolution of the plot and its overarching narrative structure are to be primarily Tatyana's, and, for Dostoevsky and others, represent the discovery of her destiny and, thereby, a triumph of true Russian spirituality over rootless cosmopolitanism. She effects this self-discovery by a reinterpretation of Onegin, and the culture which had produced him, during her visit to his now deserted estate: 'Before her there opened another world' (7: XXX, line 14). She sees that he is perhaps a 'parody', a 'Muscovite in Harold's cloak', that the man with whom she had fallen in love is a figment of her imagination, and perhaps his too. However, as soon as this epiphanic moment is given to her, she is taken to Moscow,[41] where she will be 'given to another'. Once more, even if she herself is growing into self-consciousness, her actions and her destiny are organised by the sociolect; it is precisely the same procedure which had been enacted for her mother, her nurse and countless others, and from which there is no escape. To use another fairy-tale analogue, this provincial Cinderella may go to the ball, but her pre-ordained encounter is not with Prince Charming, but with 'that fat general' (7: LIV, line 14). And, even if her final rejection of Onegin *is* a victory, it is certainly not the one for which she had wished.

3.3. Male/Female Relationships

In any novel the opening lines or chapters can be decisive,[42] and this is especially true of Chapter 1 of *Yevgeny Onegin*, given the *brio* with which it is written and which marks it off from the rest of the work. Onegin's education and adolescent behaviour are portrayed with ironic admiration, but the time, skill and attention devoted to his activities by the narrator justify them and lend them credibility. The first noun used to describe Onegin is 'rake' (*povesa*, 1: II, line 1), and this word permeates the whole chapter and much of the rest of the novel. Consequently, all the sexual and amorous relations outlined in the ensuing chapters come to be interpreted in terms of the 'rake's economy', which had been the dominating presence of the novel in eighteenth-century England and France[43] and which Pushkin consciously and deliberately reworked, even if in parodic form. In this economy, as in the two earlier works analysed, the male is the given and the female is the Other. Given that the 'tender science' of *liaisons dangereuses* is the game these people play, women are there to be surveyed, to have a *gaze* cast over them[44] and then to be seduced and abandoned. The essence of the relationships explored in this first chapter is role-playing. In this drama women are presented as objects, playthings, and it is clearly significant that when Onegin grows bored with life, the first thing he abandons are these toys (1: XLII). Underlying the rake's pursuit of women is a complete lack of interest in individual women as such.[45]

When the focus of the themes of sexuality and love move to the female, in Chapter 3, the presentation of them remains within the same parameters. Tatyana does not choose her own destiny, but merely the man (a complete stranger) to whom she will give herself, and her love is, we are clearly told, a product of the insidious power of the culture which has been outlined in Chapter 1. Within these terms, the Innocent Virgin is prepared to give herself to the rapacious Rake. In a comic reworking of *Clarissa*, the Russian Lovelace is somewhat startled to find he has no conquest to make.[46]

Given the power of culture as Pushkin describes it, it is hardly surprising that Tatyana acts as she does. Whether from fiction or 'real life', all her lessons have told that a woman must give herself or, more likely, be given to a man. This evolves in the course of the novel as the paradigmatic male/female relationship and is one that is central to many eighteenth- and nineteenth-century novels. Tatyana's decision, as explained in her letter, to attempt to give herself rather than wait for her destiny to be decided for her, may seem a shockingly bold act. Indeed, the narrator implies that she will be found guilty for proposing to Onegin, offering herself to him (3: XXIV). However, the precise terms of the letter hardly suggest rational, conscious, self-determining behaviour. Tatyana is almost forced to give herself by agencies beyond her control. She says it is within 'your [Onegin's] will' to despise her; if he had not arrived 'I would have been a faithful wife/and virtuous mother.' She places herself entirely at his disposal and wishes only to be possessed. 'I am yours!' she cries. Thus, she allots herself a completely traditional feminine destiny, wishing only to live through and for him. The powers of the sociolect, once more, dictate her behaviour. However, even greater forces are at work: 'Either it has been fated in a higher council/Or it is the will of heaven . . .'. As in *The Gipsies*, there is no escaping the Laws of the Fates, which in this instance too can be seen to be the Law of the Fathers. Tatyana envisages that Onegin may be her 'protector', 'sent by God', and she entrusts her Fate to him from this moment. Her action, then, reinforces rather than undermines the patriarchal paradigm, namely, that men possess women. She asks Onegin, as it were, to echo the words of Aleko and the Old Gipsy: my Zemfira, my Mariula, my Tatyana. And, indeed, Onegin does precisely this in her dream, in repeating the animals' cry of 'Mine!' (5: XIX–XX). Onegin's position in this menagerie is also clear: he is the host or, indeed, the Master (*khozyain*, 5: XVIII, line 5) to whom Tatyana, as we have seen, is led by the bear. The dream is, of course, open to all sorts of interpretations, but for present purposes it should be noted that even in her unconscious fantasies Tatyana can find no escape from the structures that bind her. He may be both 'sweet and awful to her' (5: XVII, line 11), but she gravitates to him nonetheless. The narrator, in this last quotation, captures exactly the ambiguity of the vulnerable virgin's situation, but does not suggest an alternative. Indeed, the opposite is the case, for, as we have already seen, in her own 'real life' Tatyana is taken to another Father, the general, who, we assume, also declares 'my Tatyana'. And, at the end, she announces to her one true love that she will be faithful to this husband/father,[47] finally accepting the fated laws of this dysphoric heroine's text. She makes it abundantly clear to Onegin and to us that she would gladly exchange her final situation for her former existence (8: XLVI), but she has no choice in her destiny.

3.4. Male/Male Relationships

The central organising plot of *Yevgeny Onegin* is that of sexual relations between men and women – as it was for most novels of the period – but there is also some discussion *en passant* of the relationships within the given pole of this dialectical axis, namely, men themselves. Indeed, the first two relationships between individuals in the text take place between men. In Chapter 1, the author/narrator appears as a *dramatis persona* and becomes friends with Onegin (1: XLV). They share the same cynical, blasé view of the world (particularly of the perfidious *koketki*), and are even prepared to travel abroad together (1: LI). Onegin, however, is moved to the countryside, where he will meet Tatyana. Before this, he and Lensky, although of disparate tastes and temperaments, strike up a friendship, and one of the main themes of this second chapter is this friendship of opposites. The first quarter of the novel is taken up with either men pursuing women as sex objects ('the Rake's day'), or by men befriending men. The given, expository basis of the later action, then, is men, with women appearing peripherally, quite literally as the Other. Significant male/female relationships could, at this juncture, almost be construed as a deviant pattern rather than as a norm.

As we know, these latter relationships do move to centre stage, and it is significant that the narrator persona does distance himself from men and their rakish games. In his introduction to Onegin's initial rejection of Tatyana, the narrator announces, after a review of Onegin's activities of Chapter 1: 'Thus he killed eight years/Wasting the finest flower of life.' (4: IX, lines 13–14). The narrator's adieu to men as his focus is completed before and during the second peripeteia, the duel. The dominant notes of his description of this event emphasise its complete absurdity. The pretext is trifling (although, significantly, it is caused by a *koketka*), it is fought between two alleged friends, one of whom kills the other, and the specific details are frankly and deliberately ridiculous. Onegin is so unconcerned about the impending tragedy that he oversleeps, and his second, Zaretsky, is a pointed caricature of the fashionable manners and the gentleman's code of honour which will lead one man to kill another for a mere bagatelle. Increasingly, then, the interaction between men receives a negative portrayal, and after this fateful climax no further such relationships are initiated or explored. In this sense, at least, the feminine does, indeed, become the dominant principle.

3.5. Images and Roles of Women

But what of the feminine 'true ideal' as it emerges as the novel (and the author) develops over the eight years it took to write? Do Tatyana and her sisters[48] mark a radical shift from the dichotomy of holy virgin/perfidious child of nature and passion that emerged from the two works analysed earlier?

In line with the 'rake's economy' of Chapter 1, women (referred to initially by the pejorative foreign word *damy*, 1: V, line 13) appear in terms of categories, as an undifferentiated collectivity. Onegin frequents the theatre to cast his gaze over them, as we have seen, and to pursue the demi-mondaine *aktrisy*. The narrator then goes on to lament his own rakish lost 'goddesses' (*boginy*, 1: XIX), appending, as we would expect, the proprietory 'my'. They are peripheral pawns in the games played by the two rapacious males. More specifically, they are presented as what we would call sex objects, and misogynistic disgust is apparent as we learn of the 'jealous whisper of modish wives' (1: XXVIII, line 14). The first major setpiece description of the text is devoted to a sensual account of one of the narrator's lost loves (Stanza XXXff.). However, the woman is unnamed and, indeed, fetishised, as it is her famous *nozhki* ('little feet') which arouse the narrator's nostalgic lust:

> I hold the lucky stirrup
> And the little foot I feel in my hands;
> Again the imagination seethes,
> Again its touch
> Has inflamed the blood in my faded heart.
> (1: XXIV, lines 3–7)

The initial impression of a venerated woman is filtered through the narrator's sub-pornographic gaze and touch.[49] However, the deification ellides into reified mistrust of women: 'The words and gaze of these sorceresses/Are deceitful . . . like their little feet.' What had begun as a worshipful evocation of a singular anatomy slips into the dismissal of the collectivity, linking it with one of the most common stereotypes of women, their dark powers to enslave men. These women are subsumed by the narrator, following the tradition of Radishchev,[50] into the recurrent abusive term *koketki*, the seductive, dangerous women, against whom the potentially saving virginity of the true ideal resonates, precisely as did Anyuta in Radishchev's *Journey*. The contrast is specifically drawn in an explicitly retrospective stanza (3: XXII) which begins the contrapuntal introduction to Tatyana's letter. Above their heads stands Dante's awesome warning: 'Abandon hope forever' (3: XXII, line 10), and men are duly warned against the main body of women.

However, it is not only in Chapter 1, nor only in St Petersburg, that men must beware women. Country women, too, are presented collectively. Their husbands' conversation is desperately dull, 'But the conversation of their dear wives/Was much less intelligent' (2:

XI, lines 13–14). Even these collectively silly creatures are threatening to the vulnerable male psyche: Lensky 'did not, of course/Have
any wish to carry the shackles of marriage' (2: XIII, lines 1–2). Much
later, even after the narrative focus has switched to Tatyana, women
are presented in terms of collectively negative stereotypes, whose
conversation is reduced to empty-headed trivia and nonsense, the
only topic being the 'fiancées' fair' (7: XXVI, line 10). Once in
Moscow, the image is even less flattering:

> But everyone in the drawing-room is occupied
> By such incoherent, vulgar nonsense
>
> .   .   .   .
>
> Not a single thought will flare up in a whole day,
> Even by chance, even at random.
>
>   (7: XLVIII, lines 3–9)

The first of the two sisters to emerge from this misogynistic
backcloth is, in fact, Olga, the *inamorata* of Lensky. The omens
implied by the first motifs of her portrait are not promising. Lensky,
we learn, shared her 'childish amusements' and she, echoing
exactly the women of the harem, 'flowered, like a hidden lily of the
valley' (2: XXI, line 12). This floral image of vulnerable virginity also
echoes poor Liza, for it is these emblematic flowers that she sells to
Erast, her seducer and destroyer.[51] Olga's portrait is a mere
caricature, but it remains within the traditional stereotypes of
women and, even if it is a parody of a stereotype, it is a stereotype
nonetheless. She is modest, submissive, has eyes as blue as the sky
and flaxen hair. The narrator points out, indeed, that one can find
such a portrait in any novel (2: XXIII, lines 9–12). However, it is
surely noteworthy that he cannot be bothered to expend any further
energy on this insignificant woman.

When Olga enters the plot proper (in Chapter 5) it is, of course, as
a destructive mechanism,. Her flirtatious behaviour towards
Onegin at Tatyana's name-day party leads to the duel and her
'beloved's' death. Like Liza before her, she is endowed with
contradictory stereotypes. Having begun in modest 'hidden' virginity, she now receives the iconic label of *koketka* for her perfidious
behaviour. The narrator asks in ironic horror:

> Is it possible? Scarcely out of nappies,
> The coquette, the flighty child!

> Already she knows cunning,
> Already she has learned to betray.
>   (5: XLV, lines 5–8)

In four swift lines Olga moves from the charmingly pre-sexual to the viperous sexual state in which women endanger men, and, in this instance, she literally leads to death. Even after the duel, Olga remains allied to the image of women encountered in Chapter 1. She is '*untrue* to her sorrow [my italics]' and, in disgust, the narrator expels her from the text.

Immediately after dismissing Olga as a mere novelistic, chocolate-box heroine, the narrator begs permission to occupy himself with her elder sister, Tatyana, and it is from this moment that the centre of the book begins to switch from the modern (or, rather, modish) to the traditional, from foreign to Russian, town to country, and male to female. Tatyana's initial depiction occupies several stanzas and is far more detailed than the author's previous female creations. The first notes, however, remain within age-old stereotypes for the typically feminine ideal: 'Wild, sad, silent/Timid like a forest doe' (2: XXV, lines 5–6). If Olga is compared to a flower, Tatyana is no less dehumanised in this animal-based simile. All the early nuances emphasise her sadness, solitariness and passivity. She is meditative and loves to sit alone watching the dawn rise. Another early note, also evoked by the initial simile, is a very strong, almost complete identification not merely with the country or *rus*, but with nature itself.[52] Her love of reading is also emphasised; this too underscores her solitary character, but also her old-worldness, in that the novels she reads are distinctly old-fashioned in character. Moreover, they are foreign in origin, so that the image of Tatyana we first see is much more complex than hitherto: she is foreign as well as Russian, most obviously in her letter.

Many of these adumbratory chords recur as leitmotifs which flicker as background echoes whenever Tatyana appears. When Onegin first enters the Larin household, Lensky repeats the narrator's opening lexicon: she is 'sad and silent' (3: V, lines 2–3). When she falls in love (immediately!), Olga's simile is repeated with a slight variation: Tatyana's imagination is like a 'grain' fallen on the ground, thirsting for the 'fateful food' (3: VII). She is the almost entirely passive 'maiden' (*deva*) waiting to be awoken. Habitually, she is linked with that ancient symbol of femininity, the moon, although here it suggests virginal innocence, rather than fickleness as in *The Gipsies*. For some considerable time this image barely alters – not, indeed, until Chapter 7 does Tatyana really begin to change, awaken, as we have seen, and in the interim the narrator regales us with repeated scenes of sighs, trembling, tears, fainting-fits and all the rest. Tatyana is in this instance a parallel rather than a contrast to her sister, in that this passive waiting for the arrival of the hero echoes that of poor Liza. Even after the epiphanic encounter in Onegin's home these notes linger on in Tatyana's mournful adieu, at dawn, to her Arcadian roots (7: XXVIII).

Slowly, however, other resonances gain ascendancy. We have already noted the punning epigraph of *rus/Rus'* which heralds her arrival. Foreign influences hold sway for a time, culminating in her letter. Gradually, however, the identification not only with the country (*rus*) but with Russia (*Rus'*), which Dostoevsky so acclaimed, grows stronger. 'Tatyana (Russian in her soul/Without knowing why herself)' (5: IV, lines 1–2), the narrator announces, at what can be accounted the *lyric* peripeteia of the novel. At this intersection of her development there is a triple identification between the narrator and her, centring on their shared love of the countryside, that is the *Russian* countryside, winter and the old traditions of *starina*: 'Tatyana believed in the traditions/Of the simple folk *starina*' (5: V, lines 1–2). This leads on to a fourth critical identification between author and heroine, namely the folkloric, the ways of which Tatyana had encountered at her *nyanya's* hands and which provides the raw material of her ensuing dream. However positive this link may be to the author (and to Dostoevsky), it merely locks Tatyana into yet another traditional feminine stereotype, a close identification with the irrational and intuitive.[53] Significantly, it is by using the classic irrationalist mechanism of a dream-sequence that the narrator seeks to unlock the undiscovered psyche of the pure Russian woman. She is further identified with the world of the fairy-tale in that her entire plot-line, like so many romances centred on the pre-sexual maiden, can be seen merely as a more sophisticated reworking of the Sleeping Beauty tale. Again, Tatyana evokes memories of Liza. The fact that Tatyana is often so close to collapse and unconsciousness reinforces this impression. Another scene redolent of the world of the folk story is her visit to Onegin's 'enchanted castle'.

As we have seen, it is here that she finally awakens from her dream, and as we also know it is a rude awakening. We may now turn to the specific state from which Tatyana awakens and the condition in which she then finds herself. From the opening stanzas of her portrait, she is set apart from the worldliness of other women, as they have been described in Chapter 1. She is the pure country girl as opposed to the deceitful city *koketka*. This contrast is made explicit, as we noted earlier, in the introduction to Tatyana's letter, which the narrator still keeps as 'holy' (3: XXXI, line 2). At this point she becomes an iconic object of veneration, a creature of the poetic imagination. For Radishchev's narrator, Anyuta comes too late to save the jaded narrator from the sins of his past. Perhaps this time the sanctified virgin may still guard the narrator from the curse of the *koketki*. As if to emphasise the point, Tatyana opens her plea to Onegin by claiming that he would never have known her 'shame' (*styd*) if she had not laid herself open before him. She hopes he will be her 'guardian' (*khranitel'*), but the rhyme *iskusitel'* ('tempter') immediately follows. As in the later dream, the appalling dilemma of the pre-sexual maiden is made apparent in these lurid imaginings of our virginal heroine. Indeed, Onegin's jaded palate is briefly stirred by these 'maidenly dreamings' (4: XI, line 3), although, unlike the narrator, this rake is beyond the redemption offered to him.

The primary imagery associated with Tatyana, then, locates her firmly in the pre-sexual world. It is here that she can be seen as the author/narrator's 'true ideal'. The young woman, before she becomes a sexual being, is the ideal: the woman-*child* can offer no threat, but possibly salvation from the dangerous world of sexuality. Accordingly, Tatyana is described specifically as a child throughout the tale. One such instance tellingly compares her with the scheming coquette:

> The coquette judges cold-bloodedly,
> Tatyana loves in earnest
> And unconditionally gives herself
> To love, *like a dear child*.
> (3: XXV, lines 1–4; my italics)

It is as a 'dear child' that the narrator erects the heroine as an object of worship.

It is, in this light, bitterly ironic that her mother announces in the stanza *immediately* following Tatyana's visit to Onegin's estate (7: XXIV–XXV): 'What is to be? Tatyana is not a child'.[54] From this moment she is pushed into womanhood. Given that the feminine ideal in this text is to be a child, to become a woman is not, in fact, to grow to adulthood, but to lose a cherished innocence (that is, virginality) and to enter an unwanted prison. As she awakens to this bewildering state in her new Moscow home, she sees not the open fields of the countryside, but 'stables, a kitchen and a *fence*' (7: XLIII, line 14; my italics). In the final chapter we see that Tatyana has, in one sense, successfully made the transition to womanhood, marriage and, one assumes, to being a maiden no more. Yet this is clearly not what she wants, as we have seen, and has led to a somewhat eerie refrigeration of her feelings. Self-denial and self-effacement, strict propriety replace her former spontaneity. With now sad irony the author recapitulates the former motifs. She remains, at heart, a 'simple maid' (8: XLI, line 12), and he reinforces the image in the rhyme *mechtan' ye/molchan' ye* ('dreams/silence', 8: XLII, lines 5–6). In this text, then, the awakening to womanhood is the very opposite of growth. The true woman is the child, the virgin. But if there had been hope for her, and hope that she might redeem the rake, this is lost in the weary resignation of her, and the narrator's, final state.

3.6. Themes and Values

The gloomy pessimism implicit in Tatyana's destiny is reinforced by the more general themes of *Yevgeny Onegin*. If Tatyana is unable to escape the patriarchal structures in which she is located, then, more generally, there would seem to be little chance, once more, of avoiding the 'Laws of Fate'. In other words, as in *The Gipsies*, the destinies of specific women are seen as part of broader tendencies within the culture, against which the individual may struggle, but only in vain.

The vanity of this struggle emerges in the very first chapter, as was noted above (3.1). Onegin, and later the other protagonists, are located in a specific culture from which no-one really escapes. The inherently tragic view of the book is adumbrated from the outset. The conditioning occasioned by one's education, reading and the wider sociolect, determines destiny. Perhaps the two most decisive examples of this theme are Tatyana's letter and Onegin's killing of Lensky. Neither acts, each enacts a pre-ordained pattern of existence. More specifically, the text advances a view of literature which can justifiably be termed hegemonistic. Tatyana falls in love almost as a conditioned response, according to a cultural imperative, and, in the ensuing stanzas, the narrator proceeds to explain how this has happened:

> Imagining herself a heroine?
> . . . .
> Tatyana in the silence of the woods
> Wanders alone with a dangerous book,
> She seeks in it and finds
> Her secret fire, her dreams.
>   (3: X, lines 1–7)

Heroes of old were *exemplars*, vice was punished, virtue rewarded. Under the aegis of modish, 'misty Romanticism', morality may have suffered, but literature remains just as 'dangerous', because it is such a powerful model for behaviour.

The narrator reiterates this view throughout the first three chapters and reinforces it with a more general proposition – that human nature is equally determined by convention, or even habit: 'Habit is a despot amongst people' (1: XXV, line 4), and by generalising the mores of town and country dwellers alike the narrator accords them an air of immutability. Worse still, they seem even to be so by pre-ordination: 'Habit is given to us from on high:/It is a substitute for happiness'. (2: XXXI, lines 13–14) Inevitability seems to dominate everything, from falling in love to killing a friend, to *rozy* rhyming with *morozy* ('roses' and 'frosts'). 'La morale est dans la nature des choses' reads the epigraph to Chapter 4, and, like the other two epigraphs already discussed, it is singularly well chosen. If this is so, can one do anything? does the narrator offer women, or indeed anyone, an alternative to pre-ordained structures, which, as we have seen on every level, are those of patriarchy? The answer would seem to be 'No'; men and women must accept their lot and 'reconcile' themselves to it as best they can.

The clearest illustration of this moral tale comes in the two future lives Lensky might have lived. In Chapter 6, Stanza XXXVII, Lensky writes his own obituary, as it were. Using the style employed to convey Lensky's romantic nonsense, the narrator speculates that perhaps a great poetic destiny awaited him:

> Perhaps he for the good of the world
> Or even for fame was born;
> His now silent lyre
> Might have raised a thundering
> Uninterrupted ringing through the ages.
>   (6: XXXVII, lines 1–5)

This is Lensky still living by the book, imagining himself to be a 'hero of a novel', just as Tatyana had imagined herself a heroine in falling in love and then writing to Onegin, or the latter imagined himself a 'Muscovite in Harold's cloak' (7: XXIV, line 11). In the next stanza, however, the narrator dismisses such lofty hopes from Lensky's breast, and in his own new style of 'humble prose'[55] outlines what *he* thinks would have happened to young Vladimir had he lived: 'An ordinary lot awaited the poet', 'he would have parted company with the Muses, married':

> In the country, happy and cuckolded
> He would have worn a quilted dressing-gown
> He would have discovered *life as it really is*.
> (6: XXXVII, XXIX, lines 1–9; my italics)

The force of the mature style, as opposed to the mockingly juvenile doggerel, insists that the latter is what 'real life' holds out for Lensky and, by implication, Tatyana and the reader. She, at least, may make this discovery, unlike anyone else in the novel apart from the narrator. However, this 'moral victory' as Dostoevsky called it, merely serves to reinforce the view reached earlier. There is no way out from the prison of culture. The best one can do is to realise this, bow down and accept it, become reconciled. In terms of the sexual politics of the novel, the same applies. Women will continue to be given to men, the ideal woman is the pre-sexual innocent, childlike virgin, and women do not grow to maturity but decline from this pre-existent state. This is the nature of things, and 'la morale est dans la nature des choses'.

Alexander Pushkin's 'true ideal', then, echoes that of the Sentimentalist tradition; the 'simple country maiden' who may regenerate the jaded rake. His is, of course, a much more complex creation than that of Radishchev, Karamzin or their predecessors, and there are strong elements of parody in his imaginative re-creation of the type. However, it is precisely *because* she is a creature of the imagination, a longed for *vision*, that she can be seen as this ideal. She, for all her alleged inner strength, has no control over her destiny, and fails to achieve any of her own longings, nor is she able to save the particular former rake with whom she falls in love. But at least she is not a *koketka*, and she does discover 'life as it really is'. However, for this woman, and women more generally, life as it really is means defeat of hope and the lack of the possibility of growth.

4

Mikhail Lermontov and A Rake's Progress

> . . . it is not easy to define the attractiveness of Pechorin: perhaps it lies in his exceptional quality of combining strength of character and adventurous action with introspection and a vivid mode of expression, to which may be added a taste for flouting social conventions.[1]

No less than Pushkin's Onegin and Tatyana, Pechorin, the 'hero' of Lermontov's only completed novel, *A Hero of Our Time*, has become a seminal figure in nineteenth-century Russian literature and the criticism of it. Perhaps more than any other single literary character in the language, the young travelling army officer who seeks adventure and challenge (and much else besides) in the Caucasus has given rise to a wide variety of different and often conflicting interpretations and opinions.[2] His portrait has also been acclaimed as the first psychological study in Russian, and the novel as revolutionary in form, structure and theme.[3] The depiction of women and their destinies in the novel has received less serious attention, and such characters as Princess Mary, Bela and Vera are often seen simply as foils to an illumination of the central figure, or as mere victims of this 'alarming type, that of the predatory man'.[4] All this may be as true as any set of generalities about a 'classic' text and a deeply influential novel. However, a closer reading of the work from the present perspective reveals that the novel *as a whole*, and not simply Pechorin's character and his treatment of women, is a deeply misogynist account of the female (and, specifically, the *feminine*) character. In Pushkin's terms it could well be called a 'dangerous book', or, in Mary Daly's terms, a particularly notable example of what she calls 'The Sado-Ritual Syndrome: The Re-Enactment of Goddess Murder'.[5] As in the previous chapter, I begin with a briefer analysis of another work by the same author, *The Demon*, which was eventually completed (after more than a

53

decade's work) in the year the final version of *A Hero of Our Time* appeared.[6] Although rather more abstract than the novel, the *poema* illustrates many of the same problems.

1. THE DEMON

1.1. Images of the Male

Like many of Lermontov's male protagonists, the Demon is an exile, an outcast from society, who both rejects and is rejected by the commonality of humanity.[7] His description and 'biography' opens the poem (indeed, his name is the first noun), and, accordingly, acts as the exposition to the plot. As with Girey in *The Fountain of Bakhchisaray*, he thereby takes on the status of the *given*,[8] the force, in this case an elemental power of evil, who will organise the discourse, and the destiny of the Other, the pure heroine, Tamara, a Georgian princess. He is an outcast not merely from society, but from life itself, operating beyond good and evil: indeed, he is bored by the limitless power for evil that he has at his disposal:

> . . . but the proud spirit
> Cast a contemptuous eye
> Over the creation of his God
> And on his high brow
> Nothing was reflected.   (p. 506)

Once more, the masterful male controls his world by the power of the *gaze*. His contempt and lofty pride, as well as his eternal isolation and will to evil, create around him the perfect iconic image of the Byronic hero.[9] By the implications of the literary code in which he functions, only the perfect image of goodness, the purest of virgins could redeem him. This is to be precisely the image and function of Tamara, although she will fail. The Demon is an abstract symbol, a metaphysical hypothesis, but, as in *The Gipsies*, the abstraction of the initial premise lends general application to the conclusions.

1.2. Setting

In line with the two principal inspirations for the work, Byron's Eastern Tales and Pushkin's Southern Poems,[10] the locus of the

poem is as vague, generalised and non-specific as is the characterisation. It is set in Georgia (as well as in eternal space), but it is a
Georgia of the imagination, an exotic, romantic frontier, the scene
for adventure and mystery. The essentially abstract setting reinforces the algebraic, formulaic nature of the characterisation.
Furthermore, the expository setting is given at some length, so that
it operates not merely as wild local colour, but provides a crucial
ingredient to the ensuing conflict between Evil and Good, Male and
Female. The mountain peaks, covered with '*eternal* snows' [my
italics], the animised torrents and the untamed animals, and so on
(pp. 505–6), are not mere *topoi* of Romantic scene-setting, but give
the 'relationship' between the Demon and Tamara a truly cosmic
significance. The poem, that is, explores the two poles as elemental
signifiers.

1.3. Plot and Narrative Structure

The plot, then, deals in highly abstract terms or, rather, archetypes,
dramatising an eternal conflict. The problematics of this are usually
considered to be Miltonic in essence – can pure goodness redeem
absolute evil? However, unlike many previous works within this
Christian tradition, the two participants are not both male. Consequently, the emphasis shifts to provide a clash between two slightly
different principles, namely masculine and feminine. Although a
highly stylised image, the Demon can be validly interpreted as a
fallen, alienated man who searches for meaning in a world lacking in
meaning, whose quest is for authentic values.[11] Tamara, in turn, is
an emblem not so much of pure goodness, but of angelic purity, or,
in the post-Sentimentalist tradition in which Lermontov too was
writing, of virginity.

After the lengthy exposition and scene-setting, the plot begins
with the significant words: 'And the Demon saw . . .' (p. 509).
Again, the given polarity, the male, activates the plot by the power
of his gaze. Quickly, the mechanism of this plot situation is
revealed: 'And again he had attained the *sacred object*/Of Love,
goodness and beauty . . . Was this a sign of *rebirth*?' (p. 510; my
italics). Can this symbol, this incarnation of 'love, goodness and
beauty', regenerate the fallen male?: precisely the paradigm we
have already examined in Radishchev's *Journey* and Pushkin's
Yevgeny Onegin. The woman is an object of the male gaze and has
her destiny, at this initial stage, defined by it and by his perspective,

or point of view. Beneath the high level of abstraction, the theme of the pure virgin redeeming the jaded Rake is unmasked. The religious lexicon noted above may seem to be simply in keeping with this particular work and its symbolic system, but it too echoes and reinforces the theme of the veneration of the (female) virgin from the male point of view.

The complication of the plot and its narrative structure is also activated by a male persona. Tamara is betrothed to an earthly *zhenikh* ('fiancé') and his imminent arrival nudges the plot into motion. However, he is never to arrive to claim his bride, and his wayside death would clearly seem to be through the malign agency of the Demon. Although a minor incident in the overall development of the plot, this casualty illustrates two more familiar situations. Two rival males compete for the trophy of the possession of the maiden, and love and death are inextricably interwoven.[12] Following on from this is a long section detailing Tamara's seduction by, and capitulation to the Demon, to which we may return. In terms of the plot, however, it should be noted that Tamara acts even less consciously than Liza or Tatyana. She is *acted upon*, the completely passive recipient of the all-consuming power of the Demon.

The peripeteia illustrates another paradigm of masculinist fiction, and one which is to be replicated on several occasions in *A Hero of Our Time*, albeit in more realistic terms. Although for a long time '[he] did not dare/To break the sacred object of the peaceful shelter' (pp. 521–2), the Demon finally arrives to abduct Tamara. He conquers her by now merely token resistance and possesses her. Love and possession, as they are to be for Pechorin, are virtually synonymous for this male hero: 'Here I possess and love' (p. 524). The plot, despite the lengthy section devoted to Tamara, remains firmly within his power, and it is precisely power over her that he seeks, despite his claim that: 'You could return me with a word to goodness and to the heavens' (p. 525). In this paradigmatic plot of male and female relations, guile, seduction, self-justifying words are legitimate tools. If these are insufficient in this more brutal version of Onegin's euphemistic 'tender science', then force is used to dominate and control the virgin. 'Having *chosen* you as my sacred object' (p. 531), the Demon later declares: this line encapsulates their relationship. He chooses her destiny and shapes her fate, and has power over her life and, in the end, her death. She becomes an object of veneration, and the repeated word *svyatynya* ('sacred object') does not disguise the fact that she is nothing but an object to the male gaze. In his long *cri d'amour* (pp. 530–3), the Demon offers her everything: 'I will give you all, all earthly things –/Love me! . . .' (p. 533) – everything, that is, except her own choice or individual destiny. Indeed, within this male-controlled discourse, she is no longer even allowed a voice. Immediately after these fervent pleas, he 'Touched with his hot lips/Her trembling lips' (p. 533) and she dies. The Sadeian motif of domination and possession reducing the heroine to silence leads, as it must in this paradigm, to a necrophiliac veneration of the death of the woman.[13] Given the Romantic obsession with the proximity of love and death, male love, or rather seduction, leads not to the 'rebirth' of the hero, but to the extinction of the virgin. It is a paradigm that is to be ritually repeated in *A Hero of Our Time*.

1.4. Images and Roles of Women

Princess Tamara enters the text after the extended introduction to the Demon, and is immediately characterised in the terms of the traditional, vulnerable heroine. She is 'young' and 'covered by a white yashmak' (p. 507).[14] Her ensuing description might be considered parodic, if this were not completely at odds with the elevated, metaphysical registers of the discourse. Certainly, it is ludicrously conventional and weighted down with almost the complete gamut of feminine stereotypes. Amidst the group of her female friends (a scene redolent of the traditional harem of the Eastern Tale), she skips around playing a tambourine 'lighter than a little bird'; she has a 'divine *little foot*'.[15] Her physical appearance echoes the usual clichés of the exotic (and erotic) heroine, with a 'languid gaze' and 'black brow'. Yet she is also innocent and specifically childlike – 'full of childish happiness' (p. 508). As in *Yevgeny Onegin*, the object of veneration is a goddess *because* she is a child.

Her initial plot situation also locates her firmly within patriarchal structures. The feast at which we have just glimpsed Tamara's little foot, has been arranged because 'Gudal was marrying off his daughter' (p. 508). This is the first thing we are told of her biography. She is identified in relation to her father, and as an object of exchange. She is controlled by one male presence and is later to be conquered by another. Intervening is a third male and an implicit fourth, the narrator and his reader. Tamara, after being presented in these terms, becomes the object of his and, implicitly, our lascivious gaze. The fountain of the harem 'had never washed over a similar figure':

> As yet no earthly hand
> Wandering over this sweet brow
> Had unplaited such hair;
> Since the world had been deprived of paradise,
> I swear, such a beauty
> Had never flowered under the sun of the south.   (p. 509)

The reader is invited to look upon the virgin, to devour her virginal innocence. The lack, 'as yet', of violation is emphasised; she is, like the women of Bakhchisaray and Olga in *Yevgeny Onegin*, compared to a plant. The implicit reference to the Fall in Genesis is also later to reverberate in Tamara's own lapse, echoing Eve's, before the power of the Demon's seduction. She is the perfect *object*.

Soon the Demon arrives to share with the narrator and his reader this lustful examination. Before this, as the last notes of the expository description of the heroine, the exact nature of her image and situation is emphasised. She is the 'playful *child* of freedom' who will shortly become a 'slave', although not of her intended earthly master. After his death, a 'magical voice' (p. 515)[16] speaks in soothing tones and echoes the same motifs, so that a collective male point of view of the vulnerable goddess child is established. 'Do not cry, child!', the voice begins, and continues using all the common-places of this category of heroine: 'maidenly cheeks', 'poor maiden', 'my earthly angel'. This is, in fact, not the first time that Tamara had acquired the *bednaya* ('poor') epithet of Liza and Tatyana. On hearing of the death of her betrothed, 'She fell on to her bed/Poor Tamara sobs' (p. 514). From now on she declines into another icon, that of the wronged maiden. She is perpetually in tears, she has difficulty breathing, and so on. Her actions are comically mechan-ical, those of a marionette hanging by the strings of Romantic clichés, lacking any individuation, distinctive inner life, or differen-tiating features. The purpose here is not parodic; it is very different, but the author could well have echoed the suggestion of the narrator of *Yevgeny Onegin* when dismissing Olga, that we pick up any novel to find her portrait.[17] Here the effect may be comical, but, in terms of the poem's discourse, all this pounding emotion would seem to be aimed at exciting maximum sentimental pathos around the fate of the vulnerable heroine.[18]

Her reaction to the words of the disembodied voice take the image of quivering, feminine emotionalism even further:

> Leaping up she looks around . . .
> Ineffable confusion
> In her breast; sorrow, fear.   (p. 516)

However, the next line races her, and the reader, on to yet another stereotype. Like Liza before her, she is to be a creature of opposite stereotypes: *simultaneously* an endangered virgin and a passion-crazed whore.[19] 'Her soul broke its fetters/A fire ran through her veins' (pp. 516–7). Her dormant sexuality is awoken in the 'ardour of ecstasy' that mingles with the sorrow and fear in her agitated breast. Henceforth, according to the plot paradigm, she is fallen, lost. Once the virgin is a maiden no more, she has transgressed the patriarchal law of prohibition, and becomes an outcast herself, beyond the protection of the father. In line with the archetypes of this situation, he is a Stern Father.[20] Part 2 of the poem begins with Tamara's appeal to him: 'Father, father, leave your threats/Do not rebuke your Tamara' (p. 517). Her crime is her seduction. Now that she is spiritually given to the Demon, she no longer wishes to marry, she is tormented 'By an irresistible dream':

> I am perishing, have pity on me!
> Give to a sacred shelter
> Your irrational daughter.   (p. 518)

Each motif adds to this self-confessed irrationalism – the dream, the uncontrollable emotions. Already the Gothic frisson of the heroine's death is anticipated – by Tamara herself. The nunnery in which she begs confinement will be 'like the grave'. But even here she is defenceless. Indeed, having transgressed, she has forfeited her protection and: 'Still in a *lawless dream*/Her heart beat within her, as before' (p. 518; my italics).

The pace of the plot now slows, allowing for maximum excitement to be aroused in the reader as we await Tamara's inevitable destiny. The transposition of setting to this holy sanctuary merely overdetermines her plot still further. Not only is the virgin violated, but so too is sanctity itself. Before the Demon's arrival to possess her, all the emotionalism of her portrait is recapitulated once more to re-emphasise the irrational nature of the feminine heroine: 'She falls into madness/And weeps . . ./Her heavy sobbing' (p. 520); 'Full of anguish and trembling' (p. 521), Tamara, in a Gothic reworking of Tatyana's statuesque pose:

> Sits in solitary thought . . .
> And the whole day, sighing, she waits . . .
> Some-one whispers to her: he will come.   (p. 521)

The last two lines, with the heavy masculine rhyme *zhdyot/pridyot* ('she waits'/'he will come') act as a particularly insidious reworking of this misogynist stereotype. The beauty this time is not sleeping; she is already wide awake and actively awaits, longs for her seduction. She is, indeed, possessed by evil: 'She may wish to pray to the saints/But her heart prays *to him*' (p. 521; my italics), and her longings now become explicitly and, one might add, unashamedly sexual:

> Her breast and shoulders are on fire
> She has no strength to breathe, a mist in her eyes,
> Her embraces greedily seek a response,
> Kisses melt on her lips . . . . (p. 521)

Soon, the Demon arrives and much of the rest of the poem is taken up with their encounter. Tamara begs for pity, for him to leave her in peace, but he, in scenes we have already described, insists. It should also be noted that Tamara's part in this dialogue is minimal and her speech is emotional and chaotic, while that of the Demon is rhetorical, majestic and, of course, *powerful*. In death, Tamara finds peace. Indeed, she is, significantly, even more beautiful as a corpse than in life, and the *dead* heroine becomes the final icon of the male point of view. *This* is the perfect image of woman. Tamara is finally welcomed into paradise (after a last struggle over her possession): it is only in death that the woman can find rest. The child is awoken to womanhood and sexuality. Even more than for Tatyana, this transition is painful: indeed, for Tamara to become a sexual being is to encounter torment, misery and, in the end, death. The goddess is murdered by the Sadeian spirit of masterful, proud evil.

2. A HERO OF OUR TIME

2.1. Setting

If the scene of *The Demon* is a Georgia of the imagination, an abstract landscape to heighten the generalities of the themes, plot and characters, then the setting of Lermontov's novel, while in the same general geographical location, is a fine example of the poet's move to realistic prose.[21] From the opening lines of the novel proper, in the tale of Bela (another abducted princess), much emphasis is placed on grounding the dramatic action in a highly particularised collection of specific places – ranging from the mountain fortress where Pechorin and Maksim intermittently fight the Chechens and other tribesmen (and where Pechorin takes Bela to seduce her), to the spa towns of Pyatigorsk and Kislovodsk. However, in the context of the development of the Russian novel and its social typification, the outstanding feature of the setting is its exoticism. We find ourselves in the wild frontier country, where bandits and smugglers roam and where striking Oriental beauties seem to be commonplace. Even in the more sheltered enclaves of high society drawing-rooms, the magnificent mountains can be seen through the windows, and raids by mountaineers are expected at any moment. All this has the effect of locating the (mainly) Russian *dramatis personae* in a non-Russian setting. The action is deliberately distanced from the 'real' world of Moscow, St Petersburg or the dreary provinces. Consequently, the alienated hero seems more at home in this foreign environment (and indeed, he identifies with the wild natural scene) but, just as in Pushkin's *The Gipsies*, the morals of the tales take on a more universal application specifically because the same 'Laws' (whether or not of the Fates) seem to hold in the wild south as in the civilised north.

Other particular points related to the setting need to be noted for our present purposes. If Bela is introduced as a part of her 'savage' *milieu* (and hence her behaviour may be partly explained by it), then this is even more true of the female character in *Taman*, the unnamed undine. The setting of this adventure story is clearly foregrounded so that it all but becomes the *dominanta*. Pechorin's lodgings are 'unclean' (that is, sinister), there are no icons; the story is set at night initially, first moonlit, then overcast and then fog.

Every detail is reminiscent of the influential *école frénétique*.[22] Accordingly, the undine could be viewed as part of a semi-parodic *literary* landscape, and in line with the particular implicit references, she is *a priori* imbued with supernatural or dark powers. As in *Yevgeny Onegin*, this female character, at least, is perhaps deliberately a stereotype, because of the setting from which she emerges. (This does not, however, make her any less of a ridiculous stereotype of the 'dangerous sex',[23] as we shall see.)

In *Princess Mary*, too, the setting has a particular resonance and, as in most of the stories, acts as an integral part of the thematic exposition. As in *Bela* and *Maksim Maksimych*, the importance of the setting is emphasised by the fact that it opens the tale. This poeticised word-picture of the magnificent mountain scenery surrounding the spa town of Pyatigorsk[24] emphasises once more the exotic, non-Russian location, but now another resonance is added: the natural scene; indeed, nature becomes a value in itself. Majestic and aloof, the mountains tower not only above the town, but over the pettiness of human intrigue and emotion: 'Why are there passions, desires, regrets here?' (p. 356), Pechorin asks in rhetorical and rather naive self-justification. Later in the story Pechorin extends this view in his love of riding off alone amidst this scenery. Here he can forget the intrigues he initiates and, more particularly, he can be alone and avoid the dangerous complications which women cause him: 'There is no woman's gaze which I would not forget at the sight of the woolly mountains, bathed in the southern sun, at the sight of the blue sky' (p. 383). Nature alone stands unsullied by the venality of amorous and other affairs.

From our present perspective, however, there is one final point to note in relation to the setting of the novel. Pechorin is a young army officer, and most of the stories make some explicit reference to the military theme. In particular, the opening and closing stories, *Bela* and *The Fatalist*, are specifically set amidst scenes of army life. This setting becomes paradigmatic for the novel. It is a world exclusively of men, where they are once more without the distracting presence of women and are free to fight each other, to compete for the possession of trophies (be they horses or women) and, where necessary, or when they so wish, to kill each other. The fact that the final story, *The Fatalist* – the key-note tale in many respects – is the most militarised, and from which women are almost completely excluded, tells us much about the highly masculinised and misogynistic world of *A Hero of Our Time*.

2.2. Images of the Male

In any account of *A Hero of Our Time* it would seem perverse not to concentrate on Pechorin as the central focus for analysis. From the first reviews of the book in the 1830s and 1840s to the most recent studies,[25] the hero has naturally occupied the most attention. This is clearly comprehensible given that he is not only the central character, but also because most of the themes centre on him. All the other characters can be said, perhaps, to have little, if any existence apart from their function as buttresses to an illumination of this character. (This last factor is a major one in explaining why little attention has been paid to female characters in the novel.) Indeed, we will also have much to say about Pechorin and his relations with women, and with men. For the moment, however, I will consider the image of masculinity as it emerges on the peripheries of the novel, that is, in the series of secondary heroes who populate the tales and who cast an interesting, and frequently parodic light on Pechorin's 'heroism'. These other characters tell us much about the idea of masculinity in this fictional world.

There are two such men in *Bela*: Azamat, the heroine's brother, and the brigand Kazbich, whose beloved horse, Karagyoz, is the object of exchange for the Circassian princess. Kazbich is the man alone in the world of nature, to an extent to which Pechorin can only aspire. He has few dealings with women and resolutely refuses Azamat's offer of his sister in exchange for the horse, declaring, in quotation from an ancient song: 'Gold will buy four wives/But a dashing steed has no price' (p. 292). In the end, of course, Kazbich *does* have dealings with Bela. Just as Pechorin had earlier taken Kazbich's horse Karagyoz in return for Azamat's delivery of Bela to him, so Kazbich, replicating Pechorin's action, abducts Bela and kills her before Pechorin and Maksim can reclaim her. To Kazbich women are worth less than a prized horse. In this male economy women are merely objects of exchange between men, a vehicle for their rivalry, and Pechorin's parallel relationship with the wild brigand Kazbich says much about the 'civilised' man's equally functional attitude to women.

Yanko, the fearless smuggler of *Taman*, provides a second lesson in true *machismo* to the callow Pechorin. He fears neither the elements nor the law. Like Kazbich, he exists in a world beyond civilisation, the very image of the proud spirit of freedom. We never really see him, and his characterisation is sketchy in the extreme. Yet he acts as a rival to Pechorin, with a woman once more acting as the focus of the competition. Pechorin's aspirations to the male ideal are again shown in a stark light. Vulich, the crazy Serbian of *The Fatalist*, is the romantic hero par excellence, a man without fear (or sense!), who is prepared to risk his life for a bet and who insists on concluding a card-game in the midst of enemy bullets. Pechorin again enters a significant *competing* relationship with this image. He it is who is prepared to challenge Vulich to a duel to death and then emulates his reckless bravery. It is against this extreme form of masculinity that Pechorin assesses himself, in each case entering into a relationship of rivalry or direct competition. For him, as for them, women are at best mere functional participants in the deadly games that men play.

2.3. Plot Situations

Rivalry between men, either for its own sake or over the possession of a woman, is a recurrent plot situation in the novel. *Bela*, with its double abduction of the heroine, involving directly or indirectly four men and culminating in her death, is an extreme form of this ritualistic game perhaps. However, the simple fact that this is the lead story, and other reasons as well, renders this the principal plot paradigm. After an extended prologue, involving travellers' notes about the Caucasus and our introduction to Maksim Maksimych and Pechorin, the last two encounter Bela, or rather *see* her, at a wedding feast. Quite specifically, a plot is hatched, or rather a double plot, as Pechorin arranges a swop of a horse for the woman. He is the principal plot agent, here as elsewhere, but Azamat and, somewhat unwittingly, Maksim also connive in her abduction tied over the back of a horse. As we shall see, the link between women and horses, or other four-legged friends, is to be a common motif in the novel. To avoid detection, and presumably so she will not escape, she is imprisoned. Abduction, followed by enforced 'protection', are the first two stages in this rake's declension, to be followed by seduction. This next stage forms the peripeteia of the story. Pechorin uses every trick and artifice of his much more aggressive 'tender science' – lying, cajoling, and, in the end, threatening precisely what he is later to do, namely, abandon her. Whereas in the prototypical novel of enforced seduction, *Clarissa*, the rape is passed over in a single line,[26] this virtual rape takes several pages to be enacted. Just as Tamara's funeral is extended to titillate the voyeuristic male reader (as Bela's death also is to be), so too here. Each detail of Bela's diffidence, reluctance and resistance is dwelled over to arouse and excite his interest.

For precisely similar reasons, the denouement of the plot is delayed. After Bela has succumbed to Pechorin's carefully planned campaign, the (male) narrator declares such a happy outcome boring, as he had 'expected a tragic denouement' (pp. 302–3), presumably the death of the wronged heroine. He is not to be disappointed, but before he and the 'dear sirs' (p. 276) to whom the novel is addressed are allowed to linger over her prolonged and agonising death, there is an extended *interruptus* provided by travelogue and nature descriptions. The retardation device may be laid bare (p. 307), but it has the effect of delaying, and therefore further exciting male expectations. When we return to the plot, Pechorin soon moves to the next stage in the paradigm: seduction is followed by abandonment. Bela enters into the predetermined dysphoric heroine's text by going into a decline, sitting alone, sadly, in silence, like Tatyana and Tamara before her, and like Mary later in the novel.

The denouement is activated as one might expect in this man's world by a male agent, namely Kazbich, who has come seeking revenge. Rhyming with Pechorin's earlier plot, he steals Bela, who again is carried off on a horse covered, as before, by the emblematic yashmak. Pechorin is stung into action by his rival's temerity, but the chase is too late. The two men fight each other at a distance, but the only possible outcome of the plot is the death of the heroine. As already noted, this is no simple execution but a lingering and suffering death, involving delirium and agonising pain, all of which is described in almost Sadeian detail. Maximum pathos is aroused but, in the end, neither of the male protagonists suffers unduly over the sad fate of the woman whose destiny they have disposed of.

Taman offers a similar plot paradigm, although one with less extreme consequences. In this strange seaside town a younger Pechorin encounters several strange, almost supernaturally en-dowed creatures, including a young unnamed woman, categorised by him as 'my undine' (p. 348). The principal plot-line concerns his abortive attempts to unlock the secret of this mystery woman and, simultaneously, to wrest control over her from another male, Yanko. This latter attempt involves violence as well, in that Pechorin physically grabs her and then wrestles with her in the rowing-boat. There are many comic and parodic motifs in this engagement,[27] but the plot implications for men who come too close to women are clear. Pechorin nearly faints from the fire of her kiss and then is almost killed by her. In his (chronologically) later campaigns against women Pechorin is never caught off guard again.

The plot of seduction and conquest receives its fullest treatment in the spa-town intrigues detailed in *Princess Mary*. The eponymous heroine is not given her own story by virtue of its title: rather, she, like Bela, is announced as the target of the 'predatory man'. In Pyatigorsk, and then neighbouring Kislovodsk, two men again act in rivalry for the heroine, this time quite explicitly. For good measure, Pechorin keeps Vera in reserve, again with a rival (her husband) to provide what is perhaps the real *raison d'être* of his apparent interest in the woman. As in the eighteenth-century tradition to which both this novel and *Yevgeny Onegin* are heirs, the plots revolve around the chastity and disposability of the virginal heroine,[28] with disastrous (if not, in this instance, fatal) conse-quences for the vulnerable woman. While conquering her virtue, Pechorin also manages to eliminate his rival, Grushnitsky. Indeed, it is significant that much of the later plot (and plotting) moves away from the initial focal point of Mary towards the explicit rivalry between the two men, culminating in their duel and the death of Grushnitsky. And, as we have seen, the plot paradigm of the last story in the novel moves completely to this level, laying bare the implications of the earlier plots. Men compete in rivalry, if necessary to the death, for the control of women. They gain pleasure and satisfaction from this hunt but, in the end, the individual women are pawns in the other, even deadlier game.[29]

2.4. Male/Female Relationships

Abduction, seduction, conquest, virtual rape – these, then, are the keynotes of the plots which make up *A Hero of Our Time*. We can now look in a little more detail at the way in which men and women interact in the novel. As in both *Yevgeny Onegin* and Lermontov's *The Demon*, the first stage in male control of women is the power of the gaze. In *Bela*, Pechorin sees her at the feast and it is at this point that his rivalry with Kazbich for her begins; the significance of the male gaze as such is conveyed in Maksim's somewhat florid account of Kazbich: 'from the corner of the room two other eyes were looking at her, motionless, fiery' (p. 287). So too in *Princess Mary*: Pechorin and Grushnitsky begin their feud as they each in turn cast an appraising look over the young princess by the well. Indeed, the power of the unobserved watcher is again emphasised, as Pechorin is able to watch her behaviour concealed in the shade of a gallery. The aggressive, intrusive nature of the male gaze is again made explicit as Pechorin directs his 'impudent lorgnette' (p. 366) at Mary who sits iconically at the window, presenting herself, unwittingly, as an object of this gaze.[30] She is not amused by this ocular rape. Pechorin is not alone in his voyeurism. This function of the look is clear in *Bela* when, on at least two occasions (pp. 300 and 302), Maksim observes the seduction of Bela from a concealed position. Even by proxy, men control women and, of course, the 'dear sirs' who read the book are equally voyeuristic.

Women, in any case, are usually under male control from the outset in that they are located explicitly within patriarchal structures. Bela is first introduced to Pechorin (and to us) as 'the younger daughter of the host' (p. 287),[31] and it is significant that Bela is kidnapped while her father is away. As in the cases of Mariya (in *The Fountain of Bakhchisaray*) and Poor Liza, women are at risk without paternal protection.[32] Bela remains as filially dependent on men. Maksim loves her as if she were his 'daughter' and is deeply upset by her death, as he had been a surrogate (though finally powerless) 'father' (pp. 310 and 323). Even the rather more mature Vera (who is a mother herself) is located within the same structures, in that she had married for the sake of her son a man 'she . . . respects like a father' (p. 381).

Deprived of an independent existence (and unable even to sit unmolested at their windows!), women are often reduced to the level of objects, equivalent merely to a horse, or even inanimates. Having swopped Bela for Karagyoz, for example, Pechorin dresses her 'like a doll' (p. 311).[33] Not only are they the pawns in masculine power-games, they are also the recipients of the full blast of this aggression. We have already seen the chicanery and bribery Pechorin resorts to in order to conquer Bela. Mary is 'wooed' by more subtle manoeuvres, although the overall effect of this strategy is remarkably similar to a duel. He goes out of his way to draw a large crowd around him, simply so that she should have fewer admirers, buys the carpet she wants and then parades it before her house, draped à la Bela over a horse, once more emphasising the interchangeability of women and objects. His affair with her continues along the same lines, involving stratagems, hypocrisy, deception and mendacity, referring to his 'system', whose main object is to control and manipulate her – to treat her, in other words, like a doll or puppet.

The main metaphor that might be used to describe Pechorin's dealings with women is that of the chase, in order first to possess and then to destroy, whether literally or not. We have already seen the hunting to the death of Bela (and it is not coincidental that Pechorin is away hunting other animals when Kazbich returns), and the same dynamics operate in *Taman* and *Princess Mary*. In the earlier of the two stories, he does not achieve possession, except through the power of verbal conquest. It is '*my* undine' who sings the song, and he refers to her in this way on three more occasions, varying this appropriation with 'my mermaid' (p. 352). If men cannot control women by force (as Pechorin, of course, tries to do in this story), then they resort to the power of the rapacious gaze or word.[34]

For the third time in the novel, Pechorin attempts, and this time succeeds in conquering the resistance of a young woman, in *Princess Mary*. Indeed, every young virgin (in fact, or by implication) he encounters is ravaged in this way. As with Bela, lying, cajoling and, in the end, physical force are used to persuade Mary he loves her.[35] The scene at the water crossing is again very close to actual rape, and the description prurient. Having delighted the 'dear sirs' with mention of his embrace of 'her tender, soft waist', Pechorin goes on: 'I paid no attention to her trembling and confusion, and my lips touched her tender little cheek' (p. 422). The force used, the repeated 'tender', the diminutive in the last noun all emphasise the vulnerability of the prey. But even the plucking of this particular flower is insufficient for Pechorin's rapacious appetites. Rarely does he leave Vera alone for long, ensuring that she remains within his control and equally destroying her life and security.

However, Pechorin is not alone in this desire to control women. We have already seen Kazbich echoing his behaviour, but virtually every male in the novel expresses similar desires. Having voyeuristically watched Pechorin finally overcome Bela's resistance, Maksim declares his annoyance that no woman had ever loved him 'in this way' (p. 302), that is, slavishly. Grushnitsky, we are told by Pechorin with no trace of irony: 'is one of those people who, when talking of a woman whom they scarcely know, call her *my Mary, my Sophie*, if she has had the good fortune to please them' (p. 377). To generalise this tendency in the novel completely, we have Vera's valedictory remarks in which she refuses to blame Pechorin for his behaviour, because his predatory and destructive actions are the norm among men: 'I will not start accusing you – you have behaved towards me as any other man would have behaved: you loved me *as property*' (pp. 452–3; my italics) Indeed, the most negative aspect of the relationships between men and women in this novel is the collective masochism of the victims: they are generally portrayed as willing accomplices in their own destruction. Before she finally submits, Bela declares to Pechorin: 'I am your prisoner . . . your slave; of course you can force me' (p. 301). However, this cry is uttered not only because she is literally a captive, or simply because she is a vulnerable and afraid sixteen-year-old. Her words are repeated by Vera: 'You know that I am your slave: I have never been able to resist you' (p. 316).[36]

Given the military environment of much of the action, it is hardly surprising that martial situations and metaphors occur in the various narrators' acounts of the 'love affairs'.[37] Pechorin's pursuit of both Bela and Mary is not a casual, haphazard hunt, but is planned with all the cunning and manoeuvring of a military campaign. In the former case, Pechorin sums up his list of gifts, or bribes, to win Bela: 'Will an Asiatic beauty withstand such a *battery*' (p. 301; my italics). Similarly, when Mary dares to withstand and, indeed, to repay him in kind, Pechorin murmurs darkly to himself: 'But I have outguessed you, dear princess, beware! You wish to repay me in kind, to prick my vanity – you will not succeed! and if you declare *war* against me, then I shall be pitiless' (p. 398; my italics). He is, of course, all too true to his words.

We have before us, then, an extreme form of the 'rake's economy' of the eighteenth-century novel. Or more accurately, we have this paradigm with the euphemisms of seduction, courtship ('the tender science') removed and laid bare. One repeated motif in this recurrent plot is that of the potential of the fresh young maiden (like Anyuta or Tatyana or Tamara), that is, the unsullied virgin, to refresh the jaded palate, or even to redeem the jaded rake. Pechorin uses precisely this argument to justify his abduction and seduction of Bela. She was, he hoped, an instrument of salvation: 'When I first *saw* Bela in my home, when for the first time, holding her on my knees, I kissed her black locks, I, fool, thought that she was an *angel*, sent to me by a compassionate fate . . . I was again mistaken' (p. 316; my italics).[38] He goes on to claim that he still loves her, but is bored . . . Pechorin is the Sadeian man *par excellence*, someone who regards women merely as food, as flowers to be plucked and then cast aside. In general, within the context of the novel, he chooses his women carefully (with the exception of the undine), that is, those he knows he will be able to conquer. He had once loved a woman with character, but they had parted as enemies. His approach is summed up in his own words as a 'thirst for power', the desire to 'subordinate everything to my will' (p. 401). Having reduced Mary to the trembling confusion outlined above, he derives unbounded pleasure 'at the thought that Mary will not sleep and will weep'; 'There are moments when I understand the Vampire' (p. 423). And, as in traditional folk tales, it is precisely the blood of young virgins that invigorates.[39]

On more than one occasion, Pechorin expresses his lack of comprehension of women (a view that is implicitly shared by Maksim and, more explicitly, Dr Werner). He wishes to unlock the 'mystery' of the undine, and wonders how Vera can still love him, knowing him as she does (p. 398). Pechorin, and the other men, reveal themselves to be singularly ill-equipped for the task of understanding women, for all his vaunted depth of analysis. For, underlying his relations with women, and other men's attitudes to them, is a profound fear of this 'dangerous sex'. The undine, as we know, nearly kills him (because he cannot swim!), and the scene in the boat has distinct (even if parodic) echoes of an encounter by this latter-day St George with the Dragon. Pechorin talks of her 'fiery breath' and later of her 'serpentine nature' (p. 352). In the image of the undine he succeeds in conflating Eve and the Devil, a traditional combination, of course. More specifically, in *Princess Mary* he defends his resolute avoidance of marriage by the fortune told his mother when he was still a child by an emblematic 'old woman': 'she foretold for me *death from an evil wife*' (p. 428). Pechorin reacts to this prophecy as Herod did to his: to avoid his fate he renders harmless, or at least attempts to, all women who cross his path, and his behaviour becomes the central paradigm for all male/female relationships in the novel.

2.5. Male/Male Relationships

As already indicated, it could be argued that women are even less significant in the novel's scheme of things, that they are mere pawns in the *real* game, which is rivalry between men. There are a number of aspects to male bonding in the novel, in fact. As in *Yevgeny Onegin*[40] men, and relationships between them, can be seen to be the

given, with women (especially their dangerous sexuality) a potentially disruptive Other. This proposition is supported by the
recurrent and pervasive use of the military setting, and, in particular, by the almost complete absence of women from the final tale.
Indeed, the same is true of the last story in the chronologically
'correct' framework, *Maksim Maksimych*, in which women also play
no part. The elegiac note of this story is largely occasioned by the
collapse of the apparent friendship between Maksim and Pechorin,
which, of course, was the opening relationship in the narrative of
Bela. Even before this, in the prologue to this story, the fictional
world opens with two men, Maksim and the travelling narrator: two
men face the world together, and interact as equals, a situation in
which no woman ever finds herself in this text. The solipsistic
Pechorin does not, of course, allow anyone to be his equal, male or
female, but his closest relationship is probably that with another
man, Dr Werner (in *Princess Mary*), who acts as a kind of double to
the hero.[41] Within this story the initial, given situation is once more
between two men, Pechorin and Grushnitsky, even if they are to
echo Onegin and Lensky in the death of the less significant partner
in the relationship.

The men of the novel use their friendships to connive with each
other in the conquest of women. Twice, bets (a metaphor close to the
more central one of duelling) are struck as to whether a women will
submit (between Maksim and Pechorin), or as to who will be the
winner in the pursuit (between Pechorin and Grushnitsky).
Werner, of course, actively assists Pechorin in seducing Mary,
initially providing him with information and titillating facts concerning Mary's innocence and consequent vulnerability: 'She
[Mary's mother] told me that her daughter is as innocent as a dove
. . . I wanted to answer that she should be calm, that I wouldn't tell
anyone this!' (p. 372). However, the more prevalent attitude of one
man to another is to see him as a rival, potential or real. As we have
seen, each of the main plots is based on this paradigm. For Pechorin
the games of abduction and seduction are always sweeter if he can
simultaneously outwit another male. In these battles men also
receive support from their fellows. Maksim is at hand for, or a
witness of, each stage of Bela's sad plot, while Werner goes almost
all the way with Pechorin, parting company only after Grushnitsky
has been killed. This facet of male bonding is particularly apparent
in the later stages of *Princess Mary*. Pechorin has only the support of
Werner, but around Grushnitsky there gathers a 'hostile gang' who

form a 'plot' (p. 414) to discredit the enemy. Military metaphors again reveal the nature of this aspect of inter-male rivalry: the gang is 'under the command' of Grushnitsky, while Pechorin later eavesdrops at their 'bellicose feast' (p. 424). As with Pechorin's campaigns of seduction, this hunting pack of young braves plans a carefully contrived conspiracy and strategy, even if it fails in the end.

When Pechorin first realises that a campaign is afoot, he is moved to declare: 'that's what I call life!' (p. 414). And, indeed, as the novel unfolds it would appear that he is happiest when he is in conflict with other men. For him the central metaphors of life are the bet, the challenge, the duel. The actual duel of this story is given a very extended description, and it is also significant that the last story, *The Fatalist*, concerns metaphorical duels between first Pechorin and Vulich and then between the hero and the drunken Cossack, culminating in Pechorin taking the latter in armed combat.

Tracing this syndrome back through the novel we can see that the rivalry between men has several functions. It is partly to clear the path of competition for the heroine. In this sense, Kazbich, Yanko and even the more fully developed character Grushnitsky, are plot functions, mere obstacles in the path of the hero.[42] However, as we have noted, conflict and duelling, including the death of the rival, occur even when no woman is involved. This is because the goal of the struggle would seem to be *power*, usually for the control of women, but not necessarily. Thus, when Pechorin is still striving to force Bela into submission, he tells Maksim that his purpose (in this instance, the hiring of a woman who knows Tartar) is to get Bela used to 'the thought that she is *mine*, because *she will belong to no-one but me*' (p. 299; my italics). Women are perceived as possessions, but also as signifiers of power over other men. In the patriarchal power games which Pechorin plays with such zest (and in which all the other men actively participate[43]), there can be only one symbolic Father, or Law-Giver.[44] Men will calmly eliminate each other to attain this position, so that they can control the women and receive the power this confers. In the case of Pechorin, an extreme version of this kind of masculine hero, it would seem to be power over *all* the young women he encounters, and supremacy over *all* his rivals. His goal is *unique* power. As he discovers from his depressed state after killing Grushnitsky, there is a fundamental flaw in this highly masculinised world, for there is nothing to be won if the prize (the woman) is actively despised.

2.6 Point of View

Bonding between men and its obverse, rivalry amongst them, play an important role in this novel. It could, indeed, be argued that it is a relationship even more central to the meaning of the novel than the theme of seduction, conquest and control of women. Similarly, the point of view of the novel is resolutely male and it is a *collective* male view which dominates: as in *Yevgeny Onegin* the shared point of view (with regard to women, at least) is an important factor in linking not only the male characters in the text, but also the narrator(s) and, finally, the reader. Here we have, indeed, not an *implied* male reader, but explicitly male ones, the 'dear sirs' of the author's introduction (p. 276).

The first mention of women is highly significant. Maksim tells the listening narrator, in his account of the wedding feast: 'The women, on seeing us, hid: those whose faces we could *examine* were far from beautiful. "I had a much better opinion of Circassian girls", Grigory Aleksandrovich said to me. "Just wait", I answered' (p. 286; my italics). Women are inspected by men, purely in terms of their physical beauty; they fail to meet the required standard (according to masculine opinion); the two men share, and are bonded by, the same views. Women in turn hide from view, in implied shame. This utterance sets the tone for later assessments of women's worth (or more usually their desirability), almost all of which are male in provenance and orientation. Soon afterwards, there emerges a similarly collective male view of Bela: to her own brother Azamat, Kazbich and Pechorin she is the object of exchange, equivalent virtually to a horse (although, as we know, Kazbich considers her worth rather less than his Karagyoz). This interchangeability of the Circassian princess and the horse is reinforced by a series of similes. Bela is introduced to the narrator (and the reader) thus: 'tall, slender, with eyes as black as those of a chamois' (p. 287). Maksim proceeds to inform us that Karagyoz has 'eyes no worse than Bela's' (p. 288). Azamat, when pleading with Kazbich for this horse, offering Bela, argues: 'Surely Bela is worth your jumper' (p. 292), and finally Pechorin neatly completes the symmetry between Bela, Karagyoz and the chamois by praising the horse to Azamat as 'such a frisky one, beautiful, just like a chamois' (p. 294).[45]

Maksim, however unsophisticated he may be as a narrator, shares this view in his tell-tale words and he continues to be a member of this masculinist collective in his story-telling. 'What won't a woman do for a coloured little rag!' (p. 299) he asks the narrator rhetorically, referring later on again to her coal-black eyes. When Bela begins to pine over Pechorin's increasingly frequent and prolonged absences, Maksim jollies her along by saying that Pechorin is a young man, he likes hunting, and he'll only be bored if she keeps being so sorrowful. Men again support each other to control women, this time through their perception of them.[46]

We have already seen what Pechorin himself thinks of women, and how he treats them – as objects for his pursuit, food to be devoured, to satisfy his vanity. Indeed, he views them merely as *categories*, not as individuals. In his confession to Maksim in *Bela*, he lays before us the dichotomous appraisal of them which had long since been traditional in literature. They are either simple-hearted maidens or 'coquettes': 'the ignorance and simple-heartedness of one bores me as much as the *coquetry* of the other' (p. 316; my italics).[47] In later stories, he receives further male support for this view, most notably from Grushnitsky and Werner. The former introduces Pechorin to the charms of Pyatigorsk society with a rather feeble attempt at rakish contempt for 'the sex': 'There are feminine societies but there's little consolation from them: they play whist, dress badly and speak awful French' (p. 361). Women again fail to come up to those exigent male standards. Mary's kindly action in picking up the glass of this fake cripple calls forth the veneration: 'she's simply an angel' (p. 365), repeating exactly Pechorin's noun as applied to Bela. Later, he shows himself as ill-equipped as Pechorin to understand women, exclaiming in a prophetic paraphrase of Freud's celebrated remark: 'Women! women! who will understand them?' (p. 364). Certainly not Dr Werner, it would seem. To him women evoke memories of the enchanted forest of Tasso's *Jerusalem Delivered*, at first full of horror, although gradually the monsters disappear, allowing the intrepid male explorer to emerge into a 'quiet and light glade' (p. 421). The point of view in the novel as regards Pechorin may indeed be unusually complex. As regards women it is virtually unitary. Women are controlled not only by Pechorin, the 'predatory man', but by the narrative itself.

2.7. Images and Roles of Women

It is, therefore, hardly surprising that the view of women that emerges from this androcentric text is negative and stereotyped. All too often their depiction is a collection of banal, traditional clichés.[48] As we have seen, Bela is introduced in terms of her physical appearance, and this approach is the one favoured in first descriptions of the other female characters. The undine in *Taman* is characterised initially by her voice, and her later description verges on the bathetic with her incessant jumping, skipping, clicking of fingers and singing, as if she were an animated doll (p. 348). When Pechorin slows down the narration to cast his gaze over her in more detail, he again draws a comparison between women and horses, quite explicitly: 'There was much breeding in her . . . breeding in women, as in horses, is a great matter' (p. 349). However, the undine soon reverts to her frenetic physicality: 'She suddenly jumped, began to sing and disappeared, like a bird startled from a bush' (p. 350). She, like Bela, is explicitly animalised: later she slips from Pechorin's embrace 'like a snake' (p. 351), and in the boat clings to Pechorin's clothes 'like a cat' (p. 352). These similes are certainly banal, but nonetheless indicative. Mary, too, moves 'more lightly than a bird' (p. 364), and even Vera, the only mature woman to receive any detailed attention in the novel, is introduced in terms of her physical attributes (pp. 373 and 379).

As if in a horse-fair each of the women is paraded before the 'dear sirs' for their appraisal and possible approval. In line with this tendency, physicality occasionally slips into sub-pornographic images of women. Pechorin's account of the undine is almost as fetishistic as the narrator's description of 'little feet' in *Yevgeny Onegin*.[49] Indeed, in explicit reference to the earlier novel we learn that 'A straight nose in Russia is rarer than a small foot' (p. 349). (Princess Mary also has small feet – p. 430.) After the struggle the undine stands on the shore and we are invited to gaze over the following description: 'She was squeezing the foam from her long hair, her wet shirt outlined her supple figure and high breast' (p. 353). The initial description of Mary is even more overtly imbued with voyeuristic sensuality:

> a light silk kerchief was wrapped round her supple neck. Her couleur puce boots were gathered at her little ankle so dearly that even one not consecrated in the secrets of beauty would have gasped in surprise. Her light, but noble gait had in it something maidenly that escaped definition, but was comprehensible *to the gaze*. (p. 361; my italics)

We are even told of her aroma. In accordance with the potency and prestige invested in the male gaze, it is important to note here the *pictorial* dimension of the presentation of women. Equally, they are not infrequently represented in statuesque poses, as in the case of the undine which we have just discussed. We, the implied male readers, are continually being invited to examine these creatures, to observe them, whether in motion or repose.

Other stereotypes can be detected within the text. Bela and the undine are typical Romantic clichés of the exotic, free 'child of nature'. Both are unindividualised and little more than mechanical dolls. However, this wildness has a darker, more menacing aspect for the male, as we saw in our earlier discussion of *Taman*. Such serpentine creatures can kill the unwary. The undine, like many such literary images, is a mixture of different stereotypes. Apart from her submarine attributes, she is imbued with mesmeric qualities: 'her eyes, it seemed, were endowed with some kind of magnetic power' (p. 349). She is dangerous precisely because she is sexually alluring and, at this stage at least, the hero is not able to control this *power*. Thus, Pechorin almost passes out from her 'fiery kiss', and these demonic qualities are confirmed by yet another male (Pechorin's Cossack), who joins the misogynist collective viewpoint in his reaction to her 'irrational' behaviour: 'What a demon the girl is' (p. 351).[50] Pechorin in turn confirms this view in his description of her fighting 'with *supernatural* effort' (p. 353; my italics). Virtually every reference to her is as a *generic* creature, whether of 'wild nature', or of demonic super-nature.

This woman may be dangerous, but most of the female portraits are cast in the mould of frailty, emotionalism and passivity.[51] Bela cowers in Pechorin's room 'as timid as a chamois' (p. 299), while Mary is the epitome of the timid and emotional virgin (although she does have other stereotypes attached to her). After picking up Grushnitsky's glass at the well, she 'went terribly red' (p. 364). She likes discussing feelings and passions and her behaviour throughout the tale is typically 'feminine'. She is ready to faint from fear and disgust when accosted by the drunk at the ball. Later, while out riding, she responds to Pechorin's second confession in an almost Pavlovian manner: 'At this moment I met her eyes: there were tears running in them; her hand, resting on mine, was trembling, her cheeks burned . . .' (p. 406). Mary's eyes in particular are the object of much comment: they seem alternately to be liquefying or flashing with anger, indignation and so on. But it is not only the vulnerable maiden who behaves in this mechanical fashion. On the same promenade the other ladies 'squealed and covered their eyes' at the abrupt chasm they came to. Vera too is frequently associated with these physical displays of uncontrollable emotion. When she and Pechorin meet by chance: 'She shuddered and turned pale' (p. 379), and she too has very expressive eyes. When they meet for their nocturnal assignation, Pechorin regales his male readers with the following original vignette: 'Her heart was pounding, her hands were as cold as ice' (p. 430).[52]

The sex is also blessed with remarkable stupidity and gullibility. Both callow Grushnitsky and cynical Werner, according to Pechorin, are able to drive women 'to distraction' (pp. 359 and 367),[53] while Bela, Mary and, in a different way, Vera all believe the charades that Pechorin acts out for them. However, perhaps the most pervasive and enduring negative stereotype of women in this novel is that of the passive, suffering victim. Bela is the first to follow the path of silent, pale, mournful Tatyana. For the first few days 'she was silent'; 'she was ever sad'; 'Bela sat on the couch, her head on her chest; she shuddered'; 'She sighed'; 'She went pale and remained silent' (pp. 299–300). Once she has been seduced, and then abandoned, she becomes even more of a Sentimentalist icon of sorrowful, wounded feminity. Maksim observes her in the following motionless pose: 'Bela was sitting on the bed . . . pale, so sad that I was afraid' (p. 311). She sighs and soon moves to the next stage of the dysphoric heroine's declension – tears. Although she proudly tells Maksim that she is 'the daughter of a prince' (again an androcentric definition), she utters not a word of complaint when Pechorin returns from the hunt. Soon the paradigm of seduction/ betrayal/separation is to be completed by the last two stages of illness and death.[54] As in life, so too in death, Bela remains passive, almost inert: 'she was quiet, silent and obedient'. As in *The Demon*, the feminine ideal is in death.

Even the undine acquires some of these attributes. When she comes to accost Pechorin: 'She sat down opposite me quietly and without a word . . . .. Her face was covered with a dull pallor.' (p. 351) It is Mary, however, who is the second icon of suffering, and her tale follows almost exactly that of Bela, albeit without the final fatal stage. When we first *see* her (and, as we know, she is being observed by the narrator Pechorin), she is strolling 'pensively' (p. 364). Rather later, as she is falling in love with her seducer, 'her face became so pensive, so sad' (p. 414). We note the repetitive, limited lexicon, the use of the expressive cliché. Indeed, on the very next page, Pechorin sees Mary sitting iconically at the window again, 'pensively'. Like the undine, Mary has a 'dull pallor' on her face. She is unable to speak, her eyes, as so often, are filled with tears. Soon Mary is quite seriously ill and, yet again, we have a male narrator observing the following statuesque pose, which almost exactly replicates that of Bela: 'She was sitting motionlessly, her head resting on her chest; before her on the little table a book lay open, but her eyes, motionless and full of ineffable sadness, seemed to run over one and the same page for the hundreth time' (pp. 430–1). It may be argued that such repetitiveness is merely a mark of poor technique. Equally, however, the repeated, stock clichés reinforce the interchange-ability, the anonymity of the suffering heroine before the devouring male gaze. Mary, like Bela and many others before her, has become the perfect icon of the woman destroyed.

If anything, Vera fulfils this role even more completely. She has known Pechorin for some time, yet returns for more torment: she is not deceived by his dangerous charms, but is a willing victim to them. Women, it would appear, learn nothing from their suffering. Indeed, none of the women in this novel is allowed a life of her own, each is dependent on the men around her to bestow happiness or torment, or even life itself. Men control their destinies and have the power of life and death. Beyond the framework of the narrative proper, stand the 'dear sirs' who first received this book and who still read it. They too are asked to view women through the eyes, not only of the 'predatory man' Pechorin, but through other, equally proprietory, male gazes. Given all that has been said, we can concur with Pushkin's view of such novels: it is a 'dangerous book' and Pechorin is 'certainly no Grandison'.[55] Rather, Lovelace has found a worthy heir.

5

Nikolay Gogol: The Russian 'Malleus Maleficarum'

All witchcraft comes from carnal lust which is in women insatiable.[1]

In these recurrent fantasies the obscene details are often identical, and their identity sheds some light on the psychological connection between persecuting orthodoxy and sexual prurience. The springs of sanctimony and sadism are not far apart.[2]

That Gogol had difficulty in dealing with women, both in life and in fiction, is no secret.[3] However, in a consideration of women in Russian fiction one can hardly bypass a writer of such importance. He has acquired many reputations: as founder of the so-called 'natural school', as a champion of the oppressed, as a symbolist, a religious writer, a proto-Surrealist and many more such labels have been attached to him and his mysterious, complex works.[4] Despite his own paradoxical sexuality and the general absence of serious portraits of women in his work, much recent interest has been devoted (in the West at least) to problems of sexuality in his fiction, culminating in an extended psychoanalytical study of one short work and an elaborate hypothesis as to his own psycho-sexual motivations.[5] It is against this critical background that any survey of Gogol's female characters must be located. Nevertheless, as the two quotations above are intended to suggest, the image of women that emerges from his fiction was not merely conservative, patriarchal and misogynist, but positively and specifically medieval in orientation. While his male characters mark a new line and are fundamentally different from those of his predecessors and contemporaries (such as Pushkin and Lermontov) both in social origin and imaginative apprehension, they were as influential on the later development of Russian literature, most noticeably in the theme of the 'poor clerk' and the 'underground' of society more generally. On

79

the other hand, his women tend to flicker on the margins, both of the consciousness of the male protagonists and of the fiction itself. Yet an analysis of women from our present perspective will show that, while their role is usually instrumental, this very instrumentality and the form it often takes play a central part in Gogol's fictional world. The main focus for investigation in this chapter will be Gogol's shorter fiction, primarily *Mirgorod* and his so-called *Petersburg Stories*, but I will again begin with a brief look at early works which are relevant to the overall themes of women and sexuality.

1. WOMAN[6]

This early essay (1831) has recently received renewed attention in Gogolian criticism, being read more or less literally as a statement of the author's fundamental views of women,[7] or as a symbolic account of the interplay between the 'masculine' and 'feminine' principles in either gender.[8] Certainly, it has much to tell us that is relevant to an interpretation of the later works, and it contains in outline the image of the female that was to appear. Written in the flamboyant, rhetorical style that Gogol favoured for his essays of the 1830s, it approaches women quite explicitly in terms of archetypes, of absolute purity and goodness, or of abysmal evil. The latter polarity is first considered, in that for the rejected lover Telecles, woman is the incarnation of all evil and poison in the world: indeed, he reproaches his interloctutor, Plato, for misleading other men, for not realising fully the abysmal depths of feminine evil.

Soon, in keeping with the diadic nature of masculinist thinking, the approach lurches to the other polarity, of veneration, as Plato reminds Telecles that when he had loved her he had 'read eternity in the divine features of Alcinoe' (p. 9). This dichotomy was to become paradigmatic for Gogol's later male characters: when loved, a woman is the incarnation of celestial virtue, when the man is rejected he realises the illusion under which he had laboured and she becomes the epitome of evil. As we shall see, the latter state is the truth-seeing one.

In this incarnation, however, woman, the representative of goodness and beauty, is to be worshipped as a holy *object*; she is identified with the 'tender, meek virtues', and the true poet's aim is 'to embody the woman in man' (p. 10). Alcinoe herself now appears.

In keeping with her status as an object of veneration (but also in line with other depictions of women in the period[9]), she is represented pictorially, *iconically*. She is silent and motionless: 'all of her, it seemed, was transformed into *wordless* attention' (p. 11; my italics). Her chest is 'divine', she is the embodiment of all that is goddess-like. Indeed, she becomes virtually a statue, as we learn of her 'marble hand' (p. 11). As for the other writers of the period, the perfect feminine image is one that is petrified. Moreover, the ideal feminine is not merely passive, but instrumental to male requirements. A woman, we have already learned, is essential not in or for herself, but to facilitate *men's* growth, to soften the traditional masculine virtues of 'firmness' and 'courage' (p. 10). She stands not merely silently (indeed, she utters not a word) but, as we saw, *listening* to the words of the teacher. As in the relationship of Sophia and Starodum in *The Minor*, the perfect male/female role division is that of Master/Pupil.[10]

All of these nuances, then, are not the idiosyncrasies of this particular paradoxical writer. However, one detail signals a warning to the observant (male) reader and initiates a theme that is to be repeated. Alcinoe may be the incarnation of the beautiful, but her aura is 'blinding' (p. 11), and the stunned Telecles throws himself at her feet. He is merely the first of the Gogolian heroes to discover that feminine beauty is not redemptive, but highly dangerous. It deprives men of their senses (usually of sight and speech[11]), and is not infrequently the cataclysmic harbinger of devastation and death. Female beauty is always deceptive.

2. IVAN FYODOROVICH SHPONKA AND HIS AUNTIE[12]

2.1. Images of the Male

This early story, first forming part of *Evenings on a Farm near Dikanka*, is 'regarded unanimously by critics as offering the first major foretaste of the art of the mature Gogol'.[13] So too, it encapsulates many of the later themes of feminine evil and danger, as well as offering the first depiction of the typically Gogolian male. Ivan Shponka, like many creations of Russian fiction of the period, is initially identified with a military environment, being a retired army officer. There, in a masculine world without women, he had been rather safer than he is to be in the main body of the story. However, the army setting is initially utilised to emphasise his excessive timidity, and it is this latter trait which was to become the hallmark of the Gogolian hero, particularly those of the Petersburg Stories, most notably Akaky Akakyevich. Shponka reveals himself to be the very opposite of the dashing army officer. He had taken eleven years to be promoted, and does not participate in the usual games of male aggression and competition except that he is, for some reason, fond of setting mousetraps.

This timorousness is exacerbated once he is removed from the army by his fearsome auntie, following his mother's death. No longer safeguarded by other men, he is exposed to the outside world. So often in Gogol this removal from the safety of the enclave, of facing change itself, spells danger. More specifically, the lone male leaves the company of other men and has to encounter the female. His response is to set the pattern, in that his general timidity becomes specifically *sexual* fear. Any suggestion of contact with women of a sexual kind reduces him to confusion and a state bordering on terror. Thus, he happens to observe that the *blondinka* he meets is pretty. After exposing him to a fearsome inquisition, his auntie suggests that he is perhaps thinking of marrying her: 'This proves that you don't know me at all' (p. 207), Shponka replies. The suggestion that he even *might* engage in sexual relations with a woman is offensive. Later he is left alone with the blonde, who we now learn has the virginal name Mashenka. In a parody of the feminine heroine of the period,[14] Shponka lowers his eyes, blushes and sits in silence with her.

Although well into middle age, the Gogolian man is clearly pre-sexual and wishes to remain that way. More than once he is further characterised either directly or indirectly as specifically infantile. He, like his successors in Gogol's fiction, even has difficulty in speaking properly. In general he stammers and babbles incoherently, although he is especially incoherent when any sexual suggestion is made. More often than not he prefers to sit in silence, and when he does form a complete utterance he is 'heartily pleased by the fact that he had uttered such a long and difficult sentence' (p. 205). He is not only pre-sexual, but *pre-linguistic*. In this, too, his behaviour represents a reversal of the patriarchal norm, in which it is men who have control of the discourse, the word.[15] He may claim that his aunt does not understand him, but in this context she does, calling him several times a 'young little child' (pp. 198, 207 and 211). Significantly for our understanding of sexuality in Gogol, he is happiest remaining a child, secure in a world unthreatened by women and any worrying contact with them. So, too, he is clearly terrified of the aggressive, highly 'masculinised' bully Storchenko.

If power (whether linguistic or sexual – and the two often go together–) is removed from the male protagonist, then it is not altogether surprising that it is transferred to the woman. This tale, like so much of Gogol's work, is dominated by terror at this reversal of the norm. In more general terms, the depiction of women in this story is consistently negative.

2.2. Images of the Female

Even before the story proper begins, we have a warning of the dangerous female character. The jolly narrator of this cycle of stories, Rudiy Panko, informs us that the second half of the story will be missing,[16] as it has been destroyed by his wife when baking. She, as one would expect in Gogol, has no name, but is tellingly referred to as *starukha* ('old woman', p. 187), a noun that occurs frequently in Gogol, often as a virtual synonym of 'witch'. Thus, the story is overshadowed by the unnamed woman's destruction of the word. Although supernatural forces may be *seemingly* absent from this story (unlike the others in the collection[17]), witches are never far from Gogol's world. It is no accident that Storchenko, when threatening to thrash the innkeeper if he is bitten by bedbugs, calls her an 'old witch' (p. 193). At the other polarity are the seemingly harmless women that Shponka encounters at dinner at Storchenko's. They are characterised by irredeemable stupidity, speaking either trivial nonsense or remaining silent, as in the case of the two unnamed daughters. When Mashenka does speak in her tête-à-tête with the hapless hero, her speech is inane nonsense.

The dominant female of the story is, of course, Vasilisa Kashporovna, the sarcastically entitled 'Auntie' of the title. Her character and behaviour are also a reversal of all that might be implied in the eponymous, usually affectionate, diminutive. Even before we are offered an extended introduction to her, we learn of her cunning, aggressive behaviour when she virtually orders her nephew out of the army, using lies and deception to achieve her aim. When he arrives at his estate, over which Auntie has taken control, Shponka is physically lifted off the ground in her crushing welcome. Her activities are appropriate to her 'almost gigantic' size (p. 198), although it would seem that nature has made a mistake in rendering her a woman, as she would have been better 'suited by a dragoon's moustaches and long jack-boots' (p. 198). She likes, for example, rowing, hunting and climbing trees. So complete is this role reversal that she remains unmarried. Indeed, no-one had ever dared ask to marry her, 'because *all* men felt some sort of timidity in her presence' (p. 197; my italics). Again, we see a *collective* masculinist point of view emerging. She is, however, not merely a caricature of the dominating stepmother of the fairy-tale, but rather the incarnation of the *false* mother. Instead of caring for her 'child', she dreams up what she knows he fears most of all, namely, a dreaded wife. Again, the extra-textual norm of male/female relations is inverted. Auntie is a ferocious, emasculating harridan, a grotesquely distorted version of her predecessor Prostakova, who also had usurped the 'natural' authority of the patriarchal world and misappropriated a dependant's estate.[18] Within Gogol's own artistic world she is everything that the ideal Alcinoe is not – aggressive, ugly and loathsome, creating not divine inspiration but fear.

However, *both* types of women (and, by implication, all variations within these two poles) are offered as different, but equally terrifying *warnings* to 'all men'. Alcinoe's beauty has the power to blind, while Auntie has the true witch's power (which she shares with Panko's wife and many later variations) of transforming reality, of life and death itself. 'Vasilisa Kashporovna knew how to make *anyone at all* quieter than grass' (p. 197; my italics), we are told in her initial characterisation, which then goes on to inform the reader that she had rendered the drunken miller (the aberrant male), 'without any extraneous means [,] . . . gold, and not a man' (p. 198). Men (and it is specifically men) are turned into vegetation, or inanimate matter, by Auntie, without any external assistance. As we enter Gogol's strange world we encounter three witches, even in a story that is apparently devoid of supernatural forces. Men have been warned.

2.3. Male/Female Relationships

If this story establishes the peculiarly Gogolian version of the essential masculinist diad of destroyer/innocent, then it also offers a basic plot paradigm of his fiction, namely, the power of women to destroy the vulnerable man. Initially, we encounter an apparently 'harmless' version of the traditional theme of the 'hen-pecked' man, the emasculated Shponka being ordered out of the army by the 'masculinised' Vasilisa.[19] It is women who control the world (contrary to all the evidence!). Shponka not only offers no resistance to his aunt, but, as we have already been told, delights in such traditionally feminine activities as sewing on buttons and reading fortune-telling books.[20] He even addresses his aunt as 'gracious sovereign' (p. 192), and she exemplifies her imperial status by not allowing her nephew to interfere in certain areas of the estate. He submissively accepts all this, and this is the secondary level of the story's warning to male readers. Women are so dangerously powerful precisely because men (*'all men'*) are so weak and powerless to defend themselves against these demonic forces.

However, the danger goes even deeper. *Any* encounter with *any* woman is threatening and potentially destructive and, as we shall see, even *seeing* a woman can lead to the destruction of a man. Thus, Shponka's quiet, albeit vegetative, existence is changed on his return to the bruising embrace with Auntie, and, as we have seen, the dumb *blondinka* reduces him to iconic, virginal confusion. However, when his sinister aunt suggests that he should actually marry Mashenka, Shponka's terror is unbounded: ' "I've never been married . . . I absolutely don't know what to do with her," [he] cried in fright' (p. 211). After the blinding in *Woman*, the muting of the hero earlier, we now see a third sensory deprivation when a woman is encountered: Shponka 'stood, as if deafened by thunder' (p. 211). And there is to be no escape for poor little Ivan. He retires to bed only to be visited by a truly horrific vision of the marital state as perceived by the misogynist imagination: 'He feels strange; he doesn't know how to approach her, what to say to her, and he notices that she has a goose's face' (p. 212). He turns away, but there is another wife, grotesquely deformed in the same way. In all directions, wherever he turns, there stands another wife. In his hat, in his pocket, everywhere, wives are to be found, and the defence-less man is powerless before this host of devouring females. His auntie enters the dream to offer the lapidary comment: 'Yes, you must jump, because you're a married man now' (p. 212). Further surreal horrors await him before he awakes, drenched in sweat. There is no explanation of this terror because, of course, the tale has been deprived of its ending by the 'old woman', Panko's *wife*. Wives not only lurk in pockets to terrify men, but they also lurk behind the text itself, controlling the narrative, castrating the very text. And so we are led into Gogol's fictional world down a never-ending tunnel (as in *Taras Bulba*) where wives, or women more generally, cannot be escaped: 'Abandon all hope, ye who enter.'

3. MIRGOROD[21]

First published in 1835 (although *Taras Bulba* underwent a major revision for the *Collected Works* of 1842[22]), *Mirgorod* was the last of Gogol's major works to be set in his native Ukraine and in many ways its four stories provide a valediction to the scenes and themes of his early works. It deals explicitly with the nature of idylls and utopias,[23] and its concluding words, 'It's boring in this world, gentlemen', are an implicit recognition that the 'Golden Age' is dead – forever. The stories offer further explorations of the themes of sexuality and its dangers, and provide a rare positive female portrait, although the criteria for this last judgement are in themselves highly significant, as we shall see.

3.1. Setting

Although each of the four stories has a different physical (and, indeed, temporal) location, they share the same dynamics. A settled, secure existence, based on habitual routines, is eventually destroyed by the intrusion of a disruptive agency. The security of an habitual, placid and loving marital relationship is the given of the opening tale, *Old World Landowners*, while the other three all begin in worlds from which, initially at least, women are excluded. In the last story the scene-setting concerns the doomed relationship of *The Two Ivans*, while the middle two stories, *Taras Bulba* and *Viy*, open in paradigmatic male-only environments, enclaves of sanctuary from dangerous women.

Sexuality is absent from the initial setting of *all* the tales, even if the first one is indeed about a marriage. The marriage, however, as commentators on this story have noted, is a peculiarly, although significantly, asexual relationship.[24] The love of Afanasy and Pulcheriya is based on constancy, habit and routinised practices, especially the consumption of large amounts of food. The couple are in their middle years and have no children. Moreover, they share the same patronymic, which suggests a relationship of brother and sister rather than husband and wife. Indeed, the very success of their relationship is based on this absence of sexual passion. On the first page of the story the narrator informs us that, on entering their world, one can imagine that 'passions, desires and the unquiet issue of the evil spirit which agitate the world do not exist at all' (p. 9). It is a refuge, quite explicitly, from the travails and turmoils of sexuality that torment the world of 'modish frockcoats' (p. 10). The narrator comments later that the 'crackle from burning straw and the illumination make this entrance hall exceedingly pleasant on a winter's evening when you run into it, frozen, from pursuing some brunette or other' (p. 14). More generally, the 'old world' of the couple and their palisaded home recreates imaginatively a lost world of *pre-sexuality*, or even of an earlier age. Their rooms are low, small and very warm, especially their bedroom, so that they, and the lucky guests who are persuaded to stay the night, exist in a womb-like cocoon, which does not change as the years pass by. Their world would seem to be a sanctuary not merely from a sexual life, but from life itself.

Yet their very need to enclose themselves, to cut themselves (and their guests) off from the world of threatening sexuality, shows that their sanctuary is not safe. The secret of their success has been to remain within the enclosure, to refuse to face the dangers of life, and therefore of sexuality. In the end, they both die, for reasons to which we may return. But the paradigm is established, for just as their refuge from danger vanishes, so too the camaraderie of the all-male Cossack *sech'* is destroyed, as is the seminary world from which Khoma Brut, the male protagonist of *Viy* comes. In each of these last two cases the agency is specifically a woman/witch. All the dark forces such beings represent and contain are unleashed upon Khoma and Andriy Bulba once they dare to leave the protective womb. Paradoxically, then, to leave the womb of one woman is to be cast adrift, without defence or protection against all the wives you might find hiding in your pockets or in churches. Even these traditional places of sanctuary are invaded by the demonic monsters which surround women, and lurk within them, in both *Taras Bulba* and *Viy*. Whether men are timid like Shponka, or a scion of the great Bulba, they will be destroyed.

3.2. Images of the Male

In all but the opening story we have the same paradigm as is usual in patriarchal fiction: men are the given. This is particularly so in *Taras Bulba*, where even the female *dramatis personae* remain unnamed, while there are frequent vivid cameos of named but purely incidental male characters.[25] Similarly, the point of view is usually close to the sympathies and experiences of the male characters, as in *Viy*, where we are shown the horrors that Khoma undergoes through his perception of them. Two ideals of the male are presented in the collection, both of which implicitly or explicitly identify this ideal as a man without women. Afanasy is a positive version of Shponka. His mutism is perceived as a deliberate abnegation of the word, an avoidance of the power and self-assertion (at the expense of others) that it implies. In his grief (which we again perceive from his point of view) at the death of Pulcheriya he remains speechless. Because of a combination of his actual age and this sign of infantilism, the loving portrait of Afanasy that the narrator offers identifies the *non-sexual* male as the ideal. More specifically, he is, again like Shponka, frequently referred to as a *child*. Pulcheriya's greatest fear as she awaits death is that no-one will care for him. She begs Yavdokha to look after him 'like her own child' (p. 32), and, later, when Afanasy himself dies, he 'submitted with the will of an obedient child' (p. 40). He can be construed as one version of the ideal male precisely because he knows not women and retains the innocence of pre-sexuality.

Like Shponka also, Afanasy had once been in the army, and this *milieu* provides the other polarity of the ideal male, for, as we see in *Taras Bulba*, the warrior is the zenith of masculinity: 'in a word, the Russian character received here its powerful, wide sweep' (p. 51). Much of the exposition of this (the longest) tale is devoted to an unreserved paean to military might and prowess. In the first scene, Taras informs his sons that all they need is 'an open field and a good steed'; a sabre is 'your mother' (p. 44). For them to become real Cossack men, they must prove themselves in battle: 'it is not fitting for a sensible man to be without battle' (p. 74), the narrator later informs us. Much later we see the braves in action, fighting a doomed battle, perhaps, but fighting like supermen, and the narrator is once more unreserved in his sorrow at the deaths of these braves, whether young or old. Ostap, in particular, is set apart as the icon of the true man, slaying six of the enemy who all attack him at once (p. 174).

The image of true masculinity is not, however, without its particular nuances: it is not all blood, although much of this is shed, and, as we shall see, its shedding is glorified. These nuances, however, present a rather confused image. Taras Bulba, the archetype of the Stern Father,[26] is depicted as deeply religious, yet his Christianity is a vivid mixture of racial and religious bigotry. His sons, Andriy and Ostap, have attended the seminary in Kiev (like Khoma Brut and his friends in *Viy*), but in deference to their

parentage they had shown little interest in books. The education of
the men in the *sech'* itself is equally contradictory. Apart from
some target practice, they seem to need no military training as such,
but gain their expertise in killing from the battle itself. Yet, again,
they are presented not as mindless marauders, but positively as
educated (some of them at least) and loyal servants of the Tsar
(p. 74). But the main emphasis is on their unbridled energy, their
love of freedom, action and, in a word, *kazachestvo*, the Cossack
essence. Action can, of course, take a variety of forms. For these
men, it is usually that of a fairly traditional male type, namely,
drinking and fighting. In the opening scenes Taras, after enjoying a
few drinks with his sons, demands some action: if there is no
fighting to be done, he will go off and start some, and he then
proceeds to break bottles and plates. This motif of unrestrained male
energy, involving heavy drinking and resultant violence, is repeated several times as a positive indicator. All the men are 'as
proud and strong as lions' (p. 70). They devote most of their time to
'revelry', which is a sign of 'the wide expanse of spiritual freedom'
(p. 72). Other related motifs are used to characterise the true man.
Ostap and Andriy must hold back their tears as they part with their
mother (p. 57), while the former endures his 'hellish tortures' as a
captive 'like a giant' (p. 198). All these values may be rather
unoriginal, but they are certainly presented positively.

However, as Karlinsky in particular has noted,[27] there is a rather
darker aspect to this image of masculinity, although it is one which
is depicted just as much as part of the male ideal. Part of the
education of the true man consists of barbaric punishments for any
wrongdoers. Theft was punished by being tied to the 'post of
shame', where each passing Cossack would strike a blow until the
thief died. Others are detailed, although the one that most
impresses the sensitive Andriy (and this 'sensitivity' is to be his
downfall) is that accorded to a murderer, who is buried alive along
with a coffin containing the corpse of his victim (p. 76). Later, the
noble, free Cossacks laugh as their 'Yiddish' victims struggle against
drowning in the Dnieper (p. 91). Having enacted this pogrom, they
attack the equally 'heathen' Poles. They repay their 'former debts' by
'battered infants, breasts severed from women, skin flayed off the
lower legs of those set free' (p. 96). Not only does the narrator accept
these activities as normal manly behaviour, but explicitly states the
effect this has on the young Cossacks: 'In one month the newly
fledged young birds grew up and were completely regenerated and

became men' (p. 97; my italics). Ostap and even Andriy mature to the sights of crashing horses and flying heads.

Such is the true man in this tale, and by negative implication in *Viy* as well, when Khoma vainly tries to bolster his rapidly evaporating courage[28] by saying to himself: 'What am I afraid of? Am I not a Cossack?' (p. 259). In order for men to be such men, to behave like giants, they must avoid at all costs the agency which most weakens and dilutes their manhood, namely sexuality. Again, in the opening scene, Taras asks rhetorically: 'What *devil* should I wait for here? Should I start sowing buckwheat, run the house, look after the sheep and pigs and fool around with the wife? She can be done for: I'm a Cossack, I don't want to' (p. 48; my italics). Domesticity, especially staying in the company of women, can only prevent a man being a man: 'A Cossack is not going to mess about with women' (p. 45), Taras had announced to his weeping wife a little earlier. This motif is also reiterated: the Cossacks, as they enjoy their 'revelry' and, later, their brutal barbarism, are able to do so precisely because they have 'no relatives . . . no family, apart from the free sky and the eternal feast of the soul' (p. 72). Only one Cossack does not learn that women restrain masculinity and, indeed, will destroy it. Andriy, the sensitive son of Bulba, becomes involved with a dangerously alluring female and this contact destroys not only him, but the entire patriarchal *sech'*.

3.3. Images of Women

Although, as we shall see, this is the dominant image of women, other types do occur. In this respect, the opening tale is again markedly different from the other three. Sharing the life of the simultaneously pre- and post-sexual Afanasy is his female equivalent, the significantly named Pulcheriya. Hers is the only sort of female beauty in the collection that does not lead to general destruction and the agonising death of its male recipient. She seems to be simultaneously his sister (as we have noted) and a motherly figure, soothing away every fear and lurking anxiety by constant oral satisfaction from the delicious food she serves several times each day. Indeed, Afanasy is her 'child', and once this sustenance is removed by her death he, and the whole estate, enter a steep decline. Her motherly love is so prized within the overall scheme of the tales (and this writer's work more generally) because it is not exclusively reserved for her partner, but is generously bestowed upon guests who are often persuaded to stay the night to enjoy further her culinary expertise.

Pulcheriya stands apart from almost all the other female characters in this collection for another rather simpler reason. She is the only important female in the tales who has the honour of bearing a name. The maiden/witch in *Viy* and the three women in *Taras Bulba* (Taras's wife, the Polish maiden and her maidservant) all remain emblematically nameless, even if each in different ways plays an important part in the actual plot or the thematic dynamics of these two stories. The various narrators, that is, quite deliberately marginalise women by refusing them this simple narrative reference. This is seen at its most transparent (and ridiculous) at the death of Andriy. As his father shoots him, his lips pronounce 'someone's name' (p. 172). But even at this moment of intense drama her identity is not revealed. Women are seen, as a result, as a collective entity, interchangeable and unindividualised. They may indeed be presented as a group (the tradeswomen bickering amongst themselves at the opening of *Viy*) or as individuals, such as the old woman who becomes the witch later in the same story, but in either case they are profoundly *other*, unnamed and, therefore, unknowable and so unnatural. Consequently, whether seen as positive or negative, they represent a force that is by definition alien to men.[29] In more purely narrative terms, women are not allowed to develop their own story-lines (however much they may disrupt those of men), but are only instrumental in men's destinies and are mere plot functions. Whether mother (*Old World Landowners* and *Taras Bulba*), messenger (*Taras Bulba*), or destroyer (*Taras Bulba* and *Viy*), they flicker on the peripheries of the narrators' – and therefore the readers' – field of vision.

However, more specific images of women do emerge, although, with the exception once more of Pulcheriya, they are not portraits of individuals but stock clichés and stereotypes. The weakness of the portraiture of the female characters in Gogol's work is usually explained in psycho-biographical terms. In the light of this critical tendency it should be emphasised at once that these stereotypes are *not* 'Gogolian', but can, as Pushkin put it, be found on the pages of any novel, including Pushkin's own work, as well as most of the other writers considered elsewhere in this book.

The first such stereotype to emerge in any detail is that of Bulba's wife, who is almost a parody (however sympathetically drawn) of Pulcheriya. This 'poor mother', as she is referred to on more than one occasion, has rather more ancient antecedents in that her image is close to that of the medieval world, most notably exemplified in Russian literature by *The Lay of the Host of Igor*. Her initial presentation is suitably iconic. On hearing that her beloved boys are to stay at home for only one week: 'spoke pitifully, with tears in her eyes, the thin old woman-mother' (p. 44). She does not wish them to depart so soon and complains, but is dismissed by the imperious father Taras: 'She, a woman, knows nothing' (p. 44). While Taras is later throwing bottles and pots around, the 'poor old woman . . . watched sadly, sitting on a bench. She did not dare say anything . . . and no-one could describe all the silent force of her grief which seemed to tremble in her eyes and on her compulsively compressed lips' (p. 48). The repeated lexis, the emphasis on silence, sorrow, passivity and actual physical immobility, are all part of the *topoi* of the suffering woman.[30] She is the archetypal wife and mother of the warrior: abandoned and rejected and left to watch and weep pitifully. The Stern Father abandons her for his horse and sabre, and the sons follow. The neglect is absolute: her face and breasts are prematurely wrinkled and she suffers insults and beatings. Serious efforts are made to engage our sympathy for this 'poor' woman, but her fate is equally seen as inevitable and universal: 'Indeed she was pitiful, as any woman of that distant age' (p. 53).

The image of the mother is one that is reiterated in this story as the quintessence of suffering femininity: indeed, within the framework of this stereotype this is a tautology. As the men leave for the exclusively male domain of the *sech'* , this tautology is, in fact, laid bare: she is 'the mother, weak as a mother' (p. 56). Having established the nexus of suffering motherhood as an icon of pathos, the narrator proceeds to utilise it as a point of reference throughout the tale. Thus, when the Cossacks leave Zaporozh'e to plunder, loot and mutilate, their essential goodness is shown as they bid 'Farewell, our mother' (p. 94) to their homeland. Even the demonic Polish maiden invokes the image of her own 'old woman' mother (p. 105) to plead with Andriy for food. The iconic mother acts, that is, as the voice of conscience amidst death and destruction, whether caused by the men themselves or enacted upon them by the agency of the woman. So, too, amidst the scenes of battle, the same image is invoked to emphasise the tragic pathos of these fallen young: 'Not for one Cossack will an old mother sob, beating her decrepit breasts with her hands' (p. 162). The repeated and repetitive epithet (old), the emphasis on physical decay, merely reinforce the stereotypical nature of the image.

If this image is cleary conceived of as positive (for all the contradictions within it), then the more general view of women in the cycle is indubitably and profoundly negative. As so often,[31] women are animalised by the similes attached to them. Thus, 'old woman' Bulba, 'with fervour, with passion, with tears, like a steppe gull, hovered over her children' (p. 54). This image, again evoking the medieval tradition, is positive; the next is less flattering. When her family finally abandons her she races after them 'with all the lightness of a wild goat' (pp. 56–7). As one might expect, the 'old woman' of *Viy*, the witch, moves 'with the swiftness of a cat' (p. 222), and emphasises her unnatural animality by first riding and then being ridden by the hapless Khoma. The earlier incarnation of witchcraft, the Polish *pannochka*,[32] is no less stereotyped, although, like so many creations of the patriarchal imagination, the stereotyping is mixed and confusingly paradoxical. She appears to Andriy in a confused half-dreaming, half-conscious state, with her 'fine hands, eyes, laughing lips, thick, nut-dark hair curling down over her breasts' (p. 106). When he is led to her, she is found in a house set apart from the others, described like an enchanted castle (pp. 116–7). She is finally encountered and her description is a generalised list of stock clichés of the devastatingly beautiful woman. Andriy 'stood motionless before her' (p. 119). Despite all the emphasis on her *mature* beauty, she calls herself a 'weak woman' and later obeys him 'like a child' (pp. 119–20). Her pose is, once more, iconic: 'She lowered her eyes; the lids, framed by lashes as long as arrows, moved over them like fine, snowy semi-circles' (p. 119). The iconography is made explicit when she weeps at her future fate and, later, was 'momentarily dumbfounded, like a fine statue' (p. 125). She is called, variously, 'child', 'maid', 'statue', '*tsaritsa*'.

These clashing stereotypes are not the product simply of poor technique, but contain an important theme which is later made explicit by Taras in a powerful oxymoron. After learning of the fate that has befallen his sensitive son, he recalls the cunning deceit he has all too often encountered in women and goes on to remark: 'great is the power of a weak woman' (p. 132). Herein lies the danger for the unwary male. Just as the beauty of 'woman' is 'blinding', so the apparent frailty of the *pannochka* (or, by implication, any other woman) disguises the deadliness that underlies this mask.[33] Indeed, she is clearly a similarly dangerously beautiful woman. In a pre-prologue to the tale that is interpolated as part of Andriy's education, we learn of an earlier encounter with the 'splendid young Polish woman' (p. 63). She is, of course, unnamed, and is described in the classic iconic, statuesque pose favoured in the literature of the time:[34]

> He [Andriy] raised his eyes and saw standing at the window a beauty, the like of which he had never seen before: black-eyed and white, like snow, illuminated by the morning pinkness of the sun. She was laughing heartily and her laughter lent a glittering force to her *blinding beauty*.   (p. 62; my italics).

From the first encounter, Andriy is deprived of his senses, just as he is later to be deprived of his life. The description is absolutely stock: frozen in a fixed position, apprehended by the male gaze,[35] and although purity is hinted at in the banal simile, it is the hidden danger that is the lasting impression.

Implicitly (by her concealed power to transform human life) and explicitly, she is a demonic force. Taras refuses at first to believe the first reports of Andriy's apostasy under her influence: 'to believe . . . that his own son could have sold his faith and *his soul*' (p. 134; my italics). He curses 'the Polish woman who had bewitched his son' (p. 144), and, moreover, who had led to the destruction of the greatest good in the world, the devoted all-male brotherhood of the *sech*'. The sexually attractive woman, then, or even the heavenly beauty (*Woman*), has the power to rob men of their senses, to cause them to sell their souls (to the devil, one presumes) – in a word (as Gogol so often put it), to bewitch them. If she is only implicitly a witch, then there is no question as to the identity of the female in *Viy*, who is a mixed stereotype made manifest in that she is simultaneously an 'old woman' (p. 219) and a beautiful young woman. 'Aha, yes she's a witch' (p. 222) mutters Khoma to himself as he is ridden at a furious gallop across the fields. By turn she robs him of physical strength (his masculinity), his sanity and leads to his death. She has the power to turn night into day, and even after death controls his destiny. As the tale progresses there is much discussion of this second *pannochka* (all women are interchangeably devilish), as to whether she has had dealings with the Devil, how one can spot a witch, and tales of how the *pannochka* had eaten babies and drunk their blood. In the end the 'material concerning witches became inexhaustible' (p. 246). The story of female evil and, more specifically, of their witchcraft is a never-ending one. One character (the *named* Dorosh) claims that it is impossible to tell which woman might be a witch: 'even if you read all the psalters, you won't find out' (p. 242). By implication, then, *all* women might be witches, and, equally, there can be no defence against them for they, once more, are an unknowable force. Even the Word of the Lord cannot protect Khoma, or any other man.

In his attempts to control women, Pechorin in *A Hero of Our Time* does not seem to mind causing their deaths.[36] In this cycle of tales, because the threat to men from women is so much more elemental and universal, so too the measures that may be used against them are even more death-dealing. Taras imagines what he might do to the woman who had emasculated his son in details of shocking sadism:

And he would have fulfilled his oath; ignoring her beauty, he would have dragged her by her thick, luxuriant plait, would have dragged her behind him across the entire field, among all the Cossacks. Her wonderful breasts and shoulders, equal in their splendour to the unmelting snows that cover the mountain peaks, would have been battered against the ground, becoming bloodied and covered with dust. He would have carried off parts of her luxuriant, splendid body.   (pp. 144–5)

This description of despoiled beauty would seem to be unmatchable in its prurient intensity. Yet there is a clear echo of it in *Viy*, where several of the details replicate those attached to the *pannochka* of *Taras Bulba*: 'Before him [Khoma] lay the beautiful woman with a dishevelled luxurious plait, with lashes as long as arrows. Insensibly she had flung out on both sides her white naked arms, her eyes, filled with tears, looking upwards' (pp. 224–5). Later, as Khoma reviews her corpse at greater leisure in the church, her beauty is equally intense. As so often, the greatest beauty achieved by a woman is in death.[37] Moreover, men must torture and kill women, and we are invited to gaze on these deathly images because women must be exterminated to be controlled. However, this version of the patriarchal fantasy is even more terrifying, because even in death they return to haunt and betray men.

That women are so dangerous is emphasised by this repeated imagery and the seeming universality of witchcraft amongst women. These negative views are further reinforced by being shared by almost all men who express an opinion on the subject, including, of course, the narrators. Even in the tranquil, asexual world of *Old World Landowners*, we are reminded of the wearisome nature of sexuality by the narrator, in his comment on the *brunetka*. Taras Bulba, as we have also seen, shares this view, laughing at the alleged stupidity of his wife and noting the hidden power of 'the weak woman': 'she [woman] has ruined many strong men' (p. 133). Even the despised 'Yid' Yankel is allowed honorary membership of this collective point of view, observing that 'even if they [beauties and noblewomen] have nothing to eat, they'll still buy pearls' (ibid.).[38] The misogynist chorus is especially vocal in the discussion of women which precedes Khoma's second dreadful night alone with the dead witch. Many stories are offered about what women may do to men. The *pannochka* has had such a devastating effect on one unfortunate: 'she so bewitched him, the man was quite lost, he became a complete woman' (p. 244). Shortly, this view again becomes a general principle: 'for women are such a stupid people' (p. 245). Constantly, that is, men attempt to defuse the power of women, in this instance by ridicule and contempt. On the last page of *Viy*, bell-ringer Khalyava claims that Khoma had died because he had been afraid: if he had not been afraid the witch could have done nothing to him. He adds: 'One only has to cross oneself and spit right on her tail, and nothing'll happen. I already know all this. After all, all the women back in Kiev, who sit around at the bazar – they're all witches' (p. 263).

In theory, then, because all women are witches men should be able to deal with them. But just as Shponka cannot escape the universal presence of wives, so too the men of the old Ukraine and their entire world cannot escape the devastation that women, especially sexual women, wreak.

3.4. Plot Situations

As already briefly noted in section 3.1., the dynamics of each of these four stories are remarkably similar. An established world (usually involving only men as actants) is destroyed, never to return, and the agency is almost always female.[39] In *Old World Landowners* the initial emphasis in the exposition is on stasis, which is presented as a value in itself. It is a secure, repetitive, habitual life where life and sexuality do not seem to intrude. The generalised, typifying, narrative style, the emphasis in their economy on preserving organic matter, reinforce this mode. Mysterious pregnancies do occur, but the disruption that these might cause is avoided, in that the sexuality that is obviously involved is banished to unnamed (as always) young girls. However, this threatening note is a harbinger of things to come. The pregnancies and equally strange thefts indicate that even this safe, non-sexual environment cannot be protected against life, sexuality and, *therefore*, death.

Finally, an event – single and non-habitual – occurs, and the old world of womb-like security must go. The beloved old grey cat (female) disappears. This would have been bad enough in itself, but mysteriously and almost magically, sexuality now enters the palisade. Dangerous, rapacious male cats appear, who kill 'young sparrows in their very nests' (p. 29). The birthplace itself is destroyed: nowhere is safe. It is these sexually active and aggressive cats who have 'lured away' Pulcheriya's cat, 'just as a detachment of soldiers dupe a stupid peasant woman' (p. 29). The military motif, the implicit reference to rape, announce the peripeteia. Once more, quite incidentally, women are shown to be stupid. For no obvious reason, this small incident destroys the old world. It is, indeed, significant that the event is so insignificant. In Gogol's fiction, almost always, one transient whiff of sexuality can destroy the entire secure world. The devastating effect is emphasised here, as it is to be in *Taras Bulba*, by the prolonged expositions which had been, and will be recounted in loving, almost reverential detail. Pulcheriya realises the inevitability of her fate and declines rapidly to an unresisted death. This, too, is a point that is to be reiterated, especially in *Viy*: the destructive force of sexuality *cannot* be resisted, for all the brave words of the likes of bell-ringer Khalyava, and this is why it is so dangerous.

Taras Bulba follows a very similar set of plot dynamics, although the demonic power of the woman in the sexual scenario is laid bare. The lengthy exposition in this instance portrays the warrior clans of the *sech'* as the finest of Russians, and presents military life as the zenith of manhood. However, it could be argued that the exposition also shows that the given world of men contains within it its own destruction. Andriy's earlier encounter with the *pannochka* is outlined, as we know, and the plot mechanism is activated by Taras's blood-lust, in that he goes forth seeking a war. Nevertheless, the complication is undoubtedly caused by the agency of women. Firstly, the messenger woman comes to lead Andriy through the strange underground tunnel, and the transition to the devilish world of sexuality (and ensuing apostasy) is heavily marked. Andriy steals his own father's food, wanders as if in a trance, and at dawn no cocks crow. These ominous portents are piled on top of one another during the very lengthy and overdetermined peripeteia which now ensues. Andriy emerges into a Catholic (therefore, heathen) church, with images of the Madonna, to be met by a monk. Andriy is semi-conscious, which also reinforces the witch-like nature of the *pannochka*, whom he finally reaches and to whom he gives the food he had stolen from the one who had given him life. The extended treatment of the peripeteia emphasises how heinous Andriy's crime is: 'he became indignant at his Cossack nature' (p. 119). As the young couple finally seal their illicit passion, the shocked narrator lays bare the meaning of the previous twenty-odd pages: 'And the Cossack was lost!' Taras will curse 'both the day and the hour in which he gave life, to his own shame, to such a son' (p. 126).

The conclusion of the peripeteia is also marked by an abrupt return to the Cossack camp, which is *already* in some disarray. The peripeteia is given such detailed treatment precisely because of the devastating effects it is to have. As if by magic (or, rather, witchcraft) the contact of one man with a woman has emasculated all men. The patriarchy has been subverted and now cannot be restored. Indeed, it is precisely at this juncture that Taras and Yankel (who reports Andriy's crime) discuss the deceptive weakness of women and their concealed 'great power'. This merely confirms the central theme of this parabolic tale: a *single*, unnamed 'weak woman' destroys all the power and majesty of this marvellous patriarchy which had been so eulogised in the exposition. Men, indeed, must avoid all contact with women.

The tragic demise of the male collective is further emphasised by the heroic, but also pathetic events of the two grim battles which form the denouement. The brave Cossacks fight with superhuman strength (which is recounted in grandiose Homeric similes[40]), but, young or old, they fall one by one, while Andriy actively supports the enemy, although he too dies, as does Ostap. Towards the end of the awful account of mayhem and destruction, Taras 'looked around: all was new in the *sech*' all the old comrades had died' (p. 177). In the end, Taras, having been led through the backstreets of Warsaw to witness Ostap's gruesome death, leads a feeble uprising for vengeance and he too is caught, to be burned alive. The patriarch and his patriarchy are dead, destroyed by a witch.

Viy's plot is equally parabolic and similar in overall structure, although its rhythms are importantly different. The exposition once more details an exclusively male world (the Kiev seminary), but now the presentation is much more perfunctory and not eulogistic. Very quickly, indeed, the community is dispersed as Khoma and his young friends set off for the summer vacation. Already, away from their protective environment, they are at risk. Soon Khoma is separated and alone, exposed, with no protection whatsoever, to the 'old woman'. Even his prayers are in vain against her power. After the nightmarish (and explicitly) sexual experiences with her, the plot rhythm becomes repetitive, night alternating with day, danger/sexuality giving way initially to longer periods of sanctuary among all-male company. This rhythmic nature of the plot, its dream-like repetitions and plot rhymes, emphasises the inescapability of the hero's situation and ultimate fate. Prayers, pleas for release, attempted escape, all prove futile: in the end he must return to the church to say prayers over the dead *pannochka*/witch, irrespective of his own wishes. Indeed, it is not explained why *he* was chosen to perform this ghoulish task.

Gradually the plot rhythm is eroded and then inverted. Female evil is initially locked away at night and only one man is subjected to it, but now night begins to invade day and all men seem to have had dealings with witches, or know of them. Khoma sleeps through until evening, and in the inn a game is played where the winner is allowed to ride another man, echoing the initial encounter between Khoma and the witch.[41] The tempo accelerates even more; Khoma goes grey in one night. This man is being physically destroyed, and the community of men is powerless to defend him. Indeed, it is precisely a man, the *pannochka*'s father, who returns him to his task. Even the Almighty Father, through His recited words, fails to prevent the 'hellish' night of the third visit. Khoma is killed by sheer terror, and although there is a brief, daytime epilogue in Kiev, it does not mark a return to harmony. Once again, a single initial contact with a sexual woman destroys the man and the community from which he came.

3.5. Male/Male Relationships

It is often argued that the central, unifying theme of *Mirgorod* is the collapse of the old order, the destruction of the old communities. In more specific terms, the last three tales show the devastation of what is presented as the *summum bonum*, the comradeship between men, the traditional patriarchy. *Taras Bulba* opens with the father welcoming his two sons home, and the patriarchal nature of their relationship is immediately signalled in the first scene as the older man (jokingly) fights his sons for supremacy. The three men proceed indoors and sit down to toast their martial successes, with their mother, of course, merely in attendance. The good-natured rivalry between parent and sons does not conceal the essential comradeship amongst them, and once they join the other Cossacks *tovarishchestvo* becomes the object of fulsome, and repeated eulogies. Scenes of pure joy follow as men dance and drink together (in *Viy* they kiss). Primitive communism forms part of the ethos, while disputes are settled on the spot by fist-fights.

Significantly, reiterated and almost ritualistic defences of comradeship occur mainly after the peripeteia, again emphasising the heinous crime committed. Kasyan Bovdyug speaks at a war council for the first time in years: 'The first duty and first honour of a Cossack is to observe comradeship' (p. 148). After the *sech*' has been literally split in two, the patriarch Taras addresses to his troops a highly charged paean to the same value: 'there are no bonds *holier* than comradeship' (p. 159; my italics). As the battle reaches its tragic conclusion, he is saved from capture by the heathen Poles by a 'faithful comrade' (p. 177), while his only concern now is to attempt to save Ostap. In a plot rhyme with Andriy, he too goes into Poland, thereby illustrating the contrast between comradeship and his errant son's treachery.

Andriy's crime has many dimensions to it, as we have seen. He abandons himself to the witch and sexuality, which leads to his own death and, by the power of witchcraft, to the destruction of the patriarchy. His transgression, though, has a more specific locus, in that he contravenes the Law of the Father, the implicit authority that underlies and is implicit within the patriarchy. As Tony Tanner puts it (in a discussion of *Mort D'Arthur*): 'The breaking of one bond (by adultery) portends the dissolution of all bonds. From then on, everything in Arthur's kingdom does, indeed, fall apart. Individual transgression leads ultimately to social disintegration.'[42] And this is precisely what happens here. Andriy steals bread from his own father, and once he has known the *pannochka* he explicitly rejects his father and the social order the latter embodies: 'But what to me are my father, my comrades and fatherland? . . . My fatherland is you!' (p. 125). At first Taras refuses to believe that his 'own son' (p. 134) could have done this, but once he is convinced, he disowns him and hunts him down. The errant son must be punished by the Stern

Father. Finally they meet on the field of battle and the oedipal implications are made clear. Andriy returns to an earlier age 'like a schoolboy': 'And he saw before him only his fearful father' (p. 172). Like an icon of femininity, Andriy stands silently, with his eyes cast down. Taras in turn, lays bare the power of the stern patriarch: 'I gave you life, I too will kill you!' (p. 172). The gesture, however, is pyrrhic. Even though the father sheds the blood of the son, this biblical echo is not enough to save the doomed community.[43] Indeed, man is now destroying man: the radiant scenes of singing, drinking and dancing are inverted. It is fitting, therefore, that the final tale concerns the feud between two men who fall out over a mere bagatelle. Women play some part in this,[44] but, as in *A Hero of Our Time*, the concluding story is primarily devoted to men who are left alone to decide the affairs of the world. Far from restoring the lost brotherhood, they destroy their friendship and man is set against man. *Mirgorod* is, indeed, a valedictory work, a sad farewell to the lost world of the patriarchy.

4. ST PETERSBURG TALES[45]

Although most of these tales were written at much the same time as *Mirgorod*, they present a fundamentally different world. Country is replaced by city, the south by the north, the Ukraine by Russia, the past by the present. The former work laments the loss of traditional communities (particularly the patriarchy), while the latter presents the debased and trivialised world of individuals. There are no communities in this harsh modern world and the individual man is abandoned to face (or escape) reality alone.[46] However, for all the fundamental differences between these two groups of stories, the image and devastating power of women remains much the same. Witches are as common in St Petersburg as in Mirgorod and men are as frequently destroyed.

The image of St Petersburg itself acts as a powerful motif in all the stories. From the opening description of Nevsky Prospekt in the keynote story of that title, we find ourselves in a place of fragmentation. On this boulevard one encounters not even entire people, but metonymical parts of them – moustaches, side-whiskers, ladies' smiles and attractive waists. It is on this thorough-fare that Piskaryov is to be bewitched, while Akaky Akakyevich loses his beloved overcoat on one of the seemingly endless, immense squares of this artificial city. Both these events occur at night, and the dim nocturnal settings, 'when the devil himself lights the lamps' (p. 57), are another recurrent, distorting motif. The basic given of all the stories is, as was usual in *Mirgorod*, men, although this time it is usually a solitary, lonely male who lacks family and friends, let alone the larger world of comradeship. Women flicker on the margins, and even in the longest story, *The Portrait*, they play a minimal (if negative) role and are absent from the second part with its important messages about art and purity. Indeed, what scenes of fellowship that do exist between men are parodies of the grand world of the *sech'*. After the extended evocation of the city's dominant thoroughfare, *Nevsky Prospekt* opens with two men strolling together in the evening. However, Pirogov and Piskaryov have almost nothing in common and they go their separate ways at once, never to meet again. Their only unifying link is, significantly, that they each see a woman on the avenue whom they then pursue, the one to his death, the other to a sound thrashing. What links these two men is their susceptibility to female charms (in both the original and more modern meanings of this word) and to the dysphoric denouement to which this susceptibility inevitably leads. Two of the stories, *The Diary of a Madman* and *The Overcoat*, are set in the alienating world of the St Petersburg bureaucracy. Again the image of male fellowship is debased. Poprishchin, the madman, is isolated from his fellows and has no apparent contact with them at all, while one of the most celebrated scenes in *The Overcoat* is the persistent tormenting of the male protagonist Akaky Akakyevich by his colleagues, culminating in the 'humanitarian' cry against this cruelty by a new clerk. The scene of the party to toast Akaky's new overcoat is also a bathetic parody of the 'revelry' of *Taras Bulba*. In this latter version, the *bonhomie* is forced, hypocritical and very short-lived as Akaky finds his precious new possession on the floor as he leaves. If *Mirgorod* is a valediction to the apparently lost (or rather destroyed) patriarchy, then, logically enough, there are only pathetic vestiges of it in the present. So, too, the image of the Stern Father so notably represented by Taras receives a degraded modern version in the Important Personage, whom Akaky petitions for his lost overcoat, and who achieves a minimalist kind of spiritual redemption at the end of the story.[47] Just as Taras disowns and then slays his son for sexual treachery, so too the Important Personage demands to know whether Akaky has visited a 'disorderly house' (p. 24); indeed, he *had* been guilty of an equally minimalist transgression of the sexual order to which we may return. There is a more noble representative of the type in the artist's father who appears in Part Two of *The Portrait* to utter lapidary statements on the need for purity and integrity in the artist. In general, however, these tales merely confirm the elegiac tone at the end of *Mirgorod*. Man is set against man: the patriarchy is dead. Nevertheless, as we shall see, women are still very deadly for the *individual* male.

4.1. Plot Situations

According to Karlinsky: 'When catastrophes do overtake the men in the St. Petersburg stories, women (real ones or surrogates) are indirectly responsible in four cases out of six.'[48] Given the 'magical' way we have seen witchcraft work, and as it continues to work even in this modern world, the word 'indirectly' may need to be reconsidered. Even in *The Nose*, the most 'illogical' of the stories, where there appears to be no explanation for this male's ('Major' Kovalyov) misfortune, a woman may be implicated, in the shape of Mrs Podtochina. Certainly, Kovalyov himself is of the opinion that it was 'none other' (p. 86) than this mother of the daughter he did not wish to marry who had 'punished' him in this way.

The more common plot paradigm that occurs in these tales is, however, a variant of that of *Taras Bulba* and *Viy*. In *Nevsky Prospekt* and *The Diary of a Madman*, in particular, men pursue women and suffer for it. The plot of the first of these two opens with a perverted version of the quest for pure beauty, and although the plot almost immediately bifurcates, the dynamics remain much the same. When Piskaryov sees the apparently divine beauty on Nevsky Prospekt: 'He trembled all over and did not believe his eyes' (p. 20). Again, we have an inverted form of the power of the male gaze: instead of giving him control of the woman, he begins virtually to hallucinate: 'The pavement moved beneath him, the carriages with their galloping horses seemed motionless, the bridge stretched out and broke at its arc, a house stood upside down' (p. 20). 'And all this was produced by one glance, one turn of a pretty head' (p. 20). The surreal images are enough to tell us, the watchful male readers, that Piskaryov is already lost, *bewitched*. The aftermath of this encounter reinforces the magical nature of the event. Piskaryov follows the unnamed woman to her 'home', which turns out to be a brothel. Piskaryov, echoing other male recipients of these fateful and fatal charms, is first deprived of his senses: 'Not hearing, not seeing, not listening, he was carried after the light trace of these splendid *little feet'* (p. 20; my italics). He attempts to stop himself, but even his will, his control of his body, has been stolen from him: *'An irresistible force* and the alarm of all his feelings hurried him on' (p. 20; my italics). And all this had happened 'in one instant' (p. 21). One look, one second of contact with a woman, and the man is doomed.

The bewitchment motif is further underscored as he reaches the brothel: 'The staircase whirled and his swift dreams whirled with it' (p. 21). They enter the house together and the magical transition, strange images, the as yet unexplained identity of the nameless apparition, all lend these scenes not only on air of mystery but of enchantment. Piskaryov 'at this moment was pure and chaste, like a maidenly youth' (p. 21). He is like a medieval knight, pursuing the divine image of feminine beauty into an enchanted castle, where he hopes to find the very Holy Grail. The fairy-tale resonances of these scenes are to be later replicated in the actual dream sequence which follows Piskaryov's epiphanic discovery. A liveried lackey appears to collect this parody Cinderella to take him to a ball in the waiting carriage. The hapless and powerless male is carried off at the behest of the waiting woman, and the ball is then depicted in generalised, literally dream-like, terms.

The peripeteia, then, is framed by two equally dream-like sequences, each with strong fairy-tale resonances. This framing device shows how central this event is, and how devastating its consequences are to be. As in *Taras Bulba,* one contact with a woman reshapes the rest of the entire story. Similarly, the event centres on the question of much of eighteenth- and nineteenth-century literature, the issue of a young woman's virtue.[49] In the usual paradigm of this plot, the principal issue at stake is whether the virtuous heroine will withstand the assaults upon her. Here the question is stated in a rather different way. The discovery involves a simple 'truth' adumbrated in earlier works: female beauty and apparent innocence are a mask for sexual danger. Here the reversal, which is, of course, the key element in any peripeteia, could hardly be more absolute. The Madonna is a whore. It is also highly significant that this discovery on the part of the bewitched Piskaryov involves the two polarities that had long been traditional in diadic patriarchal thinking.[50] This reversal is explicitly stated in the narrator's sympathetic relation of Piskaryov's point of view: 'She could have been an invaluable pearl, the whole world, all the richness of her passionate spouse: she would have been a splendid quiet star in the unnoticed family circle' (p. 24). Instead, she is specifically a demonic emanation: 'but alas! she was some awful will of the infernal spirit which desires to destroy the harmony of life' (p. 25).

Piskaryov's harmony of life is, indeed, devastated. The enchantment, followed by the discovery that the pure woman masks a drunken, grinning whore, deprives him of his sanity and in the end his life. His decline is rapid. He cannot bear reality any longer, procures opium to induce a dream-like state which is now the only one he can tolerate, and finally cuts his own throat with an apparently trembling hand. There follows a brief, pathetic epilogue which laments the lot of 'poor Piskaryov', 'the victim of insane passion'. Nothing, of course, is said of the future life of the woman produced by the 'infernal spirit', who, as in *Viy* and *Taras Bulba*, remains unnamed, a mere cypher of the destructive female sexuality which can turn the whole world upside down and destroy a man by 'one glance, one turn of a pretty head'. There then ensues a contrapuntal coda where we are offered a low-life farcical variation on this tragic theme. Although Pirogov escapes with nothing worse than a sound thrashing, the theme and plot-structure are the same. On Nevsky Prospekt a named man, Pirogov, espies an unnamed, unknown woman who takes his fancy, and, consequently, is open to pursuit. The *blondinka* turns out to be the wife of a German Schiller. Unperturbed by her marital status, the parody rake Pirogov continues his amorous pursuit, only to be caught *in flagrante*, about to kiss her 'fine little foot'.[51] Both plots illustrate a similar point: men who deal with available (or even unavailable) pretty young women will be punished.

Other stories in the cycle offer further variations in different keys. In *The Portrait* there is no amorous intrigue as such, but the agent of the destruction of Chartkov's talent is the unnamed, aristocratic *dama*. We are told later in the story that the 'strange portrait [of the title] was the cause of his perversion' (p. 142), but there is a clear peripeteia in his attitude to his art after the intervention of this woman who commissions him to paint a flattering portrait of her daughter, the empty-headed Lise. The mother is another witch in disguise: 'The aristocratic lady completely *charmed* him' (p. 125; my italics). Again the change is made explicit. Previously he had looked on such 'creatures' and their world as inaccessible. Now he was invited into their homes, was painting a society portrait. Soon he has completely betrayed his talent, 'the most precious gift of God' (p. 170). When it is already far too late he realises what he has done and, like Piskaryov, he goes insane and dies. The demonic portrait may be the ultimate cause of his destruction, but the agent of his downfall is, once more, an unnamed feminine cypher.

The Diary of a Madman returns to the tragic plight of the man who is the victim of feminine charms. The female look is again the catalyst. The director's daughter Sophie is glimpsed by the narrator and protagonist Poprishchin, alighting from her carriage: 'How she glanced to right and left, how she flashed her brows and eyes . . .. O Lord, my God! I was lost, quite lost' (p. 238). This contact acts not as a peripeteia in this story but as the starting-point. His obsession is specifically with Sophie. He is reprimanded for having the audacity to pursue the director's daughter, and it is when he learns that she is to be married that he finally topples over into complete insanity. It is at this point that he creates the compensatory fantasy of Spain, of which he imagines he is the missing king. A central feature of his ravings is his virulent denunciation of Sophie for her 'treachery', to which we may return. Eventually Poprishchin finds himself in 'Spain', that is, a lunatic asylum, and the pathetic denouement and the plot which has preceded it are thus strongly reminiscent of the first section of *Nevsky Prospekt*. A lonely, vulnerable man glimpses a woman in a public place (a locus of danger as in *Mirgorod*); she 'bewitches' him and then 'betrays' him for not conforming to his idealised image. Men in the world of St Petersburg may wish to control women, but are instead destroyed by them and their dangerous charms, ending up dead, thrashed or insane.

4.2. Images and Roles of Women

The majority of female characters in these tales share the same rather odd common factor as those in *Mirgorod*: they have no names. Both targets for male fantasy in *Nevsky Prospekt* are nameless, as are the mother in *The Portrait*, and Akaky Akakyevich's mother and landlady in *The Overcoat*. Their identity is consequently either purely instrumental to male goals or visions, or else defined by their relationship to a named male character. Groups of women, which are significantly very rare in this fictional world, are equally unnamed, as are the whores who share the brothel with Piskaryov's nemesis. Consequently, women as a collective unit are quite deliberately marginalised, removed to the periphery of the text and the reader's perception so that it is difficult even to remember them, let alone talk about them. They are, virtually by definition, the

Other, pure signs of either the ideal or the unknowable chaos that lurks both behind the façades of the St Petersburg buildings or, more dangerously, within men themselves.[52]

When women are accorded the same status as men in being named, there is quite often a hidden insult in that the names are frivolously foreign.[53] The empty-headed daughter in *The Portrait* is Lise (which even appears in Roman script in the Russian text), while the object of Poprishchin's fantasies is named with bitter irony Sophie (also in Roman script). Effectively these two women are denounced as of dubious merit by their very names. In *The Overcoat* another female of dubious repute, the mistress of the Important Personage, is clearly of foreign extraction – Karolina Ivanovna.[54] As we have already noted, it is a mark of his potential redemption that he rejects her and returns to the safety of his Russian family, implicitly echoing the havens of *Mirgorod*.

A similar use of foreign as equivalent to spurious or dangerous, is the word *dama*.[55] This type of woman is peculiarly St Petersburgan, usually high society and inevitably associated with the high-society world of glamour, a world where deceit and illusion are the norm. Piskaryov imagines that his Madonna must be a 'society lady (*dama*)' (p. 16), because of the expensive cloak she wears. The attentive reader would be forewarned that her appearances flatter to deceive the young 'shy, timid' artist Piskaryov. The society woman who tempts Chartkov away from his true path is also referred to merely as *dama*. She it is who introduces a whole series of sitters, both male and female, although the majority are an undifferentiated group of *damy* who equally wish merely for a flattering portrait which, particularly within the context of this story, is the very emblem of a deceitful, glamorous (and, therefore, demonic) illusion. So, too, as Akaky goes to meet his nemesis he glances at a naughty picture, which he imagines is of French origin (p. 198), and just before the actual theft of his beloved overcoat (an event which is to lead to his death) he all but chases after 'some *dama* or other, who like lightning, passed by' (p. 200). Society women, well-dressed and deceiving, are merely a generic category, alien to the true Russian spirit and as dangerous as the equally foreign *pannochka* type of *Mirgorod*.

These tales also feature a type adumbrated in *Shponka* and equally foreign in orientation, the dumb *blondinka* (to match the tiring *brunetka* of *Old World Landowners*[56]). This group is less glamorous than the *dama*, but no less deceptive or dangerous. Their chocolate-box prettiness (the prototype in Russian literature being Olga in *Yevgeny Onegin*) lures not the sensitive artist, but the vulgarians. Thus, the German Frau that Pirogov pursues is referred to not by name, of course, but by this generic category. The narrator's account of her echoes Pirogov's own pejorative appraisal: 'This blonde was a light, quite interesting little creature' (p. 40). Kovalyov in *The Nose* is enamoured of a similar type. Before he remembers that he has no nose and therefore is ineligible to court anyone, he approaches a young woman 'as light as a pastry', glimpsing beneath her hat 'her bright white little chin and part of her cheek, shadowed by the first spring rose' (p. 68). As in the opening description of *Nevsky Prospekt*, women are atomised and the repeated lexis ('light') emphasises the interchangeability of these objects of the predatory male.[57]

Just as the *damy* are the essence of deceitful feminine charms, the *blondinki* represent women in love with appearances, particularly objects, clothes and social events. Pirogov's *blondinka* is first espied by the greedy male gaze looking into shop-windows at 'sashes, kerchiefs, earrings, gloves and other bagatelles, ceaselessly twirling round' (p. 40). Her rotating movements emphasise her empty-headed appraisal of the mere surface of *things*. The two types often, indeed, go in pairs, as in this case or as in the mother and daughter of *The Government Inspector*. Just such a pair visit the artist Chartkov. The daughter Lise, to the 'connoiseur of human nature' (p. 123), shows all the signs of a 'childish passion for balls . . . the desire to run around in a new dress' (p. 123), while she has clearly spent so much time at these social gatherings that she has become virtually an object herself: both mother and daughter, indeed, 'had become almost waxen' (p. 124). Reification of women is not, of course, uncommon in literature, and these tales are no exception. Akaky's overcoat is described as a 'pleasant [female] friend' (p. 192), and, by implication, this particular object is more important in the plot and thematics of the story than any woman. So, too, more attention is paid to the tailor Petrovich's big toe than to his wife. Like Lise, Sophie betrays her eponymous artificiality on her first appearance. In the view of the narrator, Poprishchin, her outing in pouring rain is a clear sign that women have 'a great passion for all this finery' (p. 238). Later, when Poprishchin reads of her conversation with her suitor (in the dogs' letters), its contents are predictably confined to such feminine concerns as balls, clothes and appearances more generally. Even the dog is driven to exclaim: 'Ah, ma chère, what rubbish they talked about!' (p. 251). Sophie's portrayal illustrates another tendency common in the literature of the period, namely the use of similes which compare women to animals or, more particularly, birds.[58] Sophie drives up in search of 'all this finery' and 'jumped out of her carriage like a little bird' (p. 238). Like her movements, her voice is reduced to that of a lower creature. Poprishchin exclaims: 'Ay, ay, ay! what a voice! A canary, truly, a canary!' (p. 241). Pirogov has the same view. On seeing his prey he murmurs to himself: 'You, my little dove, are mine!' (p. 40).[59]

If the danger of sexually attractive women is warded off by these type of categorisation, then their antithetical type is viewed in no less stereotypical terms. Following the pattern set by Shponka's Auntie (although this tradition is, of course, far older), women who are deemed unattractive from the male point of view are dismissed as frightening, ugly harridans. The wife of the barber, Ivan Yakovlevich, who finds Kovalyov's nose in his morning roll, at least has a name, Praskov'ya Osipovna. However, her brief characterisation (she plays virtually no part in the plot) shows her to be a nagging, bad-tempered, dominating wife. On learning of Ivan's misfortune, she accuses him of cutting off the nose and threatens to denounce the 'swindler, drunkard . . . brigand' (p. 79) to the police. Another shadowy background wife is that of Petrovich in *The Overcoat*. The narrator speaks of her almost with reluctance, commenting briefly on her antiquated dress, her bad temper and the fact that 'she could not, so it seems, boast of her beauty' (p. 184). Indeed, only guards' officers (completely undiscriminating, one assumes) bother to peer beneath her 'cap'.

At first it may seem that the marginalised, denigrated women of St Petersburg are of no real interest to the male narrators except as symbolic, lurking presences denoting stupidity, anonymity, ugliness and so on. It has been said that 'The women are not witches or manipulators, they mean no harm.'[60] However, although they are perhaps less visible than in the Ukraine of *Mirgorod* and the earlier *Evenings*, witches *do* hide behind the appearances of St Petersburg in the same way as Shponka's Auntie can be construed as a witch in disguise. As we noted earlier, in almost every story there is at least a suggestion that women exercise mysterious 'charms' over men, and the word in Russian (*chary*) has the same origins in witchcraft. In *The Nose* Kovalyov accuses Mrs Podtochina, as we know, of stealing his nose 'by means of witchcraft, produced by you or others who exercise in the same noble activities' (p. 86). If Mrs Podtochina is a witch, then she has accomplices, the 'old women-witches' (p. 80), which Kovalyov earlier claims she has hired. As so often, the use of a generic category implicates *all* women. So, too, the society *dama* 'completely charmed' (p. 125) Chartkov away from his true path. Another unnamed, marginal woman is similarly linked with demonic powers. It is Petrovich's wife who releases the smoke to make the kitchen such a hellish place. She urges Petrovich to raise his price, calling her husband a 'one-eyed devil' to such an extent (p. 185) that Akaky resolves not to return when she is there. Piskaryov too is explicitly bewitched, following the beauty 'who had cast a spell upon him and carried him away on Nevsky Prospekt' (p. 23). Old or young, attractive or ugly – all types of women belong to the dark sisterhood. Poprishchin in his vindictive ravings sums up the implications of this motif which runs through all the stories. He denounces not only Sophie but all women: 'O this is a perfidious creature – women! . . . Up to now no-one has found out with whom she is in love: I discovered it first. Woman is in love with the Devil' (p. 257). However, he is wrong. This discovery had long been known to man, since 1486 at least.[61]

Not all stereotypes of women in these stories are negative. Alongside these images the men in the stories (both narrators and *dramatis personae*) create positive portraits of women, although these have a similar impact in that the gross idealisation involved equally reduces women to anonymous, interchangeable categories. Piskaryov, on his first glimpse of the prostitute, perceives not her as such but an artistic image: 'Did you see, a wonderful being, just like Perugini's Bianca' (p. 15). She becomes the Ideal of Beauty, who cannot, of course, exist in reality. The narrator shares this view of women. In the brothel he laments that the 'pitiful creatures' (p. 23) are not what they should be – 'a woman, this beauty of the world, the crown of creation' (p. 24). Women should be weak, fine, distinctive, but all too often are not. Piskaryov's dreams reveal another idealised vision of womanhood. In the traditions of Sentimentalism he imagines them living quietly in the country, while the woman strikes up one of the most common iconic poses of the period:[62] 'O, how nicely she sits by the window of a bright little house in the country! Her dress emanates such simplicity . . . .. The cut of her hair . . . .. Creator, how simple her hair is and how it suits her!' She becomes, and should be, demure, virginal. This type of woman is associated with all that is holy, and divinisation of the pure woman is another long established, indeed, Christian tradition which these stories follow. Bianca, it seemed, 'had flown down from heaven' (p. 17). She possesses 'divine features': 'how could he lose this deity and not even discover this holy thing' (p. 19).[63] Quasi-religious terminology is also to be found in the description of Sophie's bedchamber, at least in Poprishchin's image of it: 'there I think, are miracles, right there, I think, is a paradise which doesn't exist even in the heavens' (p. 245).

But the religious terminology merely makes even more of a mockery of the truth. The ideal is always, and is in essence an illusion, and these apparently divine allures are just another form of witchcraft to deceive pathetic innocents like Piskaryov and Poprishchin. And the greater the idealisation, the more brutal is the truth about women. A woman may seem to be a virgin, a country maiden, even a goddess, but in reality she is a whore, or a witch (or both) who lurks in the city to destroy men. The reality of women and 'all the low, all the despised life' (p. 38) they lead are loathsome.

These stories, then, run through a wide range of traditional stereotypes, occasionally positive, usually negative. In the end, it matters little as *all* women are dangerous. They deprive men of their senses, they inspire terror, particularly if they are sexually attractive. On the whole, the women do not usually actively harm men, as Karlinsky has noted. Indeed, such activity is not necessary because they are not in any sense real characters but abstract symbols of the danger that lurks within men themselves, the uncontrollable, dark, chaotic Other, the *chora* which threatens always to destroy. Men may denigrate women to suppress this force, but it will always return. And so, women must be controlled either by denigration, divinisation or virtual exclusion from the text, because of the dark powers they both represent and possess. The witches must be hammered out of existence.

6

Ivan Turgenev and the 'New Eve'

Yelena's transformation into a young woman dedicated to her own moral liberation as well as that ideal of national liberation which she shared with Insarov is one that summarised the younger generation's appetite for revolutionary change more fully, if only by implication, than any portrayal to date.[1]

The strong-willed Elena indeed became a symbol of women's emancipation in Russia.[2]

On the Eve is the story of Elena's choice, and also, more generally, of the process of a Russian woman choosing a man to love.[3]

Such recent comments are the common currency of Turgenevan criticism. From Dobrolyubov's challenging review of *On the Eve*, *When Will the Real Day Come?*, which appeared in the same year as that novel (1860), Turgenev has been acknowledged as one of the first in Russian literature to give an accurate and sympathetic account of the 'new woman'. The novel was also acclaimed in Turgenev's own lifetime as a prophecy of the later 'Going-To-The-People' movement of the 1870s.[4] Certainly, the characters of Yelena Stakhova and, to a lesser extent, Natalya in *Rudin* (1856), mark a dramatic change in the depiction of women in Russian literature. The suffering victims or demonic temptresses are replaced by energetic, independent and active women, who at least strive to determine their own destinies. However, as Ripp indicates, the choices available have their limitations: 'choosing a man to love' (as Natalya also does) is not the same as choosing a life. Moreover, if we look at Turgenev's female portraits more generally, his work must be seen as only a transition to the 'real day' of Chernyshevsky and other radical writers of the 1860s and 1870s. The present chapter will examine four key works of this period, noting the very strong residue of traditional images as well as this portrait of the 'new woman', looking at the shorter works *Asya* (1858) and *First Love* (1860) before considering the two novels *Home of the Gentry* (1859) and *On the Eve* itself.

1. ASYA[5]

Both *Asya* and *First Love* are narrated by middle-aged men recalling powerful, transcendent, erotic experiences of their youth. In each tale the central male protagonist relates a moment in his life which was never to be repeated and in which a woman was the focal point. In both stories the young, relatively inexperienced hero encounters an enigmatic, alluring young woman, the unlocking of whose riddle forms the main thread. Although the two women, the eponymous Asya and Zinaida, are presented as attractive if not bewitching presences, the stories remain profoundly androcentric in their orientation. Woman is a mystery, and however hard, or even desperately, the questing hero strives to fathom her secrets, she remains unobtainably the Other.

1.1. Setting

The exotic (and erotic) nature of the early experiences of the narrator of *Asya* (the unnamed N. N.) is emphasised by its location in a spa town on the Rhine where he is recuperating from an unhappy love affair with a 'perfidious widow' (p. 73). At each stage of his attempts to learn the secret of the heroine and to establish an unspecified relationship with her, the setting plays an important, emblematic part in denoting her identity, underscoring both her role as a symbolic presence in his life and her essential unknowability.

The initial setting is virtually a cliché: a young Russian abroad in an idyllic setting, full of Romantic potential. He is staying near a small town on the banks of the Rhine; it is June, the moon shines down on him and the town, and the students' revelry (p. 74) emphasises the youthful gaiety and sense of exhilarating, carefree liberty. It is in this town that he encounters Asya and her half-brother Gagin, and the story then proceeds on and around the fairy-tale river: 'the nearby ferry is, as it were, the gateway fron N. N.'s real world in Z. to the enchanted kingdom where Asya and her brother are staying, the twin spa of L.'[6] Asya is presented as the

centre of this 'enchanted kingdom', the princess the parody knight
(N. N.) must capture. We see her scrambling over picturesque ruins
(p. 80), and when Gagin unfolds her peculiar biography to N. N. the
two men are sitting near the emblematic statue of the Madonna,
emphasising, as O'Toole again notes, her 'purity, femininity,
childish innocence, sadness and potential martyrdom.'[7] Asya's
image is further mythicised by the setting of the discussion of life and
love between her and the narrator, which takes place overlooking the
Lorelei, the folkloric Siren who eventually commits suicide after a
career of luring men to their destruction. Through these literary/
mythic associations provided by the setting, the heroine symbolises
both danger (and potential death) to the unwitting hero, and
eventual female self-destruction. As the story approaches its fateful
denouement, the setting again takes on almost comically iconic
overtones. Asya suggests a tryst at the classic Sentimentalist locus,
the ruined chapel,[8] only to transfer it to the even more doomladen
interior of the house of Frau Louise, the grotesque, witch-like figure
who haunts the background. As N. N. approaches this last and
bitter (although highly erotic) encounter, evening shadows darken
his path. Inside the dwelling he finds Stygian darkness and Frau
Louise's bony fingers grab him and lead him to the assignation. The
fairy-tale resonances remain powerful and the implications of the
setting clear: the woman is a symbol, a polyvalent presence, rather
than an individual, suggesting both danger for the man and
ultimate sadness for herself.

1.2. Plot

Much of the early part of the story is devoted to elaborating the local
colour and to giving retrospective glimpses of N. N.'s life and
character, and it is only gradually that the plot-line emerges. As the
episodic narrative begins to take on a coherent form, the main
thread that appears is a traditional one: the pursuit of the young
virgin by the more experienced man.[9] Initially at least, the purpose
of this quest is not seduction as such but the establishment of the
heroine's identity, the resolution of the mystery afforded by a
bewildering series of roles, images and symbolic references surrounding Asya. When she, for once, behaves 'naturally', 'without a
shade of coquetry', N. N. comments: 'on this occasion there was no
possibility of reproaching her with unnaturalness' (p. 86). Shortly
afterwards he further remarks: 'I was observing her with curiosity'

(p. 87). As she slowly begins to conform to his desires and expectations and sheds her role-playing, N. N. comes to discover what he believes to be her essence. Asya is foregrounded, then, as the *object* both of his voyage of discovery and of the narrative itself.

The peripeteia of this pursuit/quest plot is the lengthy account of Asya's upbringing given by Gagin in Chapter 8. It is typical of the androcentric orientation of the story that we learn of Asya's past not from her own lips but from an actor from her patriarchal past. She is, indeed, a creature of this environment, in that she is the daughter of a serf-woman and the *barin*, the master, and, consequently, only a half-sister to Gagin. At least in part because of this hybrid parentage, she lacks a sense of true identity. For her, too, her plot is a quest to discover herself, and so we have within the tale two parallel plotlines. N. N.'s plot is to unravel her mystery and so possess her, while hers, which only occasionally manages to force its way through the overlying patriarchal discourses, is also to establish for herself who she 'really' is.

Apart from providing N. N. (and the implicity male reader) with the requisite insights to understand the enigmatic heroine, Gagin's retrospective narration seemingly gives N. N. permission to pursue his sister more assiduously, for it is immediately afterwards that N. N. and Asya have their first serious conversation. It is, as we have already noted, of a highly sentimental nature, concerning love and other matters. The peripeteia (the telling of Asya's background) seemingly has a magical effect. Gagin explains the riddle and Asya is immediately 'pacified' (p. 100) and begins to come under N. N.'s control. The latter patronisingly informs her: 'I am so glad that you, at last, are stopping being wild' (p. 100). They waltz together and Asya, symbolically at least, is seduced and becomes a woman.

Henceforth, her plot enters another traditional path. she is in love and so, like many other victim heroines before her,[10] she is unable to sleep and becomes ill. She appears before the narrator now in an almost bathetic pose, 'with bandaged brow, pale, thin, with almost closed eyes' (p. 106). Having induced her love, N. N. pulls back, realising, after further man-to-man talks with Gagin, that he could not possibly marry a girl with such an unconventional background. Despite these reservations of propriety, he is not averse to embracing and kissing Asya (that is, seducing her) at their final, portentous meeting. When he recalls Gagin's words, he abruptly curtails his amorous overtures (providing an unintentionally comic *interruptus*), only to reproach Asya bitterly for causing the whole affair. There then follows more bathos in that the two men provide a literal replay of the plot, physically searching for the vanished lady. After Gagin decides to remove his sister from the tempting embraces of N. N., the latter chases them as far as London, but without success. Indeed, the plot mirrors its own symbolic significance. The man, hopelessly locked in his own consciousness, can never find the true woman, the essential Asya, because such an idea is the creation of his own imagination. It is an image imposed upon the object of his never-ending, and ceaselessly futile pursuit.

1.3. Male/Male Relationships

As we have seen, the two men conspire to dispose of Asya's destiny, and, more generally, their relationship is presented as a model of 'natural', honest rapport, as opposed to the tormented complications of male/female relationships. In this sense, too, the tale is profoundly androcentric.[11]

In the early stages of the story, Gagin apologises to N. N. on several occasions for his sister's erratic behaviour, either explicitly or by gesture. As he begins his narrative, Gagin confirms this shared view of Asya: 'Tell me . . . what opinion do you have of Asya? Surely she must seem a little strange to you?' (p. 91). Having established this mutual viewpoint, he tells his tale, thereby giving N. N. the go-ahead, as we have noted. The second part of the story is marked by scenes between Asya and N. N., alternating with discussions of her and the 'situation' by the two men. As the relationship intensifies, N. N. comes to Gagin to attempt to clarify the problem. Gagin is at first unable to help: he too views his sister as half-insane, and they, as reasonable men, cannot possibly understand her behaviour: 'You and I, sensible people, cannot imagine how deeply she feels' (p. 107). Men are the rational norm, the woman is the irrational aberration. Despite the difficulties involved in dealing with such a 'madwoman' (p. 107), the two men of the world go on to discuss how best to proceed. Gagin is aware that Asya suspects that N. N. knows her 'shameful' background and wishes to escape, but with remarkable insensitivity, he ignores his half-sister's wishes: 'Perhaps you like my sister?' (p. 108), he asks, only to apologise for such an indelicate proposal. Not to be outdone in breaches of confidence, N. N. shows Gagin the *billet doux* that he had received from Asya arranging the meeting. They both agree that N. N. should keep the date, but explain to Asya that he cannot marry her. And so, the two men discuss and dispose of the woman they both claim to love as if she were an object; equally, each shows an honesty and frankness to the other which they never display to Asya herself. The pact between the men has a later significance. As Asya lays her head 'beneath my inflamed lips' and whispers 'Yours . . .' (p. 112), N. N. suddenly recalls his agreement with Gagin and steps back. Whatever Asya's wishes may be (and she makes them clear in her submissive pronoun), the deal struck between the two men must take precedence. Within the patriarchal relations that had dominated Asya's upbringing and which play such an important background role, an honourable relationship with another man is more important than taking a woman's desire into account.

1.4. Female/Female Relationships

Another recurrent feature of patriarchal literature is the isolation of women from each other, the almost complete absence of any meaningful relationships between one woman and another. This is as true of *Asya* as it was of *Yevgeny Onegin* or *A Hero of Our Time*.[12] Because of her unconventional background, Asya hardly knew her mother, and it is with some difficulty that she talks to N. N. about her. (This problematic, estranged mother/daughter relationship is to be found in all of the works by Turgenev considered in this chapter, as well as many others by him.) Asya fares no better in the wider world, inhabiting a *milieu* almost entirely organised by men and without female support or even friendship. At school she has only one friend, but this (unnamed) girl is 'unbeautiful, downtrodden and poor' (p. 96). Women, then, are presented as vulnerable victims (Asya, herself her mother and her schoolfriend) who are alone, friendless and consequently reliant on men for their purpose and definition.

1.5. Male/Female Relationships

As we have already seen, one of the central themes of these relations is the search for the woman's identity, by both the men and the woman herself. More generally, she is persistently seen as subservient, even subject to male requirements. This is most in evidence, of course, in the flashback to Asya's childhood. Her very conception can be seen as a product of patriarchal relations, with master/servant identified as the paradigm. Women are shown to acknowledge the legitimacy of this relationship, as Tatyana (Asya's mother) will not even move into her master's house, let alone marry him, because she is not a 'lady'. The child, however, does make this transition after her mother's death (and it is to be a move that leaves her lost between the two worlds), and the paradigm re-emerges in an intensified form. Asya's father is also her *barin* ('master') and now he is her teacher: the girl is triply subordinate.

In the diegetic present, she remains an inferior in her relationships with men. Although he is her brother, Gagin treats her almost like a servant, ordering her to busy herself in the kitchen and prepare meals while the men go out walking (and to discuss her). She only begins talking properly for the first time when instructed to do so by Gagin (p. 77). As Asya keeps reverting to her wild, unpredictable roles, N. N. comments that Gagin 'had grown used to indulge her in everything' (p. 83), while his shrug of the shoulders asks N. N. to be equally patronising to her: 'She is a child; be condescending' (p. 183). Until the one man gives the other tacit permission to court his sister, Gagin is always present, chaperoning her and also acting as a supervising presence with the power to ratify her behaviour, or to criticise it as beyond the comprehension of the 'sensible' man. N. N., as we know, initially perceives her as a potential love object, asking himself as early as the second chapter (p. 79) whether he might be falling in love. However, once they commence a real relationship, he assumes the power invested in him by Gagin and arrogates the right to supervise her behaviour. Indeed, he takes this right for granted even before the turning-point of Gagin's narrative. He finds Asya reading one day and comments: 'Bravo! . . . how diligent you are' (p. 87), only to add pompously, when seeing it is merely a French novel: 'However, I cannot praise your choice' (p. 88). Moreover, he constantly assumes the right to assess her behaviour, reproaching her for 'unnaturalness' or praising her once she begins to behave with more propriety.

Asya does not resist such control. Given the androcentric narrative (and her confused identity), it is hardly surprising that she actively desires supervision and direction. We first learn of this tendency, not from her, but once more from Gagin. He concludes his account by claiming that she had so far loved no-one, but that she 'needs a hero, an unusual man' (p. 96), while she later claims that she had loved N. N. at first sight. So, too, when the couple do begin to talk she, like so many of Turgenev's young heroines, asks for lessons, wants the man to be her mentor, and thereby to form her mind and also her very identity. Because of her peculiar education she has no real knowledge of herself or her capabilities: 'I myself sometimes don't know what's going on in my head' (p. 104). She pleads with N. N. (perhaps the first 'decent' man she has ever talked to) to help her: 'Tell me, what should I read? tell me what should I do? I'll do everything that you tell me.' (p. 104) She is drawn to him, clearly in desperation, because she has always had to rely on men to give her a self-image.

Given permission by Gagin, N. N. proceeds to attempt to make her his own. Immediately after the story he begins to feel sorry for her, and is indeed attracted by her past sufferings: 'I had looked into her soul' (p. 98), he reflects. Now he has the power conferred by this knowledge, he feels able to control her. The fact that she had never loved anyone (a euphemism, one assumes, for her virginity) is presumably also a powerful ingredient in N. N.'s quickening interest and desire. Precisely because she is so unsure of herself and has suffered so much, N. N. grows to love her: he is drawn by her *weakness*, because, unlike the 'perfidious', 'cruel' widow of his past, he will be able to dominate her: 'I admired her, I found a touching charm in her pallid features, in her indecisive slow movements' (p. 105). She is the suffering victim, who has asked him to be her master.

However, N. N. is no rake of the old school; he feels unable to seduce a girl he will not marry. But in his own weakness, his behaviour is tantamount to seduction. He pursues the enigma, is told her secret, conspires to make her fall in love with him, and then rejects her. In outline, at least, his behaviour is homologous to that of Pechorin in *Princess Mary*. Moreover, his sense of honour proves insufficient to prevent the climactic scene of actual seduction which, as in earlier versions of the same tale, is lingered over in near pornographic detail.[13] All his 'noble' intentions evaporate as he sees his victim before his gaze: 'I looked at her: there was something *touchingly helpless* in her timid immobility. . . .. My heart melted' (p. 112; my italics). Even more irresistible is the fact that the vulnerable woman offers herself to him; she slowly raises her eyes to him: 'They beseeched, these eyes, they trusted, were questioning, gave themselves. . . .. I could not resist their charm' (p. 112). She is charming precisely because she is so helpless and pleading before him, and his desire is aroused by this vulnerability: 'A subtle fire ran through me like burning little needles; I bent over to her hand . . .' (p. 112). There then follows an extended and evocatively detailed account of Asya's barely suppressed desire: 'her hand trembling like a leaf', 'her lips slightly parted', and as he draws her to him, her shawl falls from her shoulders as she prepares to submit to his mastery. The image is explicitly and intensely *physical*: as Asya offers herself to him, the submissive virgin is presented to the delectation of the reader. Later, after he has decided to relinquish her virginal charms, he is full of bitter self-reproach at having lost her when she had come to him 'in complete innocence of heart and feelings, she had brought to me her untouched youth . . .' (p. 116). The euphemisms barely conceal the chance he had missed – the opportunity to possess completely a willing virgin.

1.6. Point of View

If the plot paradigms present Asya as a vulnerable young heroine who has always been subservient to men (her father, then her brother) and who actively wishes to remain in a submissive role with her potential lover, then the narrative point of view, which privileges the male voice exclusively, suppresses her even more. Her very identity is mediated to the reader, usually by N. N. and occasionally by Gagin. The narrator may be a 'cliché-monger',[14] but it is *his* view that we have of Asya. We first see her through his eyes as he inspects her in the town, and she is later repeatedly presented to the reader in a series of poses, framed by a window, sitting motionlessly or scrambling about like a wild animal. Her image is highly physical, even pictorial in the emphases he gives it: 'A strange grin made her eyebrows, nostrils and lips twitch slightly; her dark eyes were screwed up half-cheekily, half-merrily' (p. 82).

However, this portraiture is far from objective, and highly interpretive. He continues the above description with his own *analysis* of what Asya's appearance and gestures seem to be saying, and saying to *him*, as he more often than not assumes that her thoughts and feelings are arranged for his own benefit: '"You find my behaviour improper", her face seemed to say, "so what: I know you admire me"' (p. 82). 'She *obviously* wanted to play a new role for me' (p. 83; my italics), he observes shortly afterwards. Obvious, perhaps, to him, but his approach to narration has the effect of depriving Asya of any autonomy. As we have seen, he is amazed when she *seemingly* tries to be unusual, pleased when she is compliant. Each thought, look, gesture is controlled and mediated by the male narrator. Even after he has 'looked into her soul', he refuses to grant her narrative independence, but continues to assume he knows what she is feeling.

His view of Asya's strangeness is not, however, a mark merely of his limitations as a psychologist. As in earlier works, a *collective* male point of view is established as regards female irrationality.[15] Gagin, her own brother, fails lamentably to understand her. To him, too, she is an unfathomable enigma: 'It's difficult to get on with her' (p. 91) he warns N. N., taking the implications of this remark even further as the couple seem to fall in love: 'She's mad and will drive me mad' (p. 107). To both of them this charming creature remains a mystery, the essence of female alterity, who cannot be comprehended and of whom men should consequently be wary.

However, Asya emerges from the narrative as a riddle incarnate not merely because the two men fail to understand her complexities and aspirations, but also because the narrator suppresses her individuality in his insistent desire to interpret her in terms of roles or pre-established images.[16] Her very relationship with Gagin is in doubt (is she his sister, or his mistress?) until he tells N. N. the details of her background. At times Asya is presented as a wild, irrational 'child of nature', at times as a demure young lady. She plays the servant and then is presented as a 'Russian girl, even a simple girl, all but a maid' (p. 85). She is equally linked to literary and mythological images, as we have seen. When she first opens up to the narrator, she 'would like to be like Tatyana' (p. 100).[17] Consequently, the heroine's text is almost completely suppressed. She only exists as defined, and we rarely hear her or see her on her own terms. Even during and after the climactic 'seduction scene', Asya hardly speaks, so we can only guess at her suffering or confusion during these, presumably, traumatic moments. After her abrupt departure from Frau Louise's house, we never see her again and have only a brief note to N. N. from which to deduce her story: 'Yesterday, when I wept in front of you, if you had said to me one word, but one word – I would have stayed. You did not say it' (p. 119). We may guess what this word would have been, but Asya's own point of view is lost forever. As a result, the eponymous heroine's image remains confused and contradictory: indeed, she is reduced to the essence of contradictoriness, because, despite its title, the story does not concern her as such, but is an extended meditation on male images of the unobtainable feminine. When

Asya flees, the situation is presented as *the narrator's* loss: the power of the male narrative perspective means that her disappearance (and who knows what later sufferings) is *his* misfortune. Everything is in and on his terms: it is his plot, his destiny and we, in the end, are invited to pity him and his missed opportunity.

Asya is a child, a madwoman, a demure lady, a speechless victim, a creature of freedom, the Madonna, the Lorelei and Tatyana. She is all these images (and many others), but, *ipso facto*, she is never herself, and remains at the level of a projection of male fantasy, a blank screen onto which anything (or, in this case, everything) may be projected.

2. FIRST LOVE[18]

This story, 'his [Turgenev's] intensely personal work',[19] is often considered to be one of the author's most perfect creations[20] and certainly one that has a central place in his *oeuvre*. Turgenev himself allegedly observed:

> There is only one story I reread with pleasure. That is *First Love*. It is perhaps my favourite work. In the others there is, if only a little, some invention, while in *First Love* is described a real event without the slightest decoration and when I reread it, the characters arise before me as if alive.[21]

Whether based on 'real life' or not, this work affords images of women which were clearly close to Turgenev, and are remarkably similar in some respects to those of *Asya*. This work, too, sheds a revealing light on the role and destiny of women in *On the Eve*.

2.1. Plot

As already noted, *First Love* is also an account by a middle-aged man (here explicitly for a male audience) of his youthful attempts to unlock the mysteries of an enigmatic woman. As the title suggests, the experience is traumatic in its novelty, but it is equally one whose intensity was never to be repeated. By the nature of the plot dynamics, the main motif is that of the archetypal quest or, more properly, and in the mode of Pechorin in *Taman*, of pursuit. '"How can I get to know them?" was my first thought' (p. 12), the youthful Volodya comments as soon as he has encountered Zinaida and her mother (although, as we shall see, he has no interest whatsoever in any greater intimacy with the grotesquely caricatured mother). His story, again resonating outwards from the title, is that of a young man awakening to passion. This passion is exacerbated by many complicating factors, not least of which is the enigmatic character of the (older) heroine. (The mythic elements of the plot are further enhanced by the admittedly rather seedy air of mystery attached to her rented home.) The title suggests a further resonance, of course, that of sexual initiation and all the terrors this may involve. After the epiphanic game of forfeits in Chapter 7,[22] during which Volodya touches Zinaida for the first time (accidentally), he returns home 'Tired and happy to the point of exhaustion' (p. 27), although, on reflection, this euphemistic description of post-ecstatic bliss is replaced by sexual anxiety: 'I grew cold at the thought that I was in love' (p. 28).

The remainder of the story details Volodya's growing infatuation, torment and despair. However, we soon become aware that another plot is being enacted behind the scenes, the awful significance of which is only revealed in the final denouement. The *fabula/syuzhet* disjunction[23] lends this sub-text the power of some primeval taboo, which ultimately explodes into the narrator's consciousness with all the significance of a classically Oedipal situation.

Indeed, it is highly significant that this suppressed plot (or *fabula*) first pokes through immediately after Volodya's father visits their neighbours. Zinaida appears at the door, already inhabiting the guise (and pose) of the dysphoric heroine's text. She comes to the door, and he sees only 'the face of Zinaida – pale, thoughtful' (p. 32). Already she is in decline. In terms of the later triangular drama, it is equally important that it is only now (Chapter 9) that Volodya chooses to declare: 'My "passion" began from that day' (p. 32). From this point in the narrative the seemingly all-powerful Siren enters the paradigmatic decline of the suffering heroine, and a powerful tension is created between the plot and the *fabula*. Volodya is tormented by her, but her physical appearance mutely displays *her* torment. Thus, as for Asya, we hear of the hero's sufferings, but the heroine's are only mediated through the controlling narrative voice, which, again, is male. Moreover, this plot/*fabula* disjunction shows the illusory (both deceptive and deceitful) nature of female power in an androcentric text, in that the true story is revealed ultimately to be on the level of the suppressed *fabula*. The tension between the two levels poses the question who will suffer the more, who will be broken, and the resolution tells us that it is the woman.

A single chapter later the retrospectively self-pitying narrator marks a new development by opening Chapter 10 with the repetitious statement: 'My real torments began from that moment' (p. 38). However, as before, the real peripeteia has occurred elsewhere and is noted with the bleak statement: 'A change has occurred in her – that was obvious' (p. 38). Still the truth behind this 'passion', these 'torments' and this 'change' is suppressed and deliberately so. But the *effects* of the peripeteia on the heroine are, indeed, 'obvious', and she continues to repeat the text declension of Bela and Princess Mary. She is silent, seeking solitude: her power is beginning to evaporate as it is gradually destroyed by the hidden, controlling presence. In narrative terms, this lends greater mystery to Volodya's pursuit of the key to her enigma, but, once more, because it is concealed, the secret takes on the air of that which cannot be spoken of, the essential taboo.

Gradually, the plot and *fabula* begin to intersect, as Volodya observes (from a distance) Zinaida with his father. This interaction becomes more and more acute, culminating, perhaps, in Chapter 16, where another epiphanic game of forfeits is played and Zinaida tells her fairy-tale.[24] All the young 'courtiers' cluster adoringly around their 'queen', but Zinaida, in the words of this fairy-tale personage, finally lays bare the true semantic structure of the text: 'But there, by the fountain . . . stands and waits the one I love, the one who possesses me' (p. 54). The *fabula* ('there') is here announced to be the essential plot, whereas the apparent, surface plot of Volodya's pursuit of love, his quest for the meaning of the riddle, is revealed as a charade, a game of forfeits, a magical tale. In the end, as the denouement approaches, the two levels finally merge as Volodya all but catches the 'queen' with 'the one'. While we are yet to discover the true significance of the *fabula*, the resolution of the plot is clearly stated. Clutching (and then dropping!) his emblematic penknife,[25] Volodya finally sees his father moving through the darkened garden. Although the narrative still deliberately suppresses the meaning of this encounter, its power for the young man in love is expressed directly. He awakens the next day with a somewhat bathetic headache and remarks: 'Yesterday's excitement had vanished. It was replaced by a heavy confusion and a kind of sorrow I had never experienced before – as if something was dying within me' (p. 61). The remaining fifteen pages are devoted to an explanation and elucidation of this loss and what lies behind it, as the *fabula* finally emerges to supplant the plot.

Shortly after his 'unsuccessful nocturnal expedition', a 'clap of thunder' descends upon him when the truth of his father's secret liaison with Zinaida is disclosed. The epilogue is signalled by the plot rhyme of Volodya's mother returning to Moscow, just as their arrival in the country had heralded his initiation into adulthood. Significantly, as for Zinaida, we are left only to guess at his mother's story from her tears and invalidism.[26] Her torment, her jealousy, and the unpleasant details of her relationship with her husband are also largely suppressed by the androcentric narrative or, at best, glossed over. So, too, Zinaida's plot (the *fabula*) still remains hidden, reflected on the surface plot once again only in iconic poses of female suffering. She and Volodya meet one last time, and she appears before him 'in a black dress, pale, her hair undone' (p. 66).

Yet this is not to be his final view of her. One day, out riding with his father (the first and only scene of real intimacy between them), Volodya is witness to an astonishing event where he finally is able to solve the riddle of this enigmatic woman. The real secret that has been suppressed for the entire narrative is not merely that 'the one', his successful rival in love, was his own father, but that the seemingly powerful 'queen' is the perfect victim. From a distance Volodya sees his father strike Zinaida with his (equally emblematic) riding-crop. Moreover, she does not resist but seems to accept, if not delight in, her own masochism: 'Zinaida shuddered, looked silently at my father and, slowly raising her arm to her lips, kissed the scarlet weal on it' (p. 70). In this voyeuristic account the *fabula* explodes through the suture of the plot to reveal the awful secrets of 'passion' and 'suffering'.

This is not yet the end of the narrative riddles that are solved by this dramatic coda to both the plot and *fabula*. Volodya's father is shown to be the controlling presence behind it all: the will of the Stern (indeed, sadistic) Father had, in retrospect, organised the text. Zinaida is later to die in childbirth, but the culmination of her plot, in narrative terms at least, had come four years earlier when poor, young Volodya had achieved his initiation into manhood by observing his father's treatment of his willing victim. It would seem that the son had learned the ways of the father well, because he does not even find the time to visit his youthful 'passion'[27] before her untimely death.

2.2. Point of View

One reason we never directly hear Zinaida's story is that the point of view of the tale is almost entirely that of its young male narrator. On a different level, *First Love* could be said to be about how men perceive women as images, that is, how they objectify them. Indeed, the brief pre-prologue consists of three men sitting around after dinner, smoking cigars and discussing and categorising their respective first loves. The tale which then is presented is that of Vladimir Petrovich (Volodya), and concerns itself with his quest (at the age of sixteen) for strong emotions. Although the '*image* of a woman, the ghost of female love' (p. 9; my italics), rarely rose before him in clear terms, it is with this *image* that he is concerned. And, because he is the 'sentient centre',[28] the whole story is mediated almost entirely through his perception of it.

Significantly, we first encounter the heroine as *observed* by the narrator and as the recipient of all sorts of image-making: 'In the movements of the girl (I saw her from the side) there was something so *bewitching*, *imperious*, caressing, mocking and tender' (p. 11; my italics). After this initial fantasy, Zinaida is never allowed to be herself but remains what she was at first – a dazzling array of paradoxical images. Woman is created by the controlling imagination of the male narrator: she is a blank screen rather than a being. And, as we have already seen, this tendency continues to the very end of the text – Volodya on numerous occasions watches and observes her behaviour (rarely comprehending it) and, consequently, presents it in terms of its outward appearance, in a series of enigmatic and iconic poses.

The two other men who had sat after dinner with the older Volodya were the first readers of this text, and Zinaida is frequently presented to them in precise, very physical detail which verges on the pornographic, not merely in the final sado-masochistic encounter with the narrator's father.

The first description of the as yet unknown young woman is prefaced by the significant remark: 'I *devoured* with my gaze' (p. 11; my italics), after Volodya had dropped his emblematic rifle in amazement. It continues, in suitably repetitive, breathless, co-ordinated syntax, to detail the sexually alluring features of this stranger. He 'devoured' 'this graceful figure, and little neck, and her beautiful arms, and slightly dishevelled blond hair beneath a white kerchief, and this half-closed intelligent eye, and these eyelashes, and her tender cheek beneath them . . .' (p. 11). Zinaida is atomised, reduced to a series of 'charming' little attributes which seem to exist not in their own right, but to be appreciated (or 'devoured') by young Volodya and, of course, the other males who read his staccato catalogue.

When he meets her shortly afterwards, she engages him in the seemingly innocuous task of winding wool. However, our intrepid hero manages to imbue this harmless vignette with the utmost sensuality and quite explicitly uses the occasion for another version of the 'ocular rape' so common in the 'rake's economy' of the patriarchal tradition.[29] 'I used the fact that she did not raise her eyes *to examine* her, at first furtively, then more and more audaciously' (p. 17; my italics). Zinaida sits, iconically framed by a window[30] and illuminated by a ray of sunlight which casts a soft light on

> her fluffy golden hair, her *innocent* neck, sloping shoulders and tender, *peaceful* breast. . . . She was wearing a dark, rather worn dress with a pinafore; I would willingly have caressed every fold of this dress and pinafore. The toes of her boots pointed out beneath her dress; with adoration I would have bent down before these boots (p. 17; my italics).

Once more we note the atomisation of the female body, the interpretation of physical details ('innocent', 'peaceful'), the overt fetishism and quasi-masturbatory fantasies. Zinaida may be sitting peacefully winding wool, but while she does so her body is 'examined' by the narrator, who then lays his sexual description before the admiring gaze of other male readers for their delectation (or whatever!).

There are many further physical characterisations of Zinaida in the course of the story. Because of this, and because the controlling narrative voice is so explicitly *male* (and predatory, for all Volodya's alleged innocence), she remains categorised, an object for his, and our, observation. We can only guess at her inner turmoil and ultimate tragedy, because the story is presented through his eyes (often literally so). So too at the end. When he finally discovers the truth and his innocence is lost, his painful transition to manhood is presented in highly poeticised language, as a matter of great sorrow: 'All was finished. All my flowers had been plucked at once and lay around me, scattered and trampled' (p. 65). This may be precisely the same sort of 'cliché-mongering'[31] beloved of N. N. in *Asya*, but the desired effect is obvious. Volodya, not Zinaida, is the focus of emotion and the reader's sympathy. She may later die in childbirth, but this merely causes Volodya to reflect on the transience of *his* youth (pp. 74–5). Because the point of view of the story is so resolutely and almost entirely his, female suffering, even death, is represented as merely a lapidary event in this tale of male initiation.

2.3. Images of Women

Just as the title of the earlier story under consideration announced that Asya was not so much to tell her own tale as to be the enigmatic object of desire, so here *First Love* suggests that woman is to be the object of memory, reverie and fantasy. However, this type of image-making applies not at all to women other than the heroine, the mothers of Volodya and Zinaida. In other words, women who are no longer sexually attractive or available are of little interest to this male imagination. Volodya's mother, we are told in her initial characterisation, 'led a sad life: she was constantly anxious, jealous, angry – but not in father's presence' (p. 9). This emotionalism is controlled, once more by the man who, as we have already seen, ultimately has power over everyone in the text. She plays little part at all in the story, and we can only guess at her suffering too. In line with her pre-ordained role, her principal reaction to the denouement is to retire to her room, unwell. Emotionalism and invalidism, so typical of nineteenth-century fictional women,[32] are the virtual sum total of her portrayal.

Zinaida's mother equally plays no active part in the story, but is the object of a harsh misogynist caricature. When Volodya first enters the Zasekins' house, he is met by a 'woman of about fifty, bare-headed, ugly' (p. 14). She has, Volodya notices, 'fat, red fingers' (p. 14). At his next encounter, he refers to this fifty-year-old as 'the old woman',[33] who takes her snuff 'so noisily . . . that I even shuddered' (p. 19). Virtually every reference to her chooses to endorse this profound male disgust at the expense of the older, no longer attractive female. His feelings are redolent of the horror experienced by Gogol's men and narrators when encountering women of 'a certain age'. Equally Gogolian is his unease at her noisy snuff-taking and her unappetising physical actions and attributes. As in the earlier writer, older women are commonly equivalent to witches – repellent physical presences and no more. This characterisation reaches its apogee towards the end when Volodya, in the throes of juvenile torment over Zinaida's dangerous liaison, comments once more on the repulsive habits of her mother, the precise physical detail serving to emphasise his casual, and gross, misogyny. Despite all that has happened, he resolves to visit Zinaida one last time and, as usual, first has to cross the path of 'the old woman'. She greets him offhandedly and 'shoving tobacco into both nostrils' (p. 66). It is no more nor less than intense physical loathing and revulsion from female flesh, if it be unattractive.

These two women conform to the grosser stereotypes of patriarchal literature. The main focus of the story is, of course, the 'first love', Zinaida. Although her characterisation is much more subtle than that of the older women, it is equally bedevilled, as we have already noted, by its tendency to conform to pre-established images. Indeed, it is precisely this – a series of images which are frequently paradoxical. Like Asya, Zinaida is presented as the essence of contradiction, an unfathomable enigma.

As Volodya first attempts to become acquainted with Zinaida, she more often than not has an 'ironic smile' on her lips; her behaviour and mood are unpredictable. Like Asya, again, she likes playing roles and games – the forfeits game, for example, at which she behaves 'like a real princess' (p. 22), foreshadowing her later identification with 'the queen' of her own fairy-tale. To Volodya at least, she is the image of passion incarnate, and his physical contact with her is wreathed in almost bathetic clichés of eroticism. In the course of the first game of forfeits, during which he kisses her hand, he is as drunk as if 'from wine'; 'her parted lips breathed hotly . . . the ends of her hair tickled and *burned* me' (p. 26; my italics). She begins (but also ends) as the mysterious object of desire: during the second game 'She smiled mysteriously and cunningly' (p. 26). She is a riddle personified: as he leaves, she presses his hand and 'again smiled enigmatically' (p. 26). These images remain to haunt his half-waking reverie as he recalls this enchanted evening: 'her lips smiled just as enigmatically, her eyes looked at me slightly askance, questioningly, pensively and tenderly' (p. 28).

Precisely because he sees her so much as a creature of his imagination rather than as an independent being, he has to rely on these external expressions of her emotion. Consequently, she must always remain a paradox, because his image-making actually inhibits any possibility of real understanding of her undoubted complexities. Yet he is hardly aware of this problem. On the contrary, he comes to interpret her *as* a paradoxical being, and not simply as someone he fails to comprehend. In Chapter 9, musing on the origins of his 'passion', he comments: 'In her entire being, alive and beautiful, was some particularly charming mixture of cunning and carelessness, artificiality and simplicity, quiet and playfulness' (p. 33). He clearly understands her, penetrates her consciousness, as well as he might a 'playful' kitten! One could, of course, simply ascribe all this to the inadequacies of his adolescent mind, but one central paradox reveals that there is something more sinister behind this duplicitous male structuration of the text, and which, as we have seen, the implications of the plot reveal. The seemingly powerful woman becomes what she always really was, powerless, indeed broken. And this is the central significance of the playing with images. The woman is a mere sign, lacking signification in herself. What she may or may not signify (what her signified is) is ascribed to her by men.

Apart from contradictoriness, naida's initial striking characteristic is her power over men. In Volodya's nocturnal imagination this is another central attribute of her personality ('In everything there was an idiosyncratic, playing power' (p. 33)), and it is certainly one that seems to be borne out by her behaviour to the motley individuals of her entourage. She even seems to believe in this role herself. She says to one of them, Lushin, shortly before jabbing a pin into his hand: 'I'm a coquette,[34] I have no heart, I have an actress's nature' (p. 33). She also believes in the dangerous qualities (for men) attaching to female power. Immediately before the 'clap of thunder' breaks over them all, she declares to the weeping Volodya: 'I'm guilty before you, Volodya . . . . There is so much evil, dark, sinful within me . . .' (p. 63). As so often, the women who are the object of male image-making come to believe in these images because they have no other form of validation.

The price that Zinaida has to pay for her notional power over some men is to be 'possessed' by 'the one' and ultimately destroyed by him. But this is also not merely a question of plot dynamics. The text is constructed in such a way that the reader is led to believe that the woman desires such a punishment, as we have seen. Much earlier, however, Zinaida had knowingly and willingly desired such an outcome. It may have been said in jest, but to her assembled entourage she declares: 'No, I don't love those that I have to look down on. I need such a one who would break me himself' (p. 34). And, as the vernacular has it, she gets what she asks for.

As we already know, the latter part of the story shows her steady decline, marked by her iconic poses of feminine suffering, culminating in submission to the Will of the Father. Women's power is as brief as is the interest they hold for the male imagination. Continually, in the latter stages of the narrative, she appears before the narrator (and the other male readers) stripped of her previous authority. She is iconically pale, tired, silent. At first these outward signs merely increase her strangeness, because, as *her* story is withheld, we, like Volodya, cannot comprehend her behaviour. In one telling moment, however, the narrator catches the essence of this process: 'Somehow I happened to see in one of the windows of the wing a pale spot . . .' (p. 66). This is what the image of Zinaida now is – an insubstantial faceless apparition. Her earlier identification with yet another persona, Cleopatra, has the same force as the links established between Asya and the Lorelei. Zinaida, like Cleopatra, is a woman of power who eventually is to die, powerless.

As they part, Zinaida sadly comments to Volodya: 'I am not as you *imagine* me to be' (p. 67; my italics). But this is precisely her problem. Even now she is unable to escape his imagination as he swears he will love her until he dies. But, as we know, it is she who is to die before the tale is out and her final destiny is to remain on the level of fantasy, to be recalled several decades later as merely a 'first love'.

2.4. Women and the Family

If Zinaida is isolated by virtue of the androcentric nature of the text, then she is no less so in her own immediate social setting, the family and her relations with other women. The family, as in much of Turgenev's work, has a somewhat ambivalent treatment. Marital relations may be strained, but the family is the unavoidable locus and source of erotic experience. The two main love affairs of this story are scarcely *à deux*. Iodya's mother (to say nothing of his father!) takes an active interest in his comings and goings. Parental opposition is a lively ingredient in this particular adolescent trauma too. Yet familial relations as described in *First Love* are far from amicable. Volodya's parents are distant from their son, and even more so from each other. Their marriage was explicitly made for money. Zinaida is perhaps even more estranged. She is said to be like neither her mother, with whom she has a very distant relationship, nor her father, who never appears. Indeed, she really has no family at all.

Equally, she has not a single female friend, or even acquaintance.

Her world is entirely that of men – Volodya, his father and her weird collection of 'admirers'. Female friendship, as in *Asya*, is rendered not merely invisible, but the implication is that it is non-existent.[35] Indeed, the few women in the story evince exclusively negative feelings for each other. Volodya's mother clearly shares her son's distaste for Zasekina mère, referring to her as 'une femme très vulgaire' (p. 20). Zinaida is, if anything, worse, dismissed by the spurned wife as an 'adventuress' (p. 57). Women, then, must rely on the male imagination for their identity, and this tendency is clearly buttressed by the text's refusal to allow any reality to female solidarity. The opposite is, in fact, the case.

2.5. Male/Male Relationships

It must also be said that relations between men are extremely fraught, although, by the end of the story, at least, one such relationship receives strong validation.

As in other respects, the opening pre-prologue should not be set aside as a mere pretext for the ensuing narrative, but given consideration for what it is: an all-male gathering where women only exist as objects of recollection. It is, in this light, significant that of the three possible stories the one that is told is the one considered 'unusual' (p. 8), although it could equally well be argued that there is nothing unusual in Zinaida's all too paradigmatic tragedy.

The initial situation that exists between men is another commonplace of patriarchal literature – the competition between men for the prize of the woman, a game in which, here, as before, there can only be one winner and which women almost always lose.[36] The rivalry is treated in parodic vein at first, when the young (and highly embarrassed) Volodya is caught staring at Zinaida: 'Is it permitted to stare like that at *other people's women?*' (p. 11; my italics), asks one of the admirers. This comic opening is developed in the game of forfeits, which is deliberately evocative of the fairy-tale antecedent. The path to the princess, or rather 'queen', is strewn with obstacles, in the shape of rivals.[37] The rivalry may be ritualised and stage-managed, but the real nature of it remains clear, as is to be later apparent in the less than friendly argument between Volodya and Lushin. Beneath the game-playing lies a bitter competition for the hand of the heroine.

As we know, lurking behind these charades is the one man who plays this game in deadly earnest, Volodya's father. Their relations, while not strained, are less than intimate. Volodya confesses that he admires him, loves him, considers him the very model of a man, but is not allowed to be close to him. Later in life he had realised the reason: 'he had not time for me, nor for family life; he loved something else' (p. 30). The identity of this 'something else' is, of course, the very crux of the story and one of the many riddles concealed by the plot/*fabula* disjunction which emerges at the end.

At the core of both levels of the narrative is the heroine and a retrospective analysis shows clearly, as we have seen, that the deliberate suppression of one half of the story was to delay the son's knowledge of the awesome Oedipal truth. His real rival for the woman was his father. Yet this revelation, in this version, does not lead to patricidal fury but the very opposite: 'it was as if he had grown in my eyes' (p. 67). There can really be only one reason for this rather extraordinary denouement to the potential conflict. His father had shown himself to be above other men, and Volodya cannot but admire the true source of power in the text. It is significant, therefore, that only now can there be a scene of true intimacy between men, between father and son, as they ride together to the scene of Zinaida's final humiliation. The last image of his father is as extraordinary as the scene which precedes it: having insisted that he had thrown away, and not dropped, the whip he had used on Zinaida, Volodya's father looks down; Volodya comments: 'And here I . . . saw how much tenderness and regret his stern eyes could express' (p. 71). The woman's suffering, then, serves not only as a marker of Volodya's maturation, but also brings the two men, father and son, to a moment of unprecedented and unrepeated intimacy.

2.6. Male/Female Relationships

From the very title to the epilogue referring to the death of Volodya's 'passion', the central concern is, of course, with 'love', that is, the complicated relations between men and women. As elsewhere in Turgenev's work, *eros* and *thanatos* are intimately connected.[38] The experience of love/passion is primarily perceived from Volodya's point of view, although there is a highly significant coda, the view of love as expressed by his father.

Although Volodya may be said to initiate the plot ('How can I get to know them?'), once he enters the magic circle of Zinaida's fairy-tale castle he loses all power. On his very first meeting with her he 'moved as if in a dream' (p. 15). Later he all but faints at her touch and, as we have seen, is almost literally intoxicated by her.[39] The sensation of love is compared to a violent explosion of energy, beyond the will or power of the individual man. Unable to sleep after the traumatic game of forfeits, Volodya listens to the approaching 'thunderstorm'. The pathetic fallacy conveys not orgiastic bliss but darkness and danger: 'the thunder grumbled angrily' (p. 28). Lighting flashes outside his window, finding an echo within him. Sexual energy is a violence *done to* the individual to which he must submit and wait for it to pass. It is an elemental force which cannot be resisted.

This particular thunderstorm may pass across the sky, but the storm of love lasts rather longer and the effects are more damaging. Once in love, Volodya sits by his window 'as if bewitched' (p. 28).[40] He falls asleep finally, 'with a valedictory and trusting adoration' (p. 29). It may be juvenile infatuation, but within the power struggle which seems to be the implicit semantic significance of this text, he has entered dangerous ground, as he has surrendered his will to a woman, and is deprived of all self-motivation. Once he realises his 'passion', he comments: 'an insuperable power attracted me to her' (p. 32). Zinaida controls him completely and the similes used show how absolutely lost he is: 'Like a spider tied by its leg . . . I sat for hours on end and stared, stared seeing nothing . . .. But Zinaida still played with me like a cat with a mouse' (p. 35). Even towards the end, shortly before the dramatic revelation, he declares: 'She did everything she wished to me' (p. 63).

But Volodya is not alone in being thus unmanned. Zinaida, until her own humiliation, plays the role formerly attached to Asya/Lorelei, that of the Siren who lures men to their doom. All men (bar one), it would seem, cannot resist her fateful power: 'all the men who visited her house were insane about her and she kept them all on a leash, at her feet' (pp. 32–3). The degeneration to the level of animals is again significant. Zinaida, at least according to our narrator, is like a widow-spider who needs so many men to satisfy her greed for power: 'Each of her admirers was necessary to her' (p. 33).

As we have seen, she pays fully in kind. It must, indeed, be said that the storm of love is a torment for *all*, men and women, through whom it passes. The Russian pun on *strast'* ('passion') and *stradaniya* ('suffering') becomes more and more overloaded with significance as the text progresses to its remarkable climax, culminating in Volodya's realisation of what it all means after the final scene between his beloved and his father: 'So that's love . . . that's passion! How, it seems, not to be indignant, how to bear the blow from wherever it might come! . . . from the dearest hand!' (p. 72). To love, it would seem, is to bear the whip.

One man 'who had not time for family life' remains relatively immune to the traumas of passion. He loved 'something else', the 'free will' (p. 31) of the individual. Even he is reduced to tears by a letter he receives towards the end of the story proper (p. 72), but he realises and learns well the lessons of love. On the very day of his stroke, he writes to Volodya: 'My son . . . beware a woman's love, beware this happiness, this poison' (p. 72). By the end of the story all the threads come together and the view of love, of women, of sexual relations, can be seen to be summed up in the Stern Father's valedictory note. Love, whether first or last, may bring happiness. This will be brief and full of mutual torment, because a woman's love is a 'poison'. Zinaida's last two appearances in the text confirm that the *text itself* implies an equally misogynistic view. The woman is whipped and, four years later, dies an archetypal death.

3. HOME OF THE GENTRY[41]

In Turgenev's own lifetime, *Home of the Gentry* was one of his most popular works, acceptable to all shades of opinion despite the rapid polarisation of Russian society after the end of the Crimean War, the death of Nicholas I, and in the years leading up to the Emancipation of 1861.[42] The heroine, Liza, was particularly liked, especially by those of a Slavophile persuasion. Certainly her spiritual purity and deep religious feeling set her apart from the deeply flawed Asya and Zinaida on the one hand, and the questing Yelena on the other. Alongside Liza, however, stands a completely different female type, the scheming and perfidious Varvara Pavlovna, wife and destroyer of the hopes of the hero Lavretsky. In this novel, indeed, we see more clearly than in any other work by Turgenev the traditional patriarchal dichotomous treatment of women, subdivided into the opposing but complementary poles of virgin and whore.

3.1. Plot and Setting

Although the central plot thread is the developing relationship between Lavretsky and Liza, the love story is much less centre-stage than in Turgenev's other novels.[43] Initially, and at the end, the work concerns a man's destiny, that of Lavretsky, the returning native, and his attempt to become a true Russian once more. After an extremely protracted exposition, their relationship does become of central importance, and, once again, the motif is the hero's (and the reader's) attempt to solve the riddle of the feminine soul. Here, too, the quest is doomed to failure, albeit for slightly different reasons. As the (for once) benevolent older woman, Marfa Timofeevna, asserts to Lavretsky's enquiries about Liza's nature: 'Another's soul, you know, is a dark forest, and a maiden's all the more so' (p. 182).[44] Lavretsky is forced to agree with this folk wisdom: '"Yes", he murmured in measured tones, "you can't unravel a maiden's soul"' (p. 182). In any event, this 'chivalric romance'[45] never quite takes over the plot, in that it is deliberately set against a much broader set of social and ideological relations and conflicts. Lavretsky, learning from his disastrous infatuation and marriage, is now rather more measured in his courtship than N. N. or Volodya. Even when already falling in love, he visits his friend, the musician Lemm, rather than rushing to call on Liza.

Once this mature, spiritual love begins to blossom, the pathetic fallacy of the setting again sets the tone. Here too there are marked differences from the two shorter works. Gone is the 'thunderstorm' to be replaced by the quintessential Russian scene – a beautiful spring day on a tranquil, somewhat run-down country estate. Here purity, quietude are the keynotes. Against an Arcadian backdrop, Lavretsky fishes and converses with his true Russian heroine. The peacefulness is underscored by repeated lexis: 'Reddish, tall reeds rustled *quietly* around them, before them the still water shone *quietly*, and their conversation was *quiet*' (p. 208; my italics). This repetition may verge on the bathetic, but the point is made. Later, as dusk descends and the visitors return to town, the evening is also 'warm and quiet' (p. 212). Lavretsky and Liza are further associated with the night, but now the nocturnal scenes are marked not by tempestuous passions but serenity.

However, as in the antecedent 'chivalric romance[s]', their love is to be thwarted by, on the one hand, male rivalry, and, then, by a grotesque *dea ex machina*.[46] The former motif is once more relatively muted, but is an important consideration nonetheless in blighting the purity of their love. Liza is already virtually promised to another, the self-seeking civil servant and caricature Westerniser, Panshin, and her intense sense of filial duty, as well as religious guilt cast a shadow over her feelings for Lavretsky. He is no longer given to the extravagant jealousy of his youth, but his ideological joustings with Panshin have a strong personal animosity as an undercurrent. This time, however, *neither* man is to win the hand of the virgin, for she is to seek out her own destiny as a bride of Christ.

It is significant that, once the relationship between Liza and Lavretsky does finally get started, the plot tempo quickens remarkably. And it is to reach an equally abrupt conclusion. Liza, as we learn from the brief biographical background given in Chapter 35, could perhaps never have found fulfilment in sexual (and, therefore, selfish[47]) love. The text underscores this by repeating yet again her key adjective in the penultimate sentence of the chapter: 'Lavretsky was the first to disturb her *quiet* inner life' (p. 244; my italics). Indeed, her plot and destiny had always been leading to another denouement, to the haven of the convent, which is, with some significance, the concluding scene of the whole novel.

Even if Liza *had* been willing to marry Lavretsky, their plot would have been thwarted by the rather cheap trick played by the novel's denouement. Lavretsky and Liza finally confess their love for each other, thinking, on extremely flimsy evidence, that Lavretsky's wife is dead.[48] The *very* next morning Varvara Pavlovna turns up in the town of O. As Lavretsky himself says to his estranged wife: 'In what melodrama is there precisely such a scene?' (p. 246). Indeed, it *is* melodramatic and the effect, which renders Lavretsky momentarily speechless, is that of a 'bolt from the blue', or 'the hand of God' or any other such theatrical cliché. But, in fact, it is not Fate, but a scheming, grasping coquette who has returned to destroy the honest Russian's happiness for a second time.

If this is fairly crude melodrama (and the laying-bare of the device does not alter the fact), then much of what ensures is grim farce. As the relationship between Lavretsky and Liza fades into bitter-sweet nostalgia, Varvara Pavlovna, not content with dashing Lavretsky's hopes, now lures Panshin into her web. The contrast between the two relationships is further exacerbated by the scherzo pace of the vulgar pair, Varvara and Panshin, as compared with the measured development of the earlier scenes of true love. In the end all four perhaps get what they deserve, although it remains the case that the logical conclusion of the 'true plot' has been thwarted, on the one hand by Varvara's venality, and on the other by Liza's spirituality. In terms of the plot, as well as type, the two women are diametrically opposed.

3.2. Male/Female Relationships

A further polarity within the text, with the two women once more as the focus, is between types of love – the spiritual and the merely carnal. As has already been noted, neither leads to much happiness, and marital discord, if not bitter enmity, would seem to have been the norm in Lavretsky's family background, to which the novel pays detailed attention. Stemming from this, and, in particular, because of the somewhat peculiar upbringing arranged for him by his father, Lavretsky is singularly ill-prepared to enter the ways of the world, still less to withstand the charms of such as his future wife. By the age of twenty-three he had never looked a woman in the eye, and when he sees Varvara at the theatre he is lost at once. Although this scene and the ensuing courtship are treated in parodic vein, the dangerous effects of the sensual woman on the inexperienced man are clear enough and can be seen as a pre-echo of Volodya's first view of Zinaida in *First Love*. He is unable to remove his 'gaze' (p. 166) from her; the fact that his only friend in Moscow enters her box seems to Lavretsky 'portentous and strange' (p. 167), and all night 'he both trembled and was aflame' (p. 167). The language is mocking but, as in the later 'melodrama', the device laid bare does not conceal the implicit sorcery performed by female flesh.

The rest of their early relationship and marriage is passed over in the same (somewhat forced), ironic style, until its collapse on Lavretsky's discovery of Varvara's infidelity with some vulgar Ernest. In the broader scheme of the novel, Lavretsky's 'education' may well be to blame, but it remains the case that it is the perfidious woman who destroys his first dreams of marital bliss: the equation of 'a woman's love' and 'poison' made by Volodya's father in *First Love* would seem to be entirely justified on this occasion.

If the text as a whole presents a diadic view of women, then this is one shared by its male protagonist, for it is precisely because Liza is so different from Varvara that Lavretsky is drawn to her. Like N. N. and Volodya he tends to perceive women in terms of *images*. The whore makes way for the virgin in his life, as he is drawn to her by her innocence and honesty. On his way to his country estate after meeting this distant (and much younger) relative, Lavretsky muses on her essence and, significantly enough, attempts to interpret the *image* created within his mind: 'A pale, fresh face, the eyes and lips are so serious, and the gaze is honest and innocent' (p. 184). The reading of the external signs may be positive, but the male problem of seeing women as creatures of their own imaginations remains.

Yet he comes to love Liza, not by responding to the 'lightning' within him, but by first becoming her friend, by attempting really to know her. Indeed, their relationship initially grows out of their shared likes and tastes (especially their love of Russia) and their mutual respect. They are friends first before they become lovers. When Liza comes to visit Lavretsky for their epiphanic moments by the water, she offers her hand 'in a friendly manner' (p. 207), almost as if they were old friends. Despite this, it cannot really be said that their relationship is one of equals. Lavretsky perceives her imaginatively, as we have seen; he is much older and, indeed, reveres her as an innocent *child*, calling her this ('my child', p. 198) as she reproaches him for leaving Varvara. Clearly, he idealises her or, more precisely, sees her as 'his true ideal', 'too pure' even to pronounce Varvara's name (p. 199).

To him she represents the future and the hope that he can live again, become what he wants to be. She can *redeem* his troubled past, because he has finally discovered in her what Varvara so manifestly lacked. As their love grows he tells her as much: 'in the course of these two weeks I have realised what a *pure* woman's soul means, and my past has moved even further away from me' (p. 220; my italics). Purity is the essence of the good woman, but this is, of course, as one-sided a view as his contempt for Varvara's infidelity. Indeed, once he realises his love for Liza he muses on the contrast between the two women, and his terms of reference show, firstly, his conception of women as polar opposites, and, secondly, how idealised and unrealistic his view of women remains. Liza will redeem him by leading him to his goal: 'But Liza cannot be compared *to that one*; she would not demand shameful sacrifices of me; she would not distract me from my work; she herself would inspire me to honest, severe work and we would both walk forward to a fine goal' (p. 226; Turgenev's italics).

Liza is, more than anything else, disturbed by her love for Lavretsky, precisely because it does distract *her* from her goal, her destiny.[49] Lavretsky, his love, and her love for him, are most definitely an intrusion: 'It's true . . . she trusted him herself and felt drawn to him; but all the same she felt ashamed, as if a stranger had entered her virginal, pure room' (p. 224). The somewhat clumsy euphemism in the last clause does not disguise what love means for Liza. To her, as to everyone else, although for very different reasons, it brings no happiness at all.

As is so often noted,[50] the joy of love in Turgenev's work is brief at best. In this novel it is virtually non-existent, because as soon as Lavretsky and Liza confess to each other their hopes are destroyed. The two variations on the theme of erotic non-fulfilment which occupy the last quarter of the novel serve to reinforce this bleak view absolutely. There can be *no* happy relations between male and female. The complicating factors vary, but the conclusion remains that of Liza: 'Love did not express itself as happiness' (p. 254). The circumstances of its development are profoundly different from those of Volodya, but the issue remains the same: love is a torment to be borne, or as Liza experiences it: 'a punishment for her . . . criminal hopes' (p. 257). However, it should once more be stated that the prime-mover in all this unhappiness is not God, as Liza might imagine, but the rather less spiritual being of Varvara.

3.3. Women and their Social World

Just as Lavretsky's idiosyncratic education had a critical effect on his relationships, so, too, Liza's background plays a crucial determinant function in the etiology of her ultimately unhappy love. Like most of Turgenev's young heroines, Liza's education, while taking place at home, is largely unsupervised,[51] and serves to produce someone who does not belong fully in her own context (nor, it could be said, anywhere in the Russian world which surrounds her[52]). Liza is initially brought up by her French governess, before the really important influence appears, Agafya, her nanny from peasant stock.[53] Under her influence Liza becomes an extremely serious child, but even more significantly, she is imbued with traditional Russian culture – not the fairy-tales of Pushkin and his Tatyana, but the *zhitiya* ('hagiographies'). From a combination of her own character, her separation from her family and her contact with Agafya, Liza develops into her own person: 'she did not have "her own words", but she had her own thoughts and she went her own way' (p. 243). Despite this, she is clearly inscribed into a particular culture, Russian and religious ('Entirely imbued with a sense of duty' (p. 243), and this certainly affects the way she relates to Lavretsky as well as to others.

If Liza *is* estranged from her immediate family ('She was afraid of her father; her feelings for her mother were imprecise' (p. 242)), then this sense of alienation is compensated for by close female friendships and support, something of a rarity in this writer's work as we have noted. Marfa, her aunt, supports her in her troubles after the collapse of her love (although she also severely disapproves of it), and the older woman's room upstairs (as well as her motley entourage) provides a refuge from the false society drawing room over which Liza's mother reigns in a pale imitation of Varvara.

Indeed, Liza's lack of an immediate familial context is further offset by very strong thematic and symbolic cultural relationships. Through music, as well as mutual respect and affection, she is linked with Lemm, and his warm praise of Liza is an important factor in Lavretsky's growing regard for the heroine. In this sense too, their love is almost a by-product of the wider themes of Russia and the West, town and country, the traditional and the superficially modern.

Certainly one of the strongest ties that bind Liza and Lavretsky is their shared sense of Russianness and their love of their native land. In this sense, it could be argued that their equally peculiar backgrounds have prepared them for each other, have sown the seeds for their love even before they meet. Yet the opposite is also the case. Precisely because of Liza's religious upbringing, her sense of belonging to another world, she cannot fully give herself to Lavretsky or any man. Varvara's return thwarts them, but, as already noted, Liza's 'own way' was in any case leading her to another life. It is, in this sense, highly significant that Turgenev's most idealised heroine does not belong in the world of everyday and, more specifically, sexual emotions.

3.4. Images of Women

Although Liza is to end up withdrawn from the world, a living icon of virginity, her characterisation does start out as a serious attempt to present not an image or type of woman, but an independent, rounded being. As we have seen, her education sets her apart, but the reader has known this from her first appearance in terms of her behaviour. Unlike the demure heroines of earlier decades,[54] and in anticipation of the later Yelena, she bears herself as a strong presence, looking directly at her male interlocutor (pp. 140, 179), and showing firm independence from the superficial society world of her mother's drawing room in her reproaches to Panshin for his treatment of the sensitive Lemm. Her relationship with the kindly old musician, as we know, is part of her characterisation, lending an important *moral* direction to her being. She is never afraid to speak the truth, she acts out no roles, plays no games. She is merely herself, with no attempt to impress. Her characterisation, then, is essentially moral rather than in terms of her physical appearance. This tendency in her portrayal does remain a constant, whatever her later changes may be. She prays for Lavretsky twice a day (p. 210), and is sharply moralistic in her reproaches to him for his unseemly joy at his wife's 'death' (p. 218).

More generally, Liza is firmly located within a value system, as witnessed by her religion, her love of Russia, as well as her rejection of the artificial world she temporarily inhabits. This is given added credence by the positive evaluation of her by the minor characters who are ranged on the side of the angels, most notably Lemm and Marfa: 'You are a very good girl' (p. 144), the former asserts, while he later confides to Lavretsky: 'Lizaveta Mikhailovna is a just girl, serious, with elevated emotions' (p. 197). She is, indeed, a person without 'her own words', but of whom much is spoken.

Yet, once she encounters Lavretsky, her characterisation begins to change. The rounded portrait that had been developing is disturbed even before she comes to recognise this disturbance within herself. Whereas she had begun as someone who would look others directly in the eyes, the narrator now begins to observe her adopting the mannerisms of the traditional demure heroine, and her behaviour becomes more and more that of this type. It is significant that this change in her *physical* demeanour occurs as soon as her 'virginal room' is entered for the first time. Suddenly, they have become very close, and Liza retreats into stereotyped iconography. In discussing Lavretsky's marriage, she asks him why he married: 'Liza whispered and *lowered her eyes*' (p. 199; my italics). As their relationship develops, they come to discuss happiness and, in his ardour, Lavretsky takes both her hands: 'Liza turned pale and almost with fright, but looked attentively at him' (p. 221). The change is not yet complete. As Lavretsky leaves she is unable to speak, 'because her heart was beating too fiercely and a feeling akin to fear caught her breath' (p. 222).

Shortly afterwards they meet by chance in Liza's garden, where they will finally kiss and be in love. The description of Liza's appearance and behaviour now takes on an even more intense degree of iconography. She is dressed in white, has unplaited hair, is carrying a candle and walks 'quietly' (p. 236). When Lavretsky calls her name, 'She shuddered' (p. 236). She comes to meet him, her face is 'pale'. When Lavretsky declares his love we are told: 'Her shoulders began to tremble slightly, the fingers of her pale hands clutched her face still more tightly' (p. 236); he hears '*quiet* sobbing'. Once more she 'shuddered', before, finally, he kisses her 'pale lips'. The repeated lexis – 'pale', 'shudder', 'quiet' – is quite possibly unintentional. Be that as it may, it leaves the independent heroine acting in the mechanistic way of many antecedents.

This climactic moment, however, had been prepared for by the increasing tendency to associate Liza with traditional stereotypes once she had entered a potentially sexual relationship. In particular, she becomes the very epitome of the 'virginal child'.[55] The visit to Lavretsky's country estate is, in this instance, the turning-point. We have already noted the repetition of 'quiet' (which is to occur elsewhere, as above). Liza, as in the later garden scene, has on a white dress, with a white belt just to emphasise her purity. Lavretsky looks at her (and so do we), in particular 'at her *pure*, somewhat severe profile . . . at her *tender* cheeks, which were hot, like those of a *child*' (p. 208; my italics). Liza here emerges as an icon: the pure child in virginal white. Like Anyuta and Tatyana before her,[56] she is the Arcadian innocent who could have redeemed the man corrupted by the city (and foreign lands) if, alas, it were not too late . . . ..

Having begun the novel as an independent being, Liza is now 'elevated, as the image of woman has so often been elevated before, to an abstraction or an emblem'[57] – for Lavretsky certainly, but also for the narrator and the reader.[58] The setting of the above scene and Liza's persona merge so that she represents spring, the country, Russia, or, more generally, a fresh beginning. Beneath the weight of this symbolisation, however, her *character* is submerged. Her role as the essence of the Russian soul is finally confirmed by the narrator's comments following the dispute between Lavretsky and Panshin concerning Russia's needs. In a virtual paraphrase of Pushkin's line about Tatyana: 'Russian in her soul, without knowing why herself', he tells us: 'It would never have occurred to Liza that she was a patriot; but she found Russian people to her liking; the Russian way of thinking delighted her' (p. 234).

Once her love affair has bloomed so briefly and must end, Liza shows great fortitude, but, equally, moves even more rapidly into the realms of iconography. Indeed, it can be argued that this is precisely where and how she finds her true identity, in her complete submission to her duty to God. In deciding to quit the world she behaves with '*quiet* solicitude on her face' (p. 284; my italics). All the implicit meaning of the adjectives applied to her earlier is now realised, as she becomes virtually a 'living relic'[59] even before she enters the convent. In her touching farewell scene with Marfa, we read the following: 'and Marfa Timofeevna could not kiss enough these poor, *pale*, enfeebled hands – and *speechless* tears fell from her eyes and from Liza's' (p. 261; my italics). The young virgin has now become an emblem, no longer of hope and the future, but of a death of feeling, transmogrified as she is into a virtually speechless statue. By the end of the plot she has left 'to lock herself away forever' (p. 286), and almost our last sight of her (and Lavretsky's) is as a *'pale ghost'* (p. 292; my italics).

If Liza's passage through the novel marks a decline from a rounded character to a symbolic presence to a living icon, then Varvara Pavlovna does not have so far to travel. She is a grotesque caricature from beginning to end. The portrayal of this female character is, indeed, full of fear and loathing.

Even before their marriage Varvara has shown herself to be a schemer and manipulator of others, a young woman on the make. Once she has established a secure income, she moves into her element. In almost every dimension she is a polar contrast to Liza. She loves the society world where she 'attracted guests like moths to a flame' (p. 172); they move abroad where she is even more at home. There is no attempt to investigate her inner world: the implication is that there isn't one to investigate.

This part of the novel (what has led Lavretsky to his present confused state) is deliberately passed over hastily, which in part, at least, accounts for the rather cardboard impression her character creates. When she does enter the plot proper (to devastating effect, of course), she is in no way redeemed, however; *au contraire*, as she would no doubt have said herself. Even before Lavretsky or we see her, she stands in bad odour, literally, as she is announced by the 'repulsive' smell of patchouli (p. 244). The narrator deliberately uses a foreign based word to dismiss her even more completely: 'this lady [*dama*] was his wife' (p. 245).[60] Each detail emphasises her non-Russianness and falsity. With a flourish worthy of a 'melodrama', she falls at his feet, calling him by the Gallicised version of his name, 'Théodore'. French words are liberally sprinkled in her macaronic speech, while their daughter speaks only French. Later she is at once at home with the unpleasant, and equally Westernised, Panshin.

While Liza was severely honest and unaffected, Varvara continues to act out roles, and from genres other than melodrama. For as long as is necessary (which is not very long) she acts the part of the repentant wife, although she soon proceeds to a role that clearly fits much better – seductress. She is told of Panshin's existence and asks: 'A young man? . . . And an artist? . . . And young?' (p. 259) The sarcasm invested in her portrait is extreme. Not content with this, the narrator explains the matter when Varvara encounters Panshin. Varvara murmurs to him: '"Venez!" – and nodded her head to the side of the piano. This one off-hand word: "Venez!" – instantaneously, *as if by sorcery*, changed the entire outward appearance of Panshin' (p. 262; my italics, French in the original). But this is not yet enough for her rapacious appetites. On the way home she travels by carriage with the hapless Gedeonovsky: 'the whole way she amused herself by placing, as if by accident, the tip of her little foot on his . . . she giggled and made eyes at him' (p. 267). And this is the repentant wife.

Varvara's portrait lacks all credibility, but serves merely as a pretext for fairly crude misogynistic abuse. As a consequence of this lapse from the novelist's objectivity, the image of women that emerges is utterly diadic, an almost perfect enactment of the virgin/ whore polarity. The two women are contrasted on almost every level. Liza is pure, child-like, natural, of the country, Russian: Varvara is adulterous (and a seductress), corrupt, artificial, more at home in St Petersburg or, even better (or worse), abroad. The conclusion of the novel reiterates these highly schematic divisions of the female character. The virgin has retreated to her spiritual home, while the whore has moved back to Paris. Unlike Zinaida, both are still alive, but, taking the novel as a whole, the female personality has been split asunder.

4. ON THE EVE[61]

This chapter began with quotations from three recent works about Turgenev, all of which viewed his most famous heroine, Yelena Stakhova, as essentially a positive type. It was certainly true, as Lavrov noted, that she did indeed become 'a symbol of women's emancipation in Russia'.[62] In part at least, this symbolisation depended on the time the novel appeared, 'on the eve' of the Emancipation of the Serfs in 1861, and of other broader changes in Russian society. To establish the extent to which this 'apotheosis of the Russian woman' (to use Dostoevsky's phrase for Pushkin's Tatyana[63]) is justified by the actual text will be the primary purpose of the concluding sections of the present chapter.

4.1. Plot and Setting

The novel opens with another 'scene that is quintessentially Russian',[64] and one that gives the impression that we may be entering an androcentric text. Two young intellectuals, Shubin the sculptor and Bersenev the philosophy student, lounge by the banks of the Moscow River on a hot summer's day, discussing the nature of human happiness, the possibility of altruism or the greater likelihood of egoism.[65] Certainly this discussion does set out the major themes of the novel, but male camaraderie (later partially shared by the Bulgarian revolutionary Insarov) is to prove to be merely a prologue and then a background to the main story, which is that of how Yelena 'found herself'.[66] In the same digressive manner used for Lavretsky in *Home of the Gentry*, it is her peculiar background and upbringing which is given in detail, for *she* is to be the sentient centre,[67] it is to be *her* story. She may at first appear to be as much of an enigma as the other heroines we have discussed, but it is for her to unravel her own mystery (and for the reader), rather than for any intrusive, predatory male. This tendency is later confirmed by the extended extracts from the diary she begins to keep shortly after meeting Insarov. One of the commonly noted defects of the novel is that Insarov lacks any real credibility as a character, precisely because we know so little about his inner life. But it is equally significant that it is specifically about the young heroine and her innermost secrets that we do learn. Certainly by comparison with all the other works studied in the present book, *On the Eve* must be considered one of the earliest attempts by a man in Russian literature to write from the female point of view, if only in part.[68]

However, just as the prologue gives the slightly misleading impression that we are entering the usual all-male world, so, too, the plot, once it begins to develop, bears strong traces of traditional story-lines. The plot is, in fact, initiated by Bersenev inviting his friend, Insarov, to stay with him in the country, of which Yelena, initially at least, is very much a part. It might seem that the outsider, the man, has come to the static enclave to rescue the trembling bird in her cage, to set her free into the broader world of men's affairs. Bersenev continues to act for a time as the principal plot agent, almost playing the part of matchmaker by eulogising Insarov and Yelena to each other. The first plot sequences also further echo Tatyana's situation in *Yevgeny Onegin*. The reader is told of Yelena's deep longings to escape, her aspirations to good, to action. Bersenev tells her of Insarov's equally noble ambitions, in particular that 'He has only one thought: the liberation of his native land' (p. 51). Yelena listens intently and comments: 'You have greatly interested me by your story' (p. 52). Is this *him* we ask? Indeed, it would appear that Yelena has fallen in love with the hero even before she meets him, although it must obviously be emphasised that Insarov is not at all the dangerous Romantic hero that Tatyana imagines Onegin to be (except, perhaps, in Yelena's dream).

The end of the prologue and exposition, as in *Home of the Gentry*, is signalled by a marked increase in narrative pace as Insarov arrives and they meet. They meet and talk as equals: Yelena is not seduced but inspired by the man of intense integrity on the day they exchange ideas: 'He . . . became for her a different person' (p. 68). Insarov further confirms his heroic status in the somewhat ridiculous scene where he throws a drunken German, who had insulted the ladies, into the water, and the change is again marked by Yelena's reactions on the way home from this peripeteia.

Up to this point the story has scarcely deviated from the broad outlines of *Yevgeny Onegin*, or, for that matter, a traditional fairytale. The harbingers of the future of their love affair (the ruined wayside chapel, the thunderstorm and other Gothic paraphernalia) are equally not very promising. Yelena's sleepless night and quivering anxiety as Insarov fails to keep their assignation are reminiscent of Liza's (and others') reactions. Yet the potential of Yelena, hinted at in the exploration of her inner life, suddenly bursts into life at their eventual meeting. Indeed, shortly prior to this scene Yelena announces this new direction. Having waited for Insarov, it is *she* who goes out to find him. Further, it is *she* who makes the first declaration as they shelter from the storm. From this second peripeteia ('my wife before people and before God!' Insarov exclaims, p. 95), Yelena takes charge of the plot. She may as yet only have got as far as 'choosing a man to love'[69] (out of the three possible suitors), but at least it is she who has made the choice.

Just what this choice implies soon becomes apparent. The narrator observes: 'That unforgettable meeting had cast her forever out of the old rut' (pp. 101–2). But the old life still lays claim to her, because, by one of the (melo)dramatic coincidences used again by Turgenev, it is at this point in the story that her father chooses to find her a suitor, the civil servant Mr Kurnatovsky (p. 105). She could, of course, have submitted to her parents' will, as Rudin advised Natalya in an earlier novel, but she now, like Liza, although in a very different style, goes 'her own way'. In choosing Insarov, and then insisting that he take her with him to the cause (which he does not wish to do), she has chosen much more than 'a man to love'. She thereby rejects her parents, the Will of the Father and, in the end, her own country.[70]

These implications are finally laid bare in the scene of confrontation between Yelena and her father, a nice parody of the stern paterfamilias. He intends to require her to abandon her plans and obey him, only to discover that his daughter has completely outflanked him by marrying Insarov in secret: 'To a monastery with you!' (p. 139) Nikolay Stakhov chokes out, neatly emphasising for the reader the difference between Yelena's road and Liza's terminus. Yelena is shaking 'from head to foot' (p. 139) during this scene, but her voice (and will) remain firm.

The young couple (although Insarov is already dying) finally go abroad and the switch to Venice[71] and the passing over of several intervening months yet further emphasises the enormity of Yelena's courageous decision. To 'find herself', Yelena must abandon everything of the 'old rut', but this she is prepared to do. Yet, as is the norm in Turgenev, love leads not to happiness but to death. After only one scene of unalloyed joy (Chapter 23), Insarov's illness and imminent death cast a shadow over the remainder of the novel. In the end, for all Yelena's decision to achieve self-determination, she has no control over the wider events. They enjoy a few moments of respite in Venice *'The Beautiful'* (p. 151; italics in the original), a good dinner, and the epiphanic performance of *La Traviata* in which the singer, as Yelena has done, *'found herself'* (p. 154; italics in the original).[72] But if Yelena can still move forward in her identification with the singer, Insarov sees in the opera his own death. The inexorable and ineluctable plot dynamics unfold. But Yelena, still less her decision to escape the old world, cannot be blamed (although she later suggests that she may be guilty) either for his death,[73] or for the grief she has caused her mother in particular. The narrator suggests that her behaviour and its consequences are part of an immutable (and rather grim) law governing human happiness: 'Yelena did not know that the happiness of each person is based on the unhappiness of another' (p. 157), returning us full circle to the opening, scene-setting debate between Shubin and Bersenev.

As Insarov lies dying, Yelena tends him as a faithful nurse. This both returns her to her childhood care for 'the poor, the hungry, the sick' (p. 33), and leads on to her decision, after Insarov's death, not to return to Russia but to join the 'Sisters of Mercy' (p. 165). This evocative phrase is the sum of her destiny: she has 'found herself' as a nurse, and through her devotion to others she will 'remain faithful to his memory, his life's work' (p. 165). By the end of the novel Yelena has moved (spiritually at least) yet further away from her native land, her family and the old life. We do not even know whether she remains amongst the living. Her destiny may be to continue the work of a man, her husband, and to fulfil the traditional female role of nurturing the needy, but at least she has chosen this for herself and on her own terms.

4.2. Male/Female Relationships

Although the opening discussion between Shubin and Bersenev has a general character, it also touches on the nature of erotic love. Shubin adopts a somewhat cynical stance, advising his rather diffident friend to 'provide yourself with a friend of the heart, and all your melancholy feelings will immediately disappear' (p. 12). Women, and love, are here presented as instrumental merely, to ward off the indifference of 'dumb' (p. 13) nature. Woman is a necessity to man. These views of the old school are soon put into a somewhat negative light by three rather different relationships, which, like this conversation itself, afford an important, contrastive background to the principal relationship of Yelena and Insarov.

Shubin himself is engaged in some sort of dilatory *amour* with Yelena's German companion Zoya (who is to marry Kurnatovsky). This briefly sketched liaison is clearly a parodic version of the rake/coquette alliances of early Romanticism, but it is an important backcloth nevertheless. Rather more significant is the marriage which has produced Yelena. This is even more of a relationship of the old type. They had met at a ball where Nikolay 'had conquered' (p. 18) his future wife, whom he had married for purely commercial reasons. They soon grew bored with each other and, by the time the novel opens, Nikolay is even bored with the German widow he has taken as a mistress. The initial impression of marital (and other sexual) relations is gloomy.

The third male/female relationship, the friendship between Yelena and Bersenev (although he probably does love her), serves a different purpose, in that it prepares the way for her relationship with Insarov. Yelena seeks out Bersenev's company, and engages him in serious intellectual conversations on a purely Platonic basis. She likes and admires him almost entirely because of his *ideas*. In particular, she is all too conscious of her lack of knowledge ('excuse my ignorance, what does "Schellingian" mean?' (p. 24)) and reproaches Shubin for his flippant approach: 'You and I need lectures a great deal' (p. 24). This has strong echoes of the mentor/ pupil relationship of Starodum and Sofya,[74] but again the important difference is that Yelena sets the terms of the relationship. She merely recognises that, given her woefully inadequate education,[75] she does, indeed, need lessons. In her quest for love, ideas are the paramount necessity. In preparing herself to fall in love with Insarov, she is looking for a *teacher* as much as a 'friend of the heart'.

However, there remain traces of the old Romanticism even within the 'new woman'. She is a little disappointed on first meeting Insarov, because he does not match up to the dashing 'image' of the revolutionary she had formed from Bersenev's account of his friend: 'Yelena, without suspecting this herself, had expected something more "fatale"' (p. 59). This slight disillusionment is a significant ingredient in the preparation for their eventual love. The fact that Yelena pursues her acquaintance (taking the lead here, as later) differentiates her from earlier heroines, who had 'loved by the book',[76] usually to their cost. Consequently, when their friendship begins to develop into something more profound, Yelena enters into it without any illusions, and as an equal. Their first meeting alone (Chapter 14) is conducted without any maidenly blushes or shudderings, and Yelena behaves as naturally as she had with Bersenev. She is neither 'quiet' nor 'pale'. He promises to bring her books about his native land, confirming the residual mentor/pupil relationship, but it is precisely Insarov's inspirational qualities (even if these are not very convincing on an artistic level) which deepen Yelena's feelings. After his 'heroic' dealing with the drunken German, the equality of their relationship is further confirmed by the same gesture as in *Home of the Gentry*, a simple shake of the hands, 'for the first time' (p. 79).

Even if her diary reveals that she *had* first dreamed of Insarov as some kind of Romantic avenger ('I dreamed of him last night with a dagger in his hand. And he seemed to say to me: "I will kill you and myself." What nonsense!' (p. 80)),[77] as she grows to know him better both her feelings and imagination become calmer. Later she notes in her diary: 'Here, at last, is a truthful man; here is someone you can rely on' (p. 81). It may be argued, as Ripp has done, that Yelena's love gives some form of 'accreditation' to Insarov, 'endowing him with the purposefulness he lacked by himself',[78] but her diary reveals that his initial attraction for her, as already noted, is precisely in these terms, but in reverse. *He*, with his 'voice like steel' (p. 82), 'how much better than I' (p. 82), is the one who gives *her* the strength to make the great decision of her life and, thereby, abandon her whole previous world. Initially, at least, Yelena does not and, in the circumstances could not, transcend the traditional role of having to wait for the man to liberate her. But, as we already know, once she has flown the cage of her family and of Russia itself she proves the stronger and, increasingly so, as Insarov weakens and slowly life ebbs from him.

Just as in *Home of the Gentry*, the plot (or some would say, the author's deterministic world-view[79]) plays a cruel trick on them, culminating in death and separation. Indeed, not only is this the case, not only does Yelena's happiness depend on 'the unhappiness of another', but their love would seem to bring nothing but grief and misery to all. The equation made by Volodya's father in *First Love* of a 'woman's love' and 'poison' would seem to be operative here as well. Unlike *Home of the Gentry*, a woman may not be to *blame* for the suffering, but erotic love itself would seem to be so inextricably linked with 'disaster', as Yelena herself feels on the morrow of her declaration to Insarov (p. 102). In fact, it could be argued that love does, indeed, weaken and then kill Insarov, if only indirectly, as it is in search of a false passport for Yelena that he contracts the virus that is to kill him.[80] Even before all this, Insarov seemed to have been aware of the danger of love, fleeing back to Moscow to avoid the inevitable. But, as in *First Love*, passion and suffering seem to be inevitably and inexorably interconnected: 'Has this love been sent to us as a punishment?' (p. 128), Insarov is to ask once he has made a partial recovery. Yelena insists that there is no logical foundation for such a view, but the same feelings had occurred to her.[81] No-one in the end is made happy by erotic love. And so, although this novel may allow a woman to choose self-fulfilment through choosing a man to love and following his cause, it simultaneously does not allow her this by the logic of the plot, which is, in turn, underpinned by the fateful intertwining of *eros* and *thanatos*.

4.3. Women and their Social World

Like Asya, Liza and most of Turgenev's heroines, Yelena is an oddity in her own family, effectively a spiritual orphan. Her parents are at odds with each other and she seems to have nothing in common with them. At first she had adored her father and had then become closer to her mother, but by the time we meet her in the novel proper she feels distant and cold to them both. In turn, they had done little to offer her a proper education, abandoning her to a Russian governess, who herself is of a somewhat mixed background, being the daughter of a ruined bribe-taker. Just as Liza had her Agafya to teach her authentic values, Yelena has her 'beggar-girl Katya', whom she had met at the age of ten. Katya it is who teaches the young Yelena about 'all God's freedom' and to care for the sick and needy. But their friendship, disapproved of by Yelena's parents, does not last long in that Katya dies. Thereafter, Yelena, having no siblings, is entirely alone in the world.[82] Admittedly, Zoya is her notional 'companion', but they have nothing in common and we never see them even talking together. However positive Yelena's plot line may be, the text itself does isolate her from all other women, so that she is forced to operate entirely within the structures of patriarchy. Moreover, from her strange background onwards, she is seen very much as an exception. Just as there are no 'real people' in Russia to keep Yelena there, the implication is that there are no other Yelenas.

Her father confirms the view offered by the novel as a whole, in that he sees his 'impudent lass' (p. 138) as a clear deviation from established norms. It could, indeed, be argued that Yelena's relationship with her father shows more clearly than any other aspect of the novel the deepest implications of her plot. Not only does she reject her country but the power of the (admittedly parodic) patriarch to shape and determine the lives of women. In this context, the melodramatic introduction to the plot of her intended fiancé, Kurnatovsky, serves a deeper function. By choosing Insarov, Yelena has challenged the fundamental assumptions of patriarchal power. At this stage, of course, her father does not know this: but the plot coincidence lays bare the threat that is to come to his authority and which he later makes explicit. Moreover, Kurnatovsky, an even worse example than Panshin of the stifling limitations of Russian official life, represents precisely what Yelena, if only intuitively, most detests and wishes to escape from.

Even at this stage, Nikolay Stakhov is aware of the implications of Yelena's behaviour and his action is clearly intended to put an end to her, in his view, childish longings: 'It is time for her to abandon her mistiness, to leave the company of various artists, scholars and all sorts of Montenegrins [sic] and *to become like everyone else'* (p. 105; my italics). He rattles on, as if his decision, the Word of the Father, will be a *fait accompli*, and envisages no opposition from either his daughter or her mother. But it is already too late. He may attempt to declaim his announcement with all the traditional power of the head of the family, but, quite apart from the ironical tone in which all this is presented, the daughter has already decided to ignore his will.

Nikolay is dimly aware of what is going on, as his further oracular utterances to his daughter indicate when they meet, only for her to tell him she is already married. He sees his authority not merely as that invested by ancient tradition in the father, but as emanating from the more formally constituted state structures:

> There was a time . . . when daughters did not permit themselves to look down on their parents, when parental power forced the insubordinate to tremble. This time has passed, unfortunately; at least, many people think so; but believe me, *there still exist laws* which do not allow . . . which do not allow . . . in a word, there still exists laws. I ask you to pay attention to this: laws exist.   (p. 137; my italics)

The three-fold repetition, the more general rambling incoherence, make it obvious that his time, the time of the authoritarian father, has indeed passed. His authority is reduced to shambling hypocrisy by the announcement which curtails this scene, namely that his mistress has unexpectedly arrived. Nikolay makes further rather desultory attempts to refer the matter to the authorities, but his 'impudent' daughter is now beyond his command, and beyond the recall of the wider structures of patriarchy.

5. WHEN WILL THE REAL DAY COME?

In many respects the character and plot of Yelena Stakhova do represent a major development in the portrayal of women in Russian literature. She is prepared to make heroic sacrifices for her self-fulfilment, rejecting her own country and the wishes (and threats) of her father. However, if we consider all the works discussed in this chapter, as well as certain aspects of *On the Eve* itself, major doubts must remain. As we have seen, Asya disappears from the face of the earth and her future must have been uncertain at best; Zinaida is humiliated, physically attacked and dies in child-birth; Liza ends her days 'locked away' in a convent; and Yelena, albeit in the cause of freedom, also vanishes at the end of her story. Moreover, within this story there are many traditional and transitional features. Her plot, until she meets Insarov and even later, is essentially that of Pushkin's Tatyana or of countless fairy-tale Sleeping Beauties before her. Yelena's destiny is not a brilliant career but to 'choose a man'. Consequently, she leaves the jurisdiction of the father for the world of another man, although she is to prove the stronger partner. Her behaviour and aspirations have other strong traces of the traditionally feminine. She is the pupil, the man is the teacher. Both in the past and the present of the novel she is given to inexplicable tears and other displays of emotionalism. Her principal aspiration is to nurture the sick and needy and she becomes a nurse. The resolution of her plot also does not bring real fulfilment as she is cheated by death.

These doubts about the extent to which the view of Maegd-Soep,[83] for example, is correct, are deepened by a glance at the other two principal female characters, Zoya and Yelena's mother, Anna. The former is presented as an empty-headed, kittenish coquette, whose physical characterisation is reminiscent of that of Asya and Zinaida. She is portrayed both by Shubin and the narrator as a very tasty morsel.[84] Her obedience to her eventual husband (Kurnatovsky) is so profound that she even stops *thinking* in German. Anna, although she has a minor triumph in persuading Nikolay not to persecute their daughter further, plays the traditional Victorian role of the semi-invalid, foreshadowing in many respects the character of Volodya's mother in *First Love*. Consequently, Yelena is seen as profoundly and utterly an exception and not the typical representative of Russian womanhood.

Dobrolyubov thought that *On the Eve* flattered to deceive, and in many ways he was right. Chernyshevsky, three years later, set out quite deliberately to take up from where Yelena left off. Her final words in the novel are contained in a letter to her parents, written the day after Insarov's death in Venice. She concludes her thoughts for the future: 'But as to returning to Russia – why? What is there to do in Russia?' (p. 165). Taking this last question as a starting-point, Chernyshevsky set out to prove that there were 'real people' in Russia. Moreover, he demonstrates that a woman can find real work to do, and that she can do it for herself, with a company of sisters. For all her aspirations, Yelena Stakhova remains stranded 'on the eve' of the real day.

7

Nikolay Chernyshevsky and the Real Day

Whatever is thought of its literary merits,[1] it would be hard not to acknowledge that *What Is To Be Done?* (1863)[2] is amongst the most famous and influential books in the Russian Language. It has been called 'a Bible for all advanced Russian women with aspirations toward independence',[3] and its impact can be said to have gone far beyond the literary or even intellectual world more generally: 'In its political effects, as a fundamental text of Russian socialism, this novel has probably changed the world more than any other.'[4] This is not an exaggerated claim; Lenin himself noted:

> Chernyshevsky's novel is too complicated, too full of ideas, to understand and evaluate at an early age . . .. But after the execution of my brother, knowing that Chernyshevsky's novel was one of his favourite books, I set about reading it properly and sat over it not just a few days but whole weeks. It was only then I understood its depth. It's a thing that can fire one's energies for a lifetime.[5]

Certainly, the novel, written in the Peter and Paul Fortress before the author was exiled to Siberia, made a profound impression on Chernyshevsky's contemporaries and became one of the central texts in the debates around the 'woman question'.[6] In turn, it prompted a series of anti-Nihilist novels and other writings for the next decade or so.[7]

Of central importance for an understanding of this reaction and of the novel itself is the issue of female emancipation. However, equally vital is the novel's relationship with previous works of literature, especially the novels of Turgenev,[8] and, even more particularly, the latter's *On the Eve*. Yelena had asked her parents: 'What is there to do in Russia?' (implying that there was no role for her in her homeland and that was why she was not returning), and, from the very title onwards, Chernyshevsky's novel is a riposte to this, in his view, defamatory rhetorical question on the part of

Turgenev's most emancipated heroine to date.[9] It is the contention
of this novel that there was much that not only had to be done in
Russia, but much that could be done. In particular, given the
opportunity, there was immense scope for women to grow and
develop to be at least the equal of men. Moreover, the novel sets out
to demonstrate that they could go beyond personal development
and find work of their own. In the process, Chernyshevsky's
account of Vera Pavlovna's life, marriages and careers sets out to
subvert many of the traditional roles and stereotypes allotted to
women, as well as their traditional plots. That is, the work is
profoundly polemical on the literary as well as the intellectual and
political fronts.

1. Plot and Setting

The very setting of *What Is To Be Done?* sets it apart from the world of
Turgenev and, in conjunction with Dostoevsky's *Notes from the
Underground* which was to appear a year later, marked a new
direction in Russian literature.[10] Although there are a few scenes
outside domestic and other interiors, the novel is deliberately
located within the modern metropolis, St Petersburg, amongst the
new *raznochintsy*, the class which was already superseding the
gentry as the leading group, at least amongst the intelligentsia.[11]
Teachers, students, doctors, sons and daughters of the merchant
class, as well as prostitutes, form the *dramatis personae*.[12] The change
from the leisured and leisurely world of Turgenev (which was about
to be given a different variation in the major works of Tolstoy) is
further indicated by the fact that most of the characters actually
work.

After the dramatic opening in the modern world (the apparent
suicide in an hotel room), the exposition would seem to be part of a
fairly traditional world and plot situation. The narrator, indeed,
draws attention to his use of the Turgenevan motifs: 'The content of
the tale is love, the main character, a woman' (p. 33). We then
encounter this woman, the heroine Vera Pavlovna and her *milieu*.
Her social circumstances differ sharply, but the plot structure is
exactly that of *On the Eve*. But if Yelena's story was about how she
would choose a man to love, Vera Pavlona's tale commences on a
much more dysphoric note. Hers is a world where women are
virtually bought and sold, a veritable 'kingdom of darkness'.[13] As
soon as she is sixteen and reasonably 'accomplished', her family

begins to make marriage plans for her. She is taken off to that traditional locus for advertising female wares, the opera, [14] where she is introduced to a variety of highly dubious young men. Her mother colludes in this display of her body, but then the male world takes over, the group betting the chief protagonist in this conspiracy, Storeshnikov, that he has not yet conquered Vera's virginal charms. Here the world in which women become the objects of male pursuit is revealed in all its hypocrisy, vulgarity and degradation, primarily through the prostitute, Julie Letellier. Vera Pavlovna, however, is even more threatened, as she is undefended by her family. On the contrary, as Serge remarks: 'You can't save her from them all when the mother wants to trade her daughter' (p. 49).

Storeshnikov, egged on by the other men, continues his pursuit, hoping to drug Vera's mother, Marya, with opium so he can have even easier access to the daughter. But this heroine will not submit so easily. Even at the opera she had pleaded a headache to avoid their lecherous attentions, and it is important to note that she begins her liberation from the 'cellar' by herself. She defiantly resists Storeshnikov when he comes to visit, as well as the suggestion from Julie that she should marry him to gain power. She may, as yet, be alone in the world, but she resolutely resists all attempts – from her family, the men, Julie – to storm or undermine her citadel, seeking refuge in the sanctuary of a room of her own, to which she retreats whenever she no longer wishes to have to deal with the forces of darkness.

However, she is still, metaphorically at least, trapped in her 'cellar', and her actual escape from the benighted kingdom once more echoes traditional plot devices, in that the mechanism for her flight is the rescuing man, Lopukhov, a medical student who helps to find her a position in the outside world, and later marries her. [15] In the process the narrator emphasises, to parodic effect, the fact that he is deliberately using a traditional plot. Marya eavesdrops on their conversation, playing perfectly the part of the wicked mother from whose clutches the dashing prince must extricate the virginal heroine. To Marya's dismay, and the reader's amusement, she overhears no love scene, but a discussion on rational self-interest!

Even if in reality Lopukhov is the device by which Vera is liberated, the plot remains hers, as is underscored by the first of her celebrated dreams. As in *On the Eve*, it is the inner life of the heroine we enter and, moreover, this dream, like the following three, has the effect and purpose of summing up the plot thus far. Here Vera dreams that she is locked away in her emblematic 'damp, dark cellar' (p. 114),[16] whence she is freed to the wide-open 'fields' (p. 114) by an allegorical woman. This last is a significant detail, emphasising once more that it is first and last a heroine's text, and, as we shall see, a story about how women help emancipate each other.

The emphasis on the heroine remains, and, at almost every stage, she generates the plot. Once she has left the 'cellar', she dictates the novel contract by which the young couple arrange their lives (and their living space). We return on three more occasions, in metaphorical form, to the deepest recesses of her inner life, in the dreams. She is the only constant character, in that Lopukhov disappears halfway through (to return, thinly disguised as Charles Beaumont), Kirsanov only appears at this point, while the most famous of all the 'new people', Rakhmetov, plays no real part at all in the plot.

Moreover, despite the ironic references to 'love' and 'woman' at the novel's opening, this is not merely a story of how a young woman chooses a man to love (or rather two men!), but also how she finds useful and fulfilling work which is very definitely her *own* and not, as for Yelena, someone else's 'cause' to which she will remain faithful. The implicit polemic of the plot is that for too long women's stories have exclusively been concerned with love and marriage, with the latter more often than not being the desired end-point of their destinies, whether achieved or not. Here Vera Pavlovna does not rest once married, but sets up her model sewing co-operative. This not only provides her with her own cause, but also helps to liberate and fulfil other women. It is a clear riposte to Yelena's question. Furthermore, the workshop is arranged largely without male intervention and becomes not only a model of how work can be organised 'intelligently' (p. 172), but how lives can be effectively run, as the co-operative also provides education, relaxation and, in one particular case, that of Nastya Kryukova, asylum.

There is yet a further polemic in Vera Pavlovna's plot, in that her marriage is not at all the end of her personal development, but the beginning. In other words, women remain of narrative interest even after they cease to be sexually available.[17] Alongside the account of the successful establishment of the co-operative is the story of the 'first love and lawful marriage'. This latter relationship lasts four years, and although the details of their affairs are passed over in a fairly perfunctory way, the polemical thrust remains strong. Vera Pavlovna's life, work and loves are to constitute a *Bildungsroman* for a woman. And then, of course, the polemic deepens with the title of

Part 3: 'Marriage and Second Love'. Firstly, the novel is deliberately unstructured, simply following the pattern of events in a life, the *heroine's* life. Secondly, this title would also seem to be a riposte, again to Turgenev. 'First love' is not the beginning and the end of life, not even for a nubile heroine. In other words, the very plot line emancipates the woman from traditional, patriarchal structures as Vera Pavlovna develops and matures. A sub-plot which is also subverted is that of male rivalry for the hand of the woman. Whereas Onegin and Lensky and then Pechorin and Grushnitsky fight duels, Lavretsky and Panshin engage in intellectual jousting, and even Bazarov fights a duel, Lopukhov and his 'rival', Dr Kirsanov, engage in prolonged debates about how best, that is, most rationally, to resolve the problem.

The fact that the 'second love' is hers, and that she therefore remains the constant narrative thread, is made even clearer after Lopukhov has removed himself, first to Ryazan and then by his fake suicide. But even her second (bigamous![18]) marriage is not yet the end, and the narrative continues to allow her to develop, both in her work and spiritually. Three more years pass and the second marriage is even more successful than the first because Kirsanov and Vera are more equal. They remain deeply in love. But as little time is devoted to their love as to the first, because the focus remains elsewhere, as is witnessed by Vera's fourth and most celebrated dream, as much a vision of a future Utopia as a reflection of her personality, and also by a crucial conversation some twenty pages earlier between the couple. In this debate they establish the causes of women's subordination to, and enslavement by, men and look to a future where all women will be free. *This* is the end-point of Vera's spiritual development which now enters the political domain. By carefully educating her through the processes of the plot, the novel is, in the end and in its own terms, very well structured. And, having reached full political consciousness, Vera Pavlovna is now able to reach her final personal development as she enters on her own career as a doctor. This, too, is surely a riposte to *On the Eve* in which Yelena had aspired no higher than the traditional feminine nurturing role as a Sister of Mercy. Vera Pavlovna moves out of her cellar into the domain of men, on fully equal terms.[19]

By now the plot has more or less finished with the heroine and concludes by broadening out to see how the other 'new people', both male and female, are developing similar enterprises, following similar paths. The interconnection between Vera and the others is emphasised by the latest workshop being declared ready immediately after the account of the fourth dream. Ideology and practice are perfectly combined: the reality mirrors the vision. Yet the novel is not as naive as this may make it sound, or as many commentators have thought, as the last major chapter, 'New Characters and Denouement', indicates. Polozova's story, contained therein, is a deliberate re-enactment of the sort of *milieu* and plot situation from which Vera Pavlovna has now so successfully been liberated. This plot within the plot details a traditional patriarchal environment, albeit a benevolent one, a rapacious rake and a young virginal heroine who languishes from thwarted love. There is, of course, a rational and harmonious resolution to this plot, primarily through the good offices of Polozova's ministering doctor, none other than Kirsanov. But the inclusion of this story in the novel and its structural position serves a very important double function. It both demonstrates how far Vera Pavlovna has travelled, but also suggests that much remains to be done.

The novel draws to a close with idyllic, quasi-futuristic scenes of the new people living their well-ordered, fulfilling and fulfilled lives. Another sewing co-operative has been established and work, study and leisure continue: 'And indeed they all live peacefully. They live in harmony and in amity, both quietly and noisily, both happily and efficiently' (p. 414).

But this is not quite the end of the matter. Firstly, it should be noted that the narrator is at frequent pains to point out that he is, to an extent, only going through the motions in writing a story with 'love' and 'a woman' at the centre. The artificial plot devices, such as the fake suicide to create suspense, and the ensuing, extremely protracted, flashback, are consistently laid bare. The essential artificiality of such intrigues and petty rivalries is mercilessly emphasised. Nothing does this more, perhaps, than the fact that about one quarter of the entire novel is taken up by a discussion of the central event, Vera Pavlovna's break with Lopukhov and her new liaison with Kirsanov. We hear what happened, how and why from Lopukhov's, Kirsanov's, Vera's and also Rakhmetov's point of view. Throughout, the narrator peppers their accounts with sarcastic asides about how ridiculous (or irrational) he finds it all. But an important point is made about the status of the plot. In the end, it is merely a device for the explication of it. This both mocks the artistry of such as the novelist's novelist,[20] but also enables the narrator to go beneath the plots and structures he is recounting to reveal their social and political significance. Thereby, the novel polemicises with the *literary* as well as the political traditions which had kept women in the 'cellar'.

2. Women and the Family

And so now we may return underground to see in a little more detail the 'kingdom of darkness' from which Vera Pavlovna arises. It is a family *milieu* which goes back in Russian literature at least to Fonvizin, developing through Gogol and the plays of Ostrovsky.[21] Like the latter, Chernyshevsky's novel begins in perhaps the least regarded of the Russian social groups, the backward merchant class. Yet again there is an implicit polemic with Yelena, in that Vera Pavlovna has so much further to go to escape.

Like the world of Ostrovsky's plays, Vera's home *milieu* is characterised not merely by ignorance and stupidity, but also by violence and crime. The servants and, at least by implication, Vera as well, are beaten. There are visits by the police, drunkenness: one particular incident is witnessed by Vera when she is only eight. Even when she is older, indeed after the theatre incident, we see her hair being pulled by her mother, although not too hard! But she does at least receive some education. Significantly, this takes place outside the home,[22] although her piano tuition is from a visiting teacher – 'a drunken, but very kind German' (p. 38). This last detail polemicises once more with Turgenev. Liza's tutor, Lemm, was also a very kind German, but certainly not a drunkard. At sixteen she even begins giving piano lessons herself.

The most important relationship in her early years is with her mother, Marya Alekseevna, who dominates her husband and household in a manner reminiscent of Fonvizin's Prostakova or Ostrovsky's Kabanova. She demands complete obedience from her family, including her spirited daughter: 'The girl must obey, she still understands nothing' (p. 42). She does not merely collude in the proposed transaction involving her daughter, but takes an active part, conducting her daughter to the theatre, inspecting her before Storeshnikov's visit. The narrator allows that she may have a good heart, but she is equally liable to fall off her chair, intoxicated, when having a heart-to-heart with her daughter. Even after Vera begins her escape and has left the house with Lopukhov, Marya scours St Petersburg in pursuit of the prodigal daughter. Other families from this world, such as Storeshnikov's, are briefly sketched in to show that Vera Pavlovna's family is the norm, not the exception. This is particularly shown by the farcical scenes where the two families attempt to force the arrangement for the marriage, which culminate in Marya slapping her husband and pulling him around by the hair (p. 69). Vera, of course, escapes, but does return with her husband and is shocked by the foul atmosphere she had once breathed: 'a terrible impression was produced on her by her cellar. Dirt, vulgarity, cynicism of every kind – all this struck her with novel abruptness' (p. 162).

She wonders how she had managed to survive, but she had, and not merely because of her own strength of character, for there are some 'rays of light'[23] in this kingdom of darkness too. As we have seen, she had at least received some education. So too had her brother: indeed, this was the means of her escape, as her brother's tutor was Lopukhov. Moreover, as her second dream sums up, her situation could have been even worse. In some ways, at least, her upbringing had prepared her to aspire to a life above ground, in that her mother's mercenary attitude to life had forced a degree of independence on Vera. The allegorical female figure addresses her: 'And your mother is a bad person, but all the same a person, she needed you not to be a doll' (p. 170). In the end the mother/daughter relationship again shows a new development. As in Turgenev's novels, the heroine is a spiritual orphan within her family, but, for all the excesses of this merchant family, Vera Pavlovna had learned something from her mother. As the dream asserts to Vera: 'without her you would not have been' (p. 170). Vera takes this admonition to heart and carries it with her into her later relationships with other women, for she is able to build on what rapport there had been with her mother to establish real friendships with other women. However 'terrible' her childhood had been, it did at least sow the seeds for later female solidarity.

3. The Image of the Heroine

We first encounter Vera Pavlovna half-way through the novel's story-line or *fabula*, when she receives news of her first husband's 'suicide'. The image of the heroine is deliberately balanced, distanced and unvoyeuristic: that is, we are not invited to gaze upon her physical charms, but to assess her as an independent being. She is at once a person, not an image.[24]

A 'young lady' (p. 29) is sitting sewing and singing a French[25] song which has a few sad notes in it, but is more generally characterised as 'animated, bold' (p. 29). She resists the melancholy undercurrent: 'It's clear, the young lady does not like to give in to sadness' (p. 30). The presentation of her is calm, rational, unsentimental. Now she receives a letter telling her (as we later learn) of the 'death' of Lopukhov. Her reaction is classically 'feminine': 'She covered her face with her hands, began to sob. "What have I done! What have I done!" – and again sobbing' (p. 31). However, the melancholy or even sentimental mood is immediately undercut by her maid's astonished reaction: '"Verochka, what's the matter with you? You're not one who's given to crying, are you? When are you ever like this? Whatever's the matter with you?"' (p. 31). Soon, indeed, Verochka returns to normal: '"At such moments one must control oneself; I have my will – and everything will pass . . . it will pass . . ."' (p. 31). There are more tears to come, but the point is made. This is no suffering, vulnerable heroine, but one possessed of rational free will. She is not immune to emotion, but can control it. By using the plot device of *in media res* to create parodic suspense, the novel also utilises this opportunity to establish the heroine as a complex but self-possessed individual, who decides her own behaviour, rather than being merely manipulated by a set of pre-determined roles, images or stereotypes. It is a startling opening to the novel, particularly in the context of a literary tradition where not even the strongest of the 'strong women' were allowed to control their own destinies.

We then return to see the circumstances and events which had produced this 'young woman', and the narrator continues his play with narrative conventions and reader expectation. At first the heroine is not really differentiated from her background and is presented as an 'ordinary' sixteen-year old, concerned that her dark complexion attracts the unflattering epithet of 'gipsy' (p. 39) and delighting in her new wardrobe, especially the rather more expensive boots her mother agrees to buy for her. Her plot situation is equally stereotyped: she is the vulnerable virgin at risk from predatory 'rakes' (p. 55), no different, apparently, from Bela, Asya or hundreds of others in the European novelistic tradition.[26]

But the reader's expectations are as swiftly thwarted as those of Storeshnikov and his gang of rakes. As we know, she prematurely quits their rapacious gaze at the opera and signals her dissatisfaction with her mother's part in this encounter by refusing to kiss her hand

and retiring to the sanctuary of her own room. She continues to differentiate herself from both her own background and traditional literary stereotypes of the feminine by a continued display of independence. Storeshnikov comes to visit and she apparently enacts the role of the willing fiancée-to-be by singing and playing the piano, only to take him aside and threaten to slap his face if he ever dares again 'to display me to your friends as your lover' (p. 51). When he beats his hasty retreat Marya is understandably furious, so Vera simply locks her door against further intrusion, insisting that she will only talk to her mother on her own terms.

So, having dispensed with a characterisation of his heroine in traditional scenes fairly promptly, the narrator proceeds to continue this portrayal in terms of her actions and *ideas*. This first becomes apparent in her rejection of Julie's suggestion that she should marry Storeshnikov. Vera already asserts her aspirations to freedom and independence *before*, it should be re-emphasised, she has even met her 'liberator'. She defiantly announces: 'I want neither to wield power, nor to be subordinate, I want neither to deceive nor pretend' (p. 60). She goes on to widen these demands to a declaration of rights for all: 'I want to do only what I wish to do and let others do the same; I do not want to demand anything from anyone, I do not want to restrict anyone's freedom and I want to be free myself' (p. 61). She is, then, characterised by her views and these are her *own* opinions. And already she is shown as someone who will affect the lives of others, especially other women. Julie withdraws her proposal, deeply moved by Vera's inspirational speech.

Once launched on this path, Vera rarely deviates from her firm commitment to principles. Her early conversations with Lopukhov show her to be a woman of ideas, sharing his opinion that many women would prefer to be men because of the greater freedom allowed to them (p. 84). Gone are the traditional frailties and uncertainties that afflict most literary heroines. At first the novel and its narrator are slightly ambivalent about Vera's status as a heroine. Is she a 'revolutionary' new breed, or is she a role model to which all women may aspire? When the narrator first digresses on the subject of her as a type (Chapter 2), he argues: 'Verochka feels fine now. The reason I am relating (with her agreement) her life is that, as far as I know, she is one of the first women whose lives have been organised well. The first instances have an historical interest. The first swallow greatly interests northern dwellers' (p. 74). But equally she is, in fact, more often than not characterised as 'ordinary'. When Lopukhov looks at her at her birthday party (a parody of Tatyana's catastrophic name-day party in *Yevgeny Onegin*), we read: 'he saw in front of him an *ordinary* young girl who was dancing enthusiastically, laughing heartily' (p. 83; my italics). After the party Vera wonders why she had never really thought about what she and Lopukhov had discussed, namely, the new ideas on women's oppression. Again the narrator intervenes, this time apostrophising his heroine. He tells her (and us) that these ideas are no longer so new, 'and now, Verochka, these thoughts are carried in the air, like an aroma in the fields . . . you have even heard them from your drunken mother . . . you have heard them from a brazen, ruined Frenchwoman' (p. 89). Increasingly, the latter view predominates. For all her striking novelty as a literary heroine, Vera Pavlovna is, in the end, 'ordinary'.

Indeed, as in the opening scenes, the narrator imparts a strong residue of traditional qualities to her. As she and Lopukhov prepare to effect her escape, she exclaims: 'How poor I am, I am unhappy!' (p. 119). Lopukhov echoes this view: 'How pale she is!' (p. 119)[27] She contemplates, at various times, becoming an actress, a governess, and even committing suicide. When Lopukhov is ill for a time she plays the devoted wife and nurse, echoing once more Turgenev's Yelena. But, as the plot reveals, the novel deliberately uses these traditional roles and activities only as a starting-point, as a springboard for Vera's ever higher development. Work, in its own right, is an important necessity to her, and a vital aspect of her portrait, as her second dream indicates (p. 165). As we know, she pursues an active working life to the very end of the novel. She is no rationalistic automaton, however, for great emphasis is also placed on her sensuality and, indeed, sexuality. She, even as an adolescent, has a penchant for fine boots, enjoys lying in her bath and a nice after-dinner nap. We see her lying sensually in bed on more than one occasion.

Perhaps the most important part of her characterisation is the fact that she is presented not as a *static image*, but as a developing personality, with a rich inner life (as represented by her dreams). And, as we have already noted, she is someone who is capable not only of developing fully on a personal level, but also of achieving political consciousness of her own position and of all women. In this sense it could, indeed, be argued that she is a programmatic heroine, in that she decides to train to be a doctor only after she has reached consciousness. But it is equally important to emphasise that it is this political development and eventual awareness that makes her largely unprecedented as a heroine in Russian literature.

166   *Women in Russian Literature, 1780–1863*

4. Other Women

As we have seen, Vera Pavlovna is deliberately characterised by the narrator as 'ordinary'. That is, she is not held up as an unobtainable image of perfection, but a normal young woman who is capable of growth and development. So, too, the other important female characters either change for the better or else their vice and evil are seen to be caused by their social circumstances. In all cases, therefore, the argument runs that female nature is not fixed, but capable of transformation, even redemption, or at least explanation.

Vera's mother, Marya Alekseevna, in the hands of a less sympathetic narrator (Volodya in *First Love*, for example[28]) could have emerged as an unredeemed misogynistic caricature. Most of her attributes are profoundly negative. On most occasions her language is appalling, full of execrations and violent threats.[29] She is also actively violent against virtually everyone in her household, family and servants alike. She is rather stupid, failing to see the real motives of Storeshnikov and the other men who scatter pidgin French in their speech. She is characterised, at least in Verochka's perception, as an animal: 'Verochka again saw the former Marya Alekseevna. Yesterday it had seemed to her that, from under the bestial shell peeped through some human features; now again there was the wild beast, and only that' (p. 50). She is drunken and mercenary and for most of the time an unredeemed termagant.

Indeed, by the time she disappears from the plot she is clearly beyond redemption, but there are rays of light even in her darkness. As the above suggests, there are 'human features' beneath the encrustations of viciousness. After the débâcle at the theatre she goes out of her way to be kind to Vera. Even if it is under the influence of three glasses of punch, her voice 'was indeed soft and kind' (p. 43). Before she passes out she is able to glimpse the truth of her own life and wish a better one for her daughter: 'Ah, my life is hard, Verochka. I don't want you to live like that' (p. 44). It may seem that these are merely the maudlin ramblings of an old drunk, but they are clearly validated by the narrator, who, we recall, whispers to Verochka that she had heard the new ideas even 'from your drunken mother' (p. 89). The narrator redeems the 'human features' of Marya even more explicitly as he bids farewell to her, just before Vera's second dream. He concedes that she is a 'coarse and very bad woman, she tormented her daughter, was ready to kill and ruin her for her own advantage' (p. 161). But that was not all; he goes on to assert: 'the mother sincerely wishes her daughter well' (p. 161). Moreover, the narrator is at pains to discuss the causes of the seemingly impossible mixture within the same person of the 'human features' and the 'wild beast'. Marya incoherently stumbles on the social factors which had led to her downfall (p. 44), and this is a theme taken up later in his valedictory account of Vera's mother:

> I would be happy to wipe you from the face of the earth, but I respect you . . . now you engage in evil deeds because such is demanded by your *situation*, but if you were given another situation, you would gladly become harmless, even useful. (p. 153; my italics)

It is too late to save Marya, but just as Vera climbs out of her 'cellar', so, too, in different ways do the two 'fallen women', Julie Letellier and Nastya Kryukova. Julie first appears in the company of the men at the theatre, and takes an active part in demeaning the physical attributes of Vera: 'this Georgian woman . . . colourless eyes, colourless, thin hair' (pp. 45–6). She seems no better than the coarse, lecherous crowd with which she associates. Yet she is spirited, even comically brave. Once she hears of the male conspiracy against Vera, she insists on rushing round to warn her, that is, to save her from her own fate. She then actively intervenes to help Vera, duplicitously offering to assist Storeshnikov in his machinations (p. 57) before calling on Vera to advise her to marry her 'suitor', as at least this will save her from a life of vice. She, too, has not lost her 'human features', even lecturing Storeshnikov on his duties, counselling him to do the decent thing. Her best energies are devoted, that is, to rescuing another woman.

And for Julie it is not too late. Even before her transformation, she shows an awareness, however paradoxically, of the enslavement that marriage can mean for a woman: 'Marriage? the yoke? prejudice? Never!' (p. 49), she exclaims. Moreover, she is clearly aware that it is social circumstances or, more particularly, men which have led to her own present position and which might entrap Vera also: ' "You're lying, gentlemen", she shouted, leaped up and banged the table with her fist, "you're talking slander! You are mean people! She is not his lover! He wants to buy her! . . . It's vile!" ' (p. 47). She goes on to implore: 'free me from these people, these vile people' (p. 48).

Her prayer is finally answered, because one of the first three

seamstresses that Vera Pavlovna takes on is Julie. Her redemption is
not of the religious kind,[30] but rather prosaic, *ordinary*. She plays no
major role in the plot later on, but her fate is once more polemical, a
demonstration that the 'fallen woman' can rise if she is allowed to by
the lecherous (or sentimental) men who had enslaved her. Even
more significant is that her 'saviour' is not divine, nor even a man,
but another woman. We leave Julie with her naive, Rousseauesque
vision of emigration to Switzerland, where she and her Serge 'will
settle in a little house amidst fields and mountains, on the shore of a
lake, they will love one another, catch fish, look after their vegetable
garden' (p. 159).

Nastya Kryukova's story is another old tale with a new emphasis.
Certainly, as with Vera, Marya and Julie, there are traditional
elements to her narrative. Like Julie she had been a 'fallen woman'
and had been rescued from her life of debauchery primarily through
the intervention of Dr Kirsanov, with whom she then lived. She too
ends up in the sewing co-operative and we first encounter her when
she is being released from work duties because of the advanced state
of her tuberculosis. This traditional story has its clear redemptive
quality. She, as other women also do, tells her *own* story and,
moreover, to another woman, Vera Pavlovna. Despite all her
suffering and exposure to vice, she too has managed to retain her
essential 'human features'. We are told that the second girl who had
offered a confession to Vera 'had preserved all the noble features of a
human being: her unselfishness, her capacity for faithful friendship,
the gentleness of soul – she had even preserved a fair amount of
naivety' (p. 204). And Nastya's story, which then follows, shows
she has managed the same. This account of the redemption of a
fallen woman is in no way sentimentalised, but is rather a
recognition of the essential humanity of all women, without any
morbid, still less Sadeian dwelling on vice as such.[31] Her narrative is
completely devoid of any salaciousness to titillate the reader.

Taking the portraits of these four women (and the others briefly
touched upon) together, the polemical purpose of the novel's
depiction of women is absolutely clear. Women may be evil, vicious
and debased, or merely ordinary young girls, but they all retain their
humanity. The conditions which led to their degradation are largely
created by men. There is much to be done for them, and, more often
than not, they do something both for themselves and for other
women.

5. Female/Female Relationships

Indeed, the very positive picture of how women relate to each other in *What Is To Be Done?* is one of the markedly new aspects of the 'new people' the novel depicts. In almost every other work considered in the present volume, the very opposite obtains, namely, that women are at best isolated from each other, or else are jealous rivals for the attention and affection of men. The freshness, indeed power, of the book is to show how people, especially women, can organise their own lives to their own advantage and to the advantage of other women. As in the personal progress of Vera Pavlovna there is a gradual progression from semi-isolation to a full flowering of 'development', in this instance, of what we would now call 'sisterhood'.

Julie Letellier is the first to show solidarity with another woman, as we have seen, and Vera responds to her gesture, first by acknowledging her good intentions by a warm embrace (p. 56) and then by remembering her when she sets up her co-operative. This, too, is marked by an impromptu celebration between the two women, involving drinking and dancing, while Lopukhov is a somewhat bemused bystander. Once the workshop is on course, it becomes a model of how women help each other, with almost no male participation. The women work in harmony and trust, distributing the profits when they arise. Vera, not a man, is the manager, but she always consults with the other women before any innovation. Finally, Vera leaves the world of the co-operatives, but this, too, is to further her work with women, in the sense that she believes a female doctor would be much better attuned to the needs of other women (p. 331). It is true that much of the plot details Vera's relationships with her two husbands, but the close bonds with other women are equally important to an understanding of the overall purpose of the novel, in particular its marked differences from its predecessors.

6. Male/Female Relationships

Although many political, social and philosophical themes emerge in *What Is To Be Done?*,[32] it is at least arguable that relations between the sexes is the dominant theme, and, certainly, the one most extensively discussed by the characters themselves.

We are first presented, of course, with sexual relations of the old school, both as a contrast with what is to come and as an explicit polemic with the novel's literary predecessors. Vera is viewed at the opera, and then her anatomy is dissected by Storeshnikov, Julie and the rest. In the course of this, the narrator impudently reveals the dubious new status of a rather illustrious antecedent, namely, the celebrated account of women's 'little feet' in *Yevgeny Onegin*. Julie mistakenly attributes this to Karamzin (Karasen as she calls him!), and is corrected by one of the men: 'Pushkin talked about little feet, – his verse was fine for its time, but has now lost a large part of its value' (p. 46). In this world, Russia's greatest poetry assumes the value of pornography.[33] The novel proceeds to reveal the further hidden undercurrents in the great tradition of Russian and European literature, in that Storeshnikov and his friends can legitimately be seen as very down-market versions of Pechorin or at least Grushnitsky and his 'gang'.[34] They are referred to as 'rakes' (p. 55) and their nasty little conspiracy does lay bare the real underpinnings of the 'rake's enconomy' of the eighteenth-century tradition,[35] as we have seen. Storeshnikov is attracted by Julie's suggestion that he should marry Vera because it will enable him 'to possess' her, having already imagined her in various 'poses' (p. 62). His desire to possess the woman again echoes Pechorin's musings on the same subject, where he uses precisely the same word.[36]

In other words, these opening scenes not only locate Vera firmly within the old world, but also deliberately set out to expose the hidden meanings of earlier works of literature in terms of their sexual politics. As the narrator says: 'Like Julie I like to call coarse things by the direct names of the coarse and vulgar language in which we all almost always think and speak' (p. 62). That is, he is not only telling his own story, but offering *readings* of earlier works of literature to show that the relations between such men as Storeshnikov and their women are not fundamentally different from those described even in the 'classics'. Indeed, he goes yet further by offering an explicit generalisation on the subject lest there be any misunderstanding, and thereby points out that sexual relations are central to his task. The narrator asserts: 'almost all of us, men, possess one of you, our *sisters*; again that's nonsense: what sort of sisters are you to us? – you're our servants!' (p. 62; my italics).

Having set the scene, then, and exposed its implications, the narrator immediately proceeds to offer an alternative, not only to the explicit or implicit predecessors of the above scenes, but also to the irrational view of love presented by the novel's main target, the works of Turgenev. This is the relationship between Vera Pavlovna and Lopukhov.

As we know, Lopukhov enters Vera Pavlovna's household as tutor to her brother, Fedya. The boy had suggested that Lopukhov might like to meet Vera,[37] an offer which the noble-minded student had turned down. When the two do meet they assess each other visually. Such a perception of the woman had become a commonplace in literature,[38] but once more the paradigm is undermined in that the gaze is returned by the heroine, and her physical consideration of him is as frank and direct as his of her (p. 74). At this stage we are also told that Lopukhov had had a couple of brief affairs (on a highly rational basis!), but 'this was a long time ago, about three years in the past, and now, for a year or two already, he had abandoned any such childishness' (p. 78).

Certainly their relationship begins on a very unromantic, even anti-Romantic note. There is no 'thunderstorm'[39] between them which they are powerless to resist. Rather, they are impressed by the actions and underlying decency of each other. Equality, even symmetry of attitude is emphasised. Moreover, particularly at the birthday party, they resist the sociolect, the pressure to fall in love. Earlier Lopukhov had been impressed by her spirit in simply getting up and leaving the assembled company to go off, as usual, to her own room (p. 81). Now, at the party, there is no irrational explosion of the senses. Indeed, Lopukhov merely makes himself agreeable by playing whist! Even when they do dance together they simply have a pleasant conversation, without any of the stereotypical responses (blushing, lowered eyes) on Vera's part. Instead, they have their first discussion on the subjection of women, and after this debate while dancing they confirm their equality by shaking hands, 'as if he were a girlfriend of hers or she were his comrade' (p. 85).[40]

They then go on, in fact, to discuss the nature of love and passion. Neither is denied, but a rational interpretation is offered by Lopukhov: 'But what is this love – as – passion? In what way does passion differ from a simple feeling? By its strength' (p. 87). The narrator then intervenes to clarify yet further the meaning of these exchanges and Lopukhov's words on love. As Vera sits and reflects that it is very strange that they have become so close so quickly, 'No, it's not strange at all, Verochka' (p. 88), the narrator insists. Why should love or closeness with another be alarming, fearful or even strange?: 'After all, people[41] think that love is an alarming feeling . . . . Alarm in love is not love itself, – the alarm in it is something not as it should be, but love itself is happy and carefree' (p. 88).

If such a rational approach to affairs of the heart may leave some readers incredulous, its polemical purpose, at least, is transparent. Moreover, as with most aspects of the novel, the narrator is careful to balance this new approach with a residue of the existing tradition. Vera and Lopukhov are not yet equals and their early relationship follows the paradigm of Yelena and Insarov and many others before them, in that the man is tutor to the woman. He brings her books, introduces her to the new ideas and begins to liberate her mind. However, it should also be noted that Vera already intuitively shares many of these views and enters debate as a disputant and does not ask for instructions, although she does say herself: 'You see, what a good pupil I am' (p. 102).

At this stage, however, most of their conversations are of a severely practical kind, as they continue to search for a way out of Vera's situation. Their 'first love' is about comradeship (as the frequent handshakes indicate) between a man and a woman; mutual assistance, not mutual torment. As they get closer to her escape and then their marriage they resume their discussion on male/female relations on a general or theoretical level. Although Vera to a certain extent has to depend on the man to facilitate her physical liberation, she does not wish to have to remain dependent on him, insisting that she should carry on giving lessons even after they are married. Economic considerations are perceived as being one of the root causes of female subjugation. Vera argues: 'he who has money has power and the law, say your books; this means, while a woman lives at the man's expense, she is dependent on him' (p. 128). Vera has learned this lesson well, and needless to say, Lopukhov agrees with her.

Furthermore, he asks *her* to sort out the practical side of their domestic arrangements, and Vera it is who draws up the contract by which they plan to (and do) live. The basic premise confirms what has already happened: 'We will be friends' (p. 129), Vera insists and proceeds to lay down the basic conditions of their future life, namely, that each shall have a separate room, neither shall have the right to enter this room without permission, nor even to inquire into the affairs of the other (p. 130). As Vera points out, they will thereby avoid the awful family life which she had endured. The deliberately prosaic, anti-Romantic note is sustained as they get married, kissing for the very first time on the way to the ceremony. Once married it is the woman again who organises their *modus vivendi*. As if to emphasise how ordinary all of this really is, the narrator finds almost nothing to say about their first days together, beginning the next stage of the story with a remarkably downbeat, generalised paragraph:

> And so in this way there passed by almost three years since the foundation of the workshop, more than three years since the marriage of Vera Pavlovna. How quietly and actively these years passed, how full they were of peace and joy and everything good. (p. 183)

'First love' as depicted here is, indeed, 'happy and carefree', the very opposite of a 'thunderstorm'. This is yet further emphasised by the narrative cutting into a particularly tranquil domestic interior: Vera Pavlovna is lying at her ease in her separate bed while Lopukhov makes the morning tea.

This section (Chapter 3) is entitled by the seeming oxymoron, 'Marriage and Second Love'. When the latter, potentially cataclysmic stage ensues, it, too, is managed in a rational manner, and the next quarter of the novel is taken up explaining all the ramifications. Kirsanov had felt strongly about Vera Pavlovna, it would appear, almost from the very beginning of the marriage, but had decided that such a feeling was inappropriate and so had gradually dissociated himself from their company. Now he is able to return and feel in control of himself: 'he was so pleased and proud that then, about three years ago, noticing in himself the signs of *passion*, he had been able to do firmly everything that had been necessary to stop its development' (p. 200; my italics).[42] Again, the existence, the reality of passion is not denied, but it can be controlled, dealt with. As he is now obliged to spend time with the Lopukhovs on a daily basis (because of Lopukhov's illness), his 'attachment was renewed and more powerfully than before; but his struggle with it did not present any serious torment, was easy' (p. 201). Once more he decides he must leave, having worked out the best course of action as if solving a scientific equation (pp. 217–8).

Before the triangular relationship is resolved in a way Kirsanov does not anticipate at this juncture, the narrator interpolates 'Kryukova's Story' to illustrate another variant on the theme of rational romances. This story demonstrates that, even if an affair commences in unpropitious circumstances, firmly located within traditional structures, it is nevertheless amenable to a new, that is, rational, resolution. It also leads to a conclusion that will have an important bearing on the explanation of the relative failure of the relationship between Vera and Lopukhov.

As we have already seen, Nastya Kryukova is rescued from her low life by Dr Kirsanov. It is an old story, but one that is treated in a new way. Kryukova at first attempts to seduce him, but he resists all her wiles: the account of this is deliberately de-eroticised. As a doctor, he advises her against wine and debauchery of other kinds, and, eventually, they do become lovers, but only after she has been transformed into an 'honest girl' (p. 208). Their passionate love is then described with feeling, almost ecstasy, but in a straight-forward, prosaic way, avoiding again salaciousness or innuendo. There is no shame or guilt. For two years they live together, and love has an almost miraculous and certainly curative effect on her as her tuberculosis remits. When it does recur, they must part. Both man and woman are in tears; they are fully equal, in sickness and in health. Yet, in the end – and this is the point – they could not have remained together (in terms of the novel's point of view at least), for the same reasons as Vera and Lopukhov. Our helpful narrator once more intervenes to explain why: 'Of course, Kryukova was not his equal because they were not equal *in terms of their development*' (p. 213; my italics). Sexual relations and an interpretation of them remain at the very centre of the text's concerns.

After this interlude, we now return to the resolution of the problem between Vera Pavlovna and Lopukhov. As one might expect by now, it is, in the end, a simple matter. She does not love him intensely enough, so their relationship must end (they are not equals), and so it does, without bitterness, acrimony, recrimin-ations, blame or guilt. Lopukhov later explains the situation, not in terms of masculine or feminine, but as a quasi-mathematical problem: their feelings were not symmetrical. He was not particu-larly sociable and had mistaken her yearning for a room of her own, for privacy, as a sign that she was the same. When he realised his mistake, that she needed more love and affection, more *passion* than he could give, it was too late. She, too, explains herself in due course. For her the main inequality had been her continuing dependence on her husband.

Their eventual separation (especially Lopukhov's rather melo-dramatic way of effecting it) causes pain, but, in the end, all three are pleased with the resolution because it suits the rational, self-interested needs of all of them. Vera and Kirsanov can develop their passion, while Lopukhov can make an exit which also fits his present requirements. Vera and Lopukhov are able to discuss the matter freely and frankly because there is 'trust' (p. 231) between them and because they are both possessed of 'high moral dignity' (p. 231). Lopukhov reflects: 'The loss is heavy, but what is to be done?' (p. 232, sic!). They consequently reach a renewed and higher perception of the meaning of love. In Vera's words: 'It means being pleased about what is good for him, finding pleasure in doing everything that is necessary so that things are best for him, no?' (p. 246). Lopukhov, of course, agrees, as his valedictory remarks to her suggest: 'And I am no less attached to you than you are to me. But to be well disposed to a person is to wish him happiness, you and I know that very well. But there is no happiness without freedom' (p. 254). Given these views they part as friends. There was no rational alternative, for, as we later learn: 'given these relationships, the denouement that occurred was inevitable' (p. 305).

All three make many general statements about relationships between the sexes. As Lampert puts it: 'Chemistry, physiology, sociology are massively directed by the characters upon each other, and even declarations of love are infused with scientific considerations.'[43] But it is the *really* new man, 'the flower of the best people, the mover of movers, the salt of the salt of the earth' (p. 273), Rakhmetov, who is brought in, as a contrastive type to be sure, but also to summarise the implications of these triangular debates. Not only does he do this, but he also argues that, however 'progressive' and 'rational' the solution may appear, all the emotional traumas are somewhat ridiculous to him, and to the narrator. Indeed, Vera Pavlovna had been considering abandoning her work, to retreat into emotionalism. Rakhmetov admonishes her sternly: 'you have been giving an argument against your principles to the defenders of *darkness* and evil' (pp. 281–2; my italics). At least, he goes on to argue, by virtue of their 'development', they had avoided the 'familial servitude which we admire in the majority of marriages' (p. 282). Rakhmetov now points out what we already know. They had ceased loving each other equally because Vera had now fully grown up and her demands as a *woman* could no longer be adequately satisfied by Lopukhov. However, no-one had any grounds for jealousy, which 'is the result of looking at a person as my possession, as a thing' (p. 286). He goes on to reproach them all for this 'completely unnecessary *melodrama*[44] with its completely unnecessary tragedy' (p. 287; my italics).

Gradually, then, as the novel develops and as its central character, Vera Pavlovna, also develops, the theme of sexual relations not only remains centre stage, but is treated in all its diversity, is rationalised and endlessly discussed, so that a treatise on the subject emerges – the need for equality, freedom, economic parity and so on. We now return (eventually!) to the plot and the second marriage, which is in many ways offered as an exemplar, along with other relationships, of the theories expounded, leading shortly to a more general overview of the historical relations between men and women – a theory, that is, of patriarchy. Increasingly it would seem to be the case that this theory is the central theme of the novel.[45]

The plot recommences with Vera and Kirsanov organising their life together, a life of ecstatic passion, mutuality and joy. Rarely does Vera regret or even remember the past: life in the present is too full of happiness and work for such sentimentality. The major difference between the past and the present for her is that her life is now almost completely merged with that of her husband. Moreover, she has realised not only herself through this intense and complete love, but also her responsibilities to the whole world: 'it was as if not she, Vera Pavlovna Kirsanova, personally felt dissatisfaction, but as if in her was reflected the dissatisfaction of thousands and millions' (p. 321). She is even more aware of the need for all-round fulfilment and shared pleasures: now they sit and read Nekrasov together! Time passes as quickly as before: soon a year has gone, then three. They preserve the poetry of their love because they respect each other and the right of each to freedom. Above all else, they are conscious of the need to be *honest* in their feelings and the expression of them (p. 338). After three years their passion for each other has strengthened, not lessened in its intensity. Furthermore, this growing passion in no way makes them selfish or isolated from the rest of the world. On the contrary: Kirsanov tells Vera that now 'more is beginning to be expected from me, people think that I will rework an entire large branch of science . . .. And I feel that I will fulfil this expectation' (p. 340). Love, intense physical love is certainly not ignored in the rational world of the novel.[46] A 'woman's love' is not 'poison'[47] but can stimulate new growth and be profoundly creative. Amongst many other things, the novel ends up by being a eulogy to the positive, life-giving power of love and physical love in particular. And this kind of loving is growing because, whereas in the earlier sections the novel concentrated on the relationship between Vera and Lopukhov, this second marriage is presented as merely one among many such in the world of the new people. As before, however, we are not to think they are special. The narrator reminds us that, although they are 'today's people', they are, nevertheless, 'ordinary people' (p. 338). Regrettably, he goes on to allow, the 'antedeluvian' folk are still in the majority.

The reasons for this preponderance of those still living in the 'kingdom of darkness' have been alluded to many times in the course of the novel, but only become fully explicit once Vera and Kirsanov are together. After their reading of Nekrasov, they proceed to an examination of why it is the 'antedeluvian' period in sexual relations had persisted so long. This seems particularly surprising to the couple because women appear to them both to be more 'intelligent by nature'. But women will not be allowed to enter fully into 'intellectual life' until the 'soverignty of crude force has passed' (p. 323). Women are deliberately kept in the 'kingdom of darkness', that is. Moreover, literature itself and other forms of communication play a central part in this process of subjugation. Women seem to be weak, but this appearance has a specific etiology. As Kirsanov argues: 'If a person thinks "I can't", – then in reality that person cannot. Women are told "you are weak" – and so they indeed feel weak and in reality appear to be weak' (p. 325). And so Vera, finally, in discussion with her husband, achieves an all-round understanding of the hegemonistic patriarchal culture:[48] 'Yes, Sasha, that's right. We are weak because we consider ourselves to be weak' (p. 325). She is no longer in any sense weak. She has, that is, incorporated this political theory into her own personal life and will now take one last step into the male world of 'intellectual life', as a doctor. The novel, and her own life, begin in the 'antedeluvian' world of sexual politics. The purpose of her personal growth, her marriages and all the other relationships described or referred to, has been to show how she has climbed out of the 'cellar' into full equality. It is a demonstration both of 'what there is to do' in Russia and how it can be done. As Stites argues: 'The novel thus becomes, among other things, a celebration of the latent power of woman, and a flattering summons to take her life into her own hands.'[49]

7. Literary and Other Polemics

'As literature the novel may be easily ridiculed. Characterisation is stilted, incident contrived, style ponderous.'[50] This remark by

Richard Freeborn is a fairly typical view of the literary merits (or otherwise) of *What Is To Be Done?* More generally, the argument (outside the Soviet Union, at any rate) runs that the fictional form is a mere pretext for the (to some people, rather tedious) sermonising on women's rights and so on. In a paradoxical way, this opinion may not be so far from the truth. As we have noted on numerous occasions, the novel deliberately lays bare plot devices, refuses conventional expectations and refers to other works of literature. But this is surely not a sign of the failure of the work taken in its totality. Rather, it has been the implicit argument of the present chapter that this is not only a work *of* literature, but also a work *about* literature. In particular, it takes issue with the way literature has played its own part in the 'sovereignty of crude force', and with the way literature has tended to tell women they are 'weak'. The novel can legitimately be read as a critique of previous literature in these terms, and a first step in redressing the balance.

The laying bare of the artificiality of many literary devices begins in the 'Foreword', which itself is deliberately displaced and does not appear first,[51] where the narrator, as we know, rather reluctantly offers us a story about 'love' and 'a woman'. He has started as he means to continue. When Lopukhov disappears, there are clear hints that he has not shot himself (p. 254). 'The denouement was inevitable' we are later told, and the extremely protracted peripeteia is ridiculed by the narrator, as is the 'melodrama' in which the characters indulge: 'life is much simpler' (p. 313) he argues. In particular, there is the recurrent device of the 'perceptive reader',[52] who is used to represent the 'public' and who cries 'immoral' (p. 313) about the goings-on of the love triangle.

This is not a literary game, but has the purpose and effect of deliberately refusing to titillate the reader, to arouse false pleasure or *jouissance*[53] in us. Nowhere is this more true than in the narrator's fierce refusal to poeticise his heroine, to hold her up to our gaze and fetishise her body in the way Bela, Asya and Zinaida, amongst many others, were.[54] Lopukhov and Kirsanov discuss Vera and her situation and the narrator suggests that the two men may seem to lack an 'aesthetic nerve' (p. 110) because they fail to talk of her appearance. Later he remarks that Lopukhov 'indeed continued to think of all the advantages instead of lofty poetic and plastic dreams' (p. 133). The explicit polemic here is precisely with those writers who had approached women (especially their bodies) from the 'poetic and plastic' angles. These adjectives are clear euphemisms for 'voyeuristic', if not 'pornographic'. This is a theme that continues to the end. When Vera decides to become a doctor, the narrator points out that this decision will do nothing for her romantic aura. He adds: 'I, without any shame, have compromised Vera Pavlovna a great deal from the poetic angle' (p. 332).

The literary polemics are on occasion much more explicit. We have already noted the parodic or sarcastic references to *Yevgeny Onegin* and *A Hero of Our Time* and implicit comment on many other works and writers, as well as the subverting of traditional situations on countless occasions. But the principal target is Turgenev. Victor Ripp argues that this novel is 'itself an elaboration of Turgenev's novelistic achievement'.[55] 'Elaboration' would hardly seem to be the right word. The references to Turgenev are legion. Explicitly, Kirsanov and 'first love' hark back to Turgenev, while Lopukhov is a clear reference to Bazarov.[56] *Vera* Pavlovna can be read as a rather more positive version of *Varvara* Pavlovna, *vera* being the Russian for 'faith'. The novel's very title, it would seem, derives from Yelena's rhetorical question in *On the Eve*. The purpose of all these allusions seems, in the end, to be twofold. Firstly, as we have argued extensively, the novel refutes the implications of Yelena's question. Secondly, and more generally, it seeks to refute the validity of the 'poetic and plastic' image of women presented in Turgenev's works, indeed, that writer's view of love and passion.

What Is To Be Done? does not, however, offer merely a critique of existing ideas, but presents a range of positive alternatives, as we now know. Vera, Lopukhov, Kirsanov and the others who organise their lives on the principles of 'rational egotism', are not exceptional (Rakhmetov alone receives that accolade). The narrator, on many occasions, makes the following sort of remark: 'I wanted to depict ordinary, decent people of the new generation of whom I meet whole hundreds' (p. 292). If they are so ordinary and there are so many of them, then the book has a clear inspirational purpose. Everyone can refuse to say 'I can't'. Indeed, the narrator addresses the readers (perceptive or otherwise) in precisely these terms: 'You can be the equal of these people whom I depict, if you wish to work on your development' (p. 294). What is more, even the lowlier of the characters, because they retain their 'human features', are capable of such development. After all, Vera has heard the new ideas even from her 'drunken mother' or a 'ruined Frenchwoman'.

Although there are many 'new ideas' in the novel, its underlying theme, as I have already argued, would appear to be a critique of, and a response to hegemonistic patriarchy. This receives its fullest and most definitive treatment in Vera Pavlovna's fourth and most celebrated dream, where the various strategies employed by men throughout history to subjugate women are explicitly discussed. Given its position in the text, it is clearly intended to be perceived as the keynote section.

The fourth dream traces various images of women as they have appeared in history. The slave girl is a great beauty, adorned with jewels, but her attractions hold no allure because she lacks even the pretence of equality. There can be no true beauty where there is no equality. The goddess Aphrodite or the Virgin are equally not true women. They may be worshipped and revered, but are not considered equal by men. The turning point is seen to be La Nouvelle Héloïse. Only now, in the period immediately before the novel was written, was equality for women being accepted by men. Echoing Rakhmetov's words, the allegorical woman of the dream asserts: 'When man acknowledges the same equality of rights for woman as for himself, he rejects the view of her as his possession' (p. 351).

This dream not only summarises and resolves the central themes of the novel, but clearly generalises them. That is, *What Is To Be Done?* sets itself the task not only of addressing the need for action in Russia in 1863, but also of understanding what the novel itself views as one of the central problems of world history. The novel, and especially the fourth dream, also offers a solution to this problem in the Utopian vision in the dream of a future transfigured by equality. But the book itself offers a solution in a more general way. As we saw earlier, Vera and Kirsanov agree that women are weak because they are told to be weak. By polemicising, explicitly or implicitly, with Pushkin, Lermontov, Turgenev and others, this novel lays bare this tendency within literature. By exposing the tendency it seeks to refute it. Thereafter, the novel attempts to give an alternative view, to present both a positive image of women and their destinies, and an overall vision of the future. Chernyshevsky said elsewhere: 'To straighten a stick which has been bent for too long in one direction, it is necessary to bend it the other way.'[57] *What Is To Be Done?* strives, that is, to straighten the bent stick of Russian literature and its generally negative representation of women.

Notes

Publication dates and places, where not mentioned, may be found in the Bibliography.

1 INTRODUCTION

1. See K. K. Ruthven, *Feminist Literary Studies, An Introduction*, p. 7.
2. Quoted in J. Fetterley, *The Resisting Reader, A Feminist Approach to American Fiction*, p. xviii.
3. See G. Greene and C. Kahn (eds), *Making a Difference*, pp. 2–3.
4. See S. de Beauvoir, *The Second Sex*, p. 162. Ruthven makes a similar point in, perhaps, more modern terms: 'To read a canonical text in a feminist way is to force that text to reveal its hidden sexual ideology which, in so far as it happens to coincide with that of the predominantly male critics who have written about it, tends not to be mentioned in non-feminist criticism.' See Ruthven, *Feminist Literary Studies*, p. 31.
5. For a discussion of this, see J. Andrew, *Writers and Society During the Rise of Russian Realism*, and *Russian Writers and Society in the Second Half of the Nineteenth Century*.
6. See H. Hartmann, 'The Unhappy Marriage of Marxism and Feminism: Towards a More Progressive Union', in L. Sargent (ed.), *Women and Revolution*, p. 14.
7. See C. Ehrlich, 'The Unhappy Marriage of Marxism and Feminism: Can It Be Saved', in Sargent, *Women and Revolution*, p. 110.
8. See S. Firestone, *The Dialectics of Sex. The Case for Feminist Revolution*, p. 16.
9. 'In the subjection of female to male, Engels (and Marx as well) saw the historical and conceptual prototype of all subsequent power systems . . . the fact of oppression itself.' See K. Millett, *Sexual Politics*, p. 121.
10. See A. Al-Hibri, 'Capitalism is an Advanced Stage of Patriarchy, but Marxism is not Feminism', in Sargent, *Women and Revolution*, p. 171.
11. See de Beauvoir, *The Second Sex*, p. 152.
12. See Fetterley, *The Resisting Reader*, p. 189.
13. C. Boggs, *Gramsci's Marxism* (London, 1976), p. 39, quoted in Sargent, *Women and Revolution*, p. 78.
14. See J. V. Femia, *Gramsci's Political Thought: Hegemony, Consciousness and the Revolutionary Process*, p. 24. Although I am in general indebted to this work for the ensuing discussion, it is also interesting to note Femia's (presumably inadvertent) hegemonistic usage of the male code.

15. See Femia, *Gramsci's Political Thought*, p. 32. This quotation is taken from *The German Ideology*.
16. See S. Ardener, *Defining Females*, p. 20. The intercourse between codes or discourses within society is not as simple or unproblematic as this discussion may suggest. As Foucault argues: 'we must not imagine a world of discourse divided between accepted discourse and excluded discourse, or between the dominant discourse and the dominated one; but as a multiplicity of discursive elements that come into play in various strategies.' See M. Foucault, *The History of Sexuality*, p. 100. I would argue, however, that there is at least a tendency to the hegemony of one discourse above all others, although Foucault is quite right to point to the polyphony of modern societies.
17. See S. M. Okin, *Women in Western Political Thought*, p. 5.
18. See T. Tanner, *Adultery in the Novel: Contract and Transgression*, p. 64. See the work of M. Daly and D. C. Cameron, in particular, for feminist attempts to rewrite the Word of the Father.
19. See W. Martin, 'Seduced and Abandoned in the New World: The Image of Woman in American Fiction', in V. Gornick and B. K. Moran (eds), *Women in Sexist Society*, p. 228.
20. See S. Gorsky, 'The Gentle Doubters: Images of Women in English-women's Novels, 1840–1920', in S. K. Cornillon (ed.), *Images of Women in Fiction: Feminist Perspectives*, p. 48.
21. See C. Blinderman, 'The Servility of Dependence: The Dark Lady in Trollope', in Cornillon, *Images of Women in Fiction*, p. 55.
22. See E. Morgan, 'Humanbecoming: Form and Focus in the Neo-Feminist Novel', in Cornillon, *Images of Women in Fiction*, pp. 189–90. Gail Cunningham makes a similar point: 'a novelist would have little chance of publishing a work which seriously challenged accepted standards of delicacy.' See G. Cunningham, *The New Woman and the Victorian Novel*, p. 3.
23. See M. R. Lieberman, 'Sexism and the Double Standard in Literature', in Cornillon, *Images of Women in Fiction*, p. 328.
24. Quoted in Fetterley, *The Resisting Reader*, p. xix.
25. See Firestone, *The Dialectic of Sex*, p. 186.
26. See K. Stewart, 'The Marriage of Capitalist and Patriarchal Ideologies: Meanings of Male Bonding and Male Ranking in US Culture', in Sargent, *Women and Revolution*, p. 300.
27. See Fetterley, *The Resisting Reader*, pp. 28–9.
28. See de Beauvoir, *The Second Sex*, p. 104.
29. See Fetterley, *The Resisting Reader*, p. ix.
30. See C. Gledhill, '*Klute* 2: Feminism and *Klute*', in E. A. Kaplan (ed.), *Women in Film Noir*, p. 121.
31. See V. Gornick, 'Woman as Outsider', in Gornick and Moran, *Women in Sexist Society*, p. 78.
32. See E. Figes, *Patriarchal Attitudes*, p. 114.
33. See Gorsky, 'The Gentle Doubters', p. 48.
34. As Foucault argues, the nineteenth century did *not* anathematise sexuality: 'On the contrary, it put into operation an entire machinery

for producing true discourses concerning it.' See Foucault, *The History of Sexuality*, p. 69.

35. See N. K. Miller, *The Heroine's Text, Readings in the French and English Novel 1722–1781*, p. 159, and also Tanner, *Adultery in the Novel*, for extended discussions on the same points.
36. See C. G. Heilbrunn, *Reinventing Womanhood*, p. 171.
37. See E. Showalter, 'Towards a Feminist Poetics', in M. Jacobus (ed.), *Women Writing and Writing about Women*, p. 31.
38. See Okin, *Women in Western Political Thought*, p. 12.
39. See Fetterley, *The Resisting Reader*, p. xii.
40. See ibid., p. xxii.
41. See ibid., pp. xx and xxiii. This type of 'resistance' can perhaps have even more far-reaching consequences, as Nelly Furman has argued: 'In this respect, a textual approach to literature guided by feminist concerns can be an effective political tool. When a textual reader steadfastly ignores an author's presumed intentions or the assumed meaning of a literary work, it is a serious act of insubordination, for it puts into question the authority of authors, that is to say the propriety of paternity' (Greene and Kahn, *Making a Difference*, p. 71).
42. See Andrew, *Writers and Society During the Rise of Russian Realism*, for a discussion of the society and literature of this period.
43. It is worth noting that much Russian Formalism and also the work of Yury Lotman have concerned themselves with this period.
44. For the work of women writers in nineteenth-century Russia, see the Bibliography, especially D. Atkinson *et al.* (eds), *Women in Russia*; N. N. Golitsyn, *A Bibliographical Dictionary of Russian Women Writers*; B. Heldt Monter, 'Rassvet and the Woman Question', C. de Maegd-Soep, *The Emancipation of Women in Russian Literature and Society*; S. I. Ponomareva, *Our Women Writers*; and R. Stites, *The Women's Liberation Movement in Russia*.
45. See the work of D. Atkinson *et al.* (eds), *Women in Russia*, and R. Stites, *The Women's Liberation Movement in Russia*.
46. See Tanner, *Adultery in the Novel*, p. xi.
47. See J. Andrew (ed.), *The Structural Analysis of Russian Narrative Fiction*, and L. M. O'Toole, *Structure, Style and Interpretation in the Russian Short Story*.
48. Quoted in J. Mitchell, *Woman's Estate*, p. 77.
49. See T. Moi, *Sexual/Textual Politics*, pp. 174–5; her italics.
50. See Chapter 7 of the present work, and Stites's monograph.

2 PRELUDE: RADICAL SENTIMENTALISM OR SENTIMENTAL RADICALISM?

1. For a discussion of this period and its culture see J. Garrard (ed.), *The Eighteenth Century in Russia* (Oxford, 1973), and H. Rogger, *National Consciousness in Eighteenth-Century Russia* (Cambridge, Mass., 1960).
2. For a discussion of these two terms, see H. M. Nebel, *N. M. Karamzin:*

    A Russian Sentimentalist (The Hague, 1967), and G. S. Smith, 'Sentimentalism and Pre-Romanticism as Terms and Concepts', in A. G. Cross (ed.), *Russian Literature in the Age of Catherine the Great* (Oxford, 1976), pp. 173–89.

3. For all references to this work, see *Nedorosol'* in D. I. Fonvizin, *Sobranie Sochineny v Dvukh Tomakh* (ed. G. P. Makogonenko, Moscow-Leningrad, 1959), Vol. I, pp. 105–78. All translations from this and other Russian works referred to are my own, unless otherwise stated.
4. See Alexander Pushkin, *Yevgeny Onegin*, Chapter 1, Stanza XVIII.
5. See D. J. Welsh, *Russian Comedy: 1765–1823* (The Hague, 1966).
6. For a discussion of the use of 'telling names', see ibid., pp. 64–6.
7. For a discussion of the schema, and other terms of narrative analysis, see O'Toole, *Structure, Style and Interpretation in the Russian Short Story*, pp. 11–36.
8. See N. K. Miller, *The Heroine's Text*, p. xi for an excellent discussion of the vulnerability of the traditional heroine.
9. No distinction is made here between *syuzhet* and *fabula* (plot and fable). Any such dislocation would be extremely unusual in a play.
10. For a discussion of the overdetermination of literary characters and plots, see N. K. Miller, *The Heroine's Text*, p. 65.
11. See note 6.
12. See J. Gallop, *Feminism and Psychoanalysis: The Daughter's Seduction*, pp. 47 and 74–5 for a discussion of the symbolic and psychoanalytical interpretation of the Father and his 'Law'. 'The law of the father' or 'the name of the father' (sometimes hyphenated so that they are effectively one-word terms) have been most fully developed by Lacan. See J. Sayers, *Sexual Contradictions: Psychology, Psychoanalysis and Feminism*, pp. 85–6, for a critical account of Lacan and his indebtedness to Lévi-Strauss. See also Nelly Furman, 'The Politics of Language: Beyond the Gender Principle', in Greene and Kahn, *Making a Difference*, pp. 59–79, especially pp. 70–1.
13. The theme of the benighted, brutal family in rural Russia was to prove enduring: see, for example, A. N. Ostrovsky's *The Thunderstorm* (1859) and Chekhov's *The Peasants* (1897).
14. For a discussion of this model of female relationships, see Okin, *Women in Western Political Thought*, pp. 43–4.
15. It should be remembered that characterisation, in the sense of the creation of individual, 'rounded' characters was virtually non-existent in Fonvizin's work, as in eighteenth-century Russian literature in general.
16. See M. Ellmann, *Thinking About Women*, pp. 74ff.
17. See Foucault, *Discipline and Punish: The Birth of the Prison*, p. 27.
18. For a discussion of this term, see ibid., pp. 195–228.
19. See Gallop, *Feminism and Psychoanalysis*, passim. It should be noted that the play provides an ideal, indeed idealised, version of the symbolic Father, whereas the only mother in the work is a grotesque parody; this contrast says much for the general tendency of the play's sexual politics.
20. Much of the 'low comedy' of the play centres on linguistic distortions,

especially in the scene where the three tutors (one of whom is German) play particular havoc with the Russian language.

21. For a discussion of labelling in literature, see Tanner, *Adultery in the Novel*, pp. 346–54.

22. For all references to this work, see *Puteshestviye iz Peterburga v Moskvu* in A. N. Radishchev, *Polnoye Sobranie Sochineny* (Moscow–Leningrad, 1938), reprinted, I. K. Lupol *et al.* (eds) (Vaduz, 1969), pp. 225–392.

23. See T. Woolf (ed.), *Pushkin on Literature* (London, 1971), p. 390.

24. For a discussion of the depiction of women in de Sade, see A. Carter, *The Sadeian Woman*.

25. For a discussion of this term, see N. K. Miller, *The Heroine's Text*.

26. Ibid.

27. For a discussion of a fairly typical eighteenth-century rake, see L. Stone on Boswell: L. Stone, *The Family, Sex and Marriage in England, 1500–1800*, pp. 350–78.

28. See A. G. Cross, *N. M. Karamzin* (Carbondale, 1971), p. 103.

29. For all references to his work, see *Bednaya Liza* in N. M. Karamzin, *Izbranniye Sochineniya v Dvukh Tomakh* (ed. P. Berkov, Moscow–Leningrad, 1964), Vol. I, pp. 605–21.

30. For a discussion of this term, in the context of eighteenth-century literature, see N. K. Miller, *The Heroine's Text*, especially the Introduction.

31. Not only is it tedious; even thirty years after its appearance the narrative had taken on a rather comic coloration. Belinsky remarked: 'Now tell me frankly, *sine ira et studio*, as our true-bred scholars say, who is to blame that *Poor Liza* is now being laughed at as much as it was once cried over?' Belinsky's comment conveys more than a change in literary taste. See Nebel, *N. M. Karamzin*, p. 122.

32. For the use of this symbolism in the iconography of the Virgin Mary, see M. Warner, *Alone of All Her Sex: The Myth and Cult of the Virgin Mary*, *passim*.

33. Showalter, *A Literature of their Own: British Women Novelists from Brontë to Lessing*, p. 117. The reference is to *Jane Eyre*.

34. Pechorin, an unreconstructed rake, makes the following illuminating comment about his relations with women: 'But surely there is a boundless pleasure in the possession of a young, scarcely burgeoned soul! It is like a flower whose finest aroma evaporates at the first ray of sunlight; one must pick it at this moment, and, breathing it in to one's fill, cast it on the road: perhaps someone will pick it up.' *A Hero of Our Time* in M. Yu. Lermontov, *Sochineniya*, Vol. IV (Leningrad, 1962), p. 401. See Chapter 4 of the present work, especially section 2.4.

35. A common trick, in that one of the usual devices of any ideology to defuse the threat of an opposing class, group or society is both to trivialise it, and, simultaneously, to depict it as dangerous. See L. Althusser, *Lenin and Philosophy and Other Essays*.

36. See E. G. Belotti, *Little Girls* (London, 1975), p. 102, quoted in A. Oakley, *Subject Women*, p. 109.

37. For an extended discussion of this interconnection, see L. Fiedler, *Love and Death in the American Novel*.

3 ALEXANDER PUSHKIN AND HIS TRUE IDEAL.

1. See F. M. Dostoevsky, *Polnoye Sobraniye Sochineny v Tridsati Tomakh* (Leningrad, 1972–), vol. XXVI, p. 140.
2. For a discussion of this contrast, see Chapter 6 of the present work, especially section 4.2, and R. Freeborn, *Turgenev: The Novelist's Novelist. A Study* (London, 1960).
3. See C. de Maegd-Soep, *The Emancipation of Women in Russian Literature and Society*, p. 124.
4. All references to works by Pushkin are to A. S. Pushkin, *Sobraniye Sochineny v Desyati Tomakh* (Moscow, 1959–62). The two long poems are in Vol. III, pp. 143–58 and 159–80, and *Yevgeny Onegin* in Vol. IV, pp. 5–198.
5. Ibid., Vol. VI, p. 343. The (unpublished) article which contains these words was written in 1830.
6. See J. L. I. Fennell, 'Pushkin', in J. L. I. Fennell (ed.), *Nineteenth-Century Russian Literature* (London, 1973), p. 17.
7. Pushkin, Vol. IX, p. 73 (from a letter dated 23 October 1823).
8. See Gallop, *Feminism and Psychoanalysis*, especially pp. 38–9 and 74–5.
9. For a discussion of the 'gaze' in cinematic terms, see E. A. Kaplan, *Women and Film: Both Sides of the Camera*, pp. 14–15. The respective power and degree of valorisation for the male and female gaze will be an important recurrent theme in the ensuing chapters. N. K. Miller sets the paradigm well: 'The dialogue of meaningful looks is a necessary preliminary to the verbal exchange. In accordance with the canons of masculine and feminine behaviour (which presuppose naivete on the part of the woman and experience on the part of the man), the man's gaze is a declaration, a communication that disconcerts; the woman's timorous . . . but compelled.' N. K. Miller, *The Heroine's Text*, p. 26.
10. See Foucault, *Discipline and Punish*, pp. 195–228.
11. See Fennel, *Nineteenth-Century Russian Literature*. For a fuller discussion of Pushkin's debt to Byron in terms of structure, see V. M. Zhirmunsky, *Byron i Pushkin. Iz Istorii Romanticheskoy Poemy* (Leningrad, 1924).
12. For a discussion of the difference between plot (*syuzhet*) and *fabula*, see O'Toole, *Structure, Style and Interpretation in the Russian Short Story*, pp. 84–6, and Andrew, *The Structural Analysis of Russian Narrative Fiction*, pp. ix–xi.
13. For the effect of her father's death on Liza's destiny, see Chapter 2, section 3.3.
14. For a discussion of the 'creative etymology' practised by some recent feminists, see Cameron, *Feminism and Linguistic Theory*, pp. 79–90. A particularly noteworthy exponent of the art is Mary Daly. See her *Gyn/Ecology* in particular.
15. For a discussion of this theme in *The Gipsies*, see section 2.2.
16. For a discussion of this theme in Pushkin's work generally, see Andrew, *Writers and Society During the Rise of Russian Realism*,

pp. 36–40, and the *Pushkin Speech* by Dostoevsky (Vol. XXVI, pp. 136–49).

17. See de Beauvoir, *The Second Sex*, especially pp. 64ff.

18. The word in the Russian original for 'resigned' (line 239) is, significantly, *smirennoy*, which can also be translated as 'reconciled'.

19. See Fennell, *Nineteenth-Century Russian Literature*, p. 15.

20. Ibid., pp. 15–25.

21. The Old Gipsy and Aleko both refer to their 'wives' in the same proprietory terms: 'my Mariula' (line 295) and 'my Zemfira' (line 371).

22. See note 15 above, and for a more general discussion of the theme (primarily in American literature), see L. Fiedler, *Love and Death in the American Novel*.

23. For a discussion of the power of giving names to others, originally conferred by God on Adam, see Ruthven, *Feminist Literary Studies. An Introduction*, p. 3. For a discussion of the female misappropriation of this power (by Prostakova in *The Minor*), see Chapter 2, section 1.1. of the present work.

24. See Fennell, *Nineteenth-Century Russian Literature*, p. 21.

25. Ibid., p. 24.

26. Ibid.

27. See Dostoevsky, p. 139. It is here that Dostoevsky adumbrates the theme of *smireniya* ('reconciliation') in his quoted words: *Smiris'*, *gordy chelovek* ('Reconcile yourself, proud man').

28. The centrality of these themes emerges not only from the present reading. Over one hundred lines (out of a total of 571 lines) are devoted to this discussion between the Old Gipsy and Aleko, lines which are located immediately before the denouement, suggesting that they do, indeed, hold the key to the meaning of the text.

29. For a brief outline of some of the more obvious interpretations, see Fennell, *Nineteenth-Century Russian Literature*, pp. 36–7.

30. For a more general discussion of the part literature plays in forming these constructs, see R. M. Brownstein, *Becoming a Heroine: Reading About Women in Novels*.

31. For a general discussion of the formative influence literature plays in this and other novels, see G. Gibian, 'Love by the Book: Pushkin, Stendhal, Flaubert', in *Comparative Literature*, Vol. VIII (1956), pp. 97–105.

32. For a discussion of this, see V. Nabokov, *Eugene Onegin. A Novel in Verse by Aleksandr Pushkin*, trans. from the Russian with a commentary, 4 vols (London, 1964), Vol. II.

33. For a discussion of the eighteenth-century novel in England and France, in these terms, see N. K. Miller *The Heroine's Text*.

34. For a discussion of the Lovelace character, theme and tradition in the original novel and since, see T. Eagleton, *The Rape of Clarissa* and Brownstein, *Becoming a Heroine*, pp. 32–77.

35. In this respect, in particular, the nearest parallel to Pushkin's novel would seem to be the work of Jane Austen. For a recent account of this theme in her novels, see Brownstein, *Becoming a Heroine*, pp. 79–134.

36. According to Viktor Shklovsky, the work can, in general, be read as 'a novel of parody and a parody of a novel' (quoted in Fennell, *Nineteenth-Century Russian Literature*, p. 37).

37. For a discussion of possible fairy-tale sources for literary plots, see Chapter 2, sections 3.1 and 3.4 of the present work.

38. In plot situation, as in character typology, *Yevgeny Onegin* acted as the fountainhead of much of Turgenev's work; see Chapter 6, section 4.1 of the present work.

39. See, for example, Tatyana's entranced state in the following lines:

> All is full of him; for the dear maiden
> Without cessation, with a *magical power*
> All speaks of him.
>
> (3: VIII, lines 5–7; my italics)

40. For a discussion of this term, see N. K. Miller, *The Heroine's Text*.

41. The fact that Tatyana is abruptly removed from her beloved country to the city of Moscow underlines the epiphanic nature of this moment.

42. For an excellent discussion of beginnings and endings in narrative fiction, see A. Shukman, 'The Short Story. Theory, Analysis, Interpretation', in *Essays in Poetics*, 2.2 (1977), pp. 27–95, especially 79–91.

43. For a discussion of these themes, see Chapter 2 of the present work, N. K. Miller, *The Heroine's Text* and Tanner, *Adultery in the Novel*.

44. Once more the power of the male gaze is referred to explicitly. Onegin enters:

> Walks amongst the stalls on people's feet,
> Directing askance his double lorgnette
> At the boxes of unfamiliar ladies;
> He cast his *gaze* over all the circles,
> And saw *everything*.
>
> (1: XXI, ll. 1–6; my italics)

45. For a discussion of the rake's view of women, see Eagleton, *The Rape of Clarissa*, and Brownstein, *Becoming a Heroine*.

46. Pushkin places Onegin quite specifically in the tradition of Richardson's heroes; see, especially, 3: XV.

47. Although no real indication is given as to the age of Tatyana's husband, it is significant that he is commonly assumed to be rather older than she is. See section 2.2 of the present chapter for a similar emphasis in *The Gipsies*.

48. I use the term 'sisters' ironically. Women as a group in this text are portrayed with contempt and there is no account given of female friendship. Indeed, we see almost no interaction at all between women apart from Tatyana's conversations with her *nyanya*.

49. After Tatyana has penned her letter to Onegin the (implicitly male) reader is invited to *gaze*, voyeuristically, at the following vignette:

> She bowed her little head to her shoulder
> Her light shift had slipped
> From her charming shoulder . . .
> (3: XXXII, 5–7)

The importance of little feet for men's perceptions of femininity is also mentioned in *A Hero of Our Time*. See Chapter 4 of the present work, section 2.7. The cultural anthropologist will not need reminding of the gruesome results of producing 'little feet' in the Chinese tradition. For a harrowing account of this, see Daly, *Gyn/Ecology*, pp. 134–52.

50. See Chapter 2 of the present work, section 2.2.
51. It should be noted that the word 'hidden' may well be a coy, sub-pornographic reference to the male perception of the female genitalia.
52. For the commonplace identification of women with the natural world, see de Beauvoir, *The Second Sex*.
53. Ibid.
54. For the lack of female solidarity in patriarchal fiction, see note 48 above, and Chapter 2, note 32.
55. Pushkin notes in 3: XIII, l. 6, that he may eventually turn to 'humble prose'. Significantly, the Russian adjective once more is *smirennoy* ('reconciled').

4 MIKHAIL LERMONTOV AND A RAKE'S PROGRESS

1. See C. J. G. Turner, *Pechorin: An Essay on Lermontov's 'A Hero of Our Time'* (Birmingham, 1978), p. 73.
2. For a discussion of the critical reception of the novel at the time and since, see ibid., especially pp. 3–10 and 73–81.
3. For a discussion of the novel's place in Russian literature, see Andrew, *Writers and Society During the Rise of Russian Realism*, p. 52–5; B. M. Eykhenbaum, *Lermontov: Opyt Istoriko-Literaturnoy Otsenki* (Munchen, 1967); and R. Freeborn, *The Rise of the Russian Novel* (Cambridge, 1973), pp. 38–73.
4. The remark of Apollon Grigor'ev in Turner, *Pechorin*, p. 75.
5. See Daly, *Gyn/Ecology*, pp. vii and 107–312.
6. All references to these two works are to M. Yu. Lermontov, *Sobraniye Sochineny v Chetyrekh Tomakh* (Moscow–Leningrad, 1959–62). *The Demon* is in Vol. II, pp. 504–41; *A Hero of Our Time* is in Vol. IV, pp. 275–474.
7. For a discussion of this theme in Lermontov's work, see T. J. Binyon, 'Lermontov, Tyutchev and Fet', in Fennell, *Nineteenth-Century Russian Literature*, p. 181, and Andrew, *Writers and Society During the Rise of Russian Realism*, pp. 63–6 and 72–4.
8. See Chapter 3, section 1.1 of the present work, and Chapter 3, note 42.
9. For a discussion of Lermontov's relationship to Byron, see Andrew,

Writers and Society During the Rise of Russian Realism, pp. 43, 50, 52, and C. M. Bowra, *The Romantic Imagination* (London, 1950), pp. 149–50.

10. For a discussion of Lermontov's debt to Pushkin and Byron in this area, see Zhirmunsky. *The Demon* is explicitly sub-titled 'An Eastern Tale'.

11. For a discussion of this theme in Lermontov, see Andrew, *Writers and Society During the Rise of Russian Realism*, pp. 42–75.

12. For a discussion of this in Pushkin, see Chapter 3, section 2.2. For more general accounts, see Fiedler, *Love and Death in the American Novel* and M. Praz, *The Romantic Agony*.

13. For a discussion of de Sade from a feminist perspective, see Carter, *The Sadeian Woman*, and A. Dworkin, *Pornography: Men Possessing Women*. One should also remember E. A. Poe's celebrated dictum: 'The death of a beautiful woman is, unquestionably, the most poetical topic in the world.'

14. The specifically Islamic context, with the implicitly subservient position of women, is an important point of reference here, as in Pushkin's *The Fountain of Bakhchisaray*: see Chapter 3, section 1.3. Bela in *A Hero of Our Time* is twice carried off, shrouded in a yashmak.

15. See Chapter 3, note 49, for a discussion of little feet in Pushkin's *Yevgeny Onegin*, as well as in a wider cultural context.

16. As in the previous note, this is an implicit reference to *Yevgeny Onegin*: see Chapter 3, note 39. One assumes that this voice is that of the Demon.

17. See *Yevgeny Onegin*, 2: XXIII, lines 9–12.

18. For a discussion of this, see N. K. Miller, *The Heroine's Text*, p. xi: 'the heroine's text is the text of an ideology that codes femininity in paradigms of sexual vulnerability.'

19. See Chapter 2, section 3.4. For a more general discussion of these lurid mixed stereotypes, see Ellmann, *Thinking About Women*.

20. Girey, in Pushkin's *The Fountain of Bakhchisaray*, is an earlier version of this admonishing figure: See Chapter 1, section 1.1.

21. See Andrew, *Writers and Society During the Rise of Russian Realism*, pp. 52–5, and Eykhenbaum, *Lermontov*.

22. For a discussion of this school in Russian literature, see V. V. Vinogradov, *Evolyutsia Russkogo Naturalizma: Gogol i Dostoevsky* (Leningrad, 1929).

23. See H. R. Hays, *The Dangerous Sex*.

24. For the significance of this particular location, see J. Mersereau, *Mikhail Lermontov* (Illinois, 1962), pp. 115–6.

25. Ibid., and Turner, *Pechorin*.

26. See Brownstein, *Becoming a Heroine*, pp. 32–78, and Eagleton, *The Rape of Clarissa*.

27. For a discussion of these points, see R. A. Peace, 'The Role of *Taman* in *A Hero of Our Times*', in *Slavonic and East European Review*, January 1967, pp. 12–29.

28. See N. K. Miller, *The Heroine's Text*, p. 4.

29. For a discussion of some of these points, see Turner, *Pechorin*, pp. 33–43.
30. The use of the inquisitive lorgnette is one of many covert references to *Yevgeny Onegin*. For Onegin's use of this phallic symbol, see *Yevgeny Onegin*, 1: XXI, 1. 3. In Freudian and post-Freudian theory the gaze is commonly interpreted as a specifically phallic (and, therefore, male) activity. Toril Moi argues (*Sexual/Textual Politics*, p. 134): 'As long as the master's scopophilia (i.e. "love of looking") remains satisfied, his domination is secure.' (Her argument here is a development of that of Luce Irigaray.) Others argue that the gaze is not necessarily male. See, for example, Sayers, *Sexual Contradictions*, p. 106: 'Similarly, and despite the cultural association of scoptophilia [sic] with masculinity expressed in stories of Peeping Toms . . . girls also seek to repeat the voyeuristic pleasure.' Indeed, in the context of the present work, it should be noted that one of the markers of the 'new woman' in Turgenev and, especially, Chernyshevsky, is their refusal to submit to the male gaze. See Chapter 6, section 4.2, and Chapter 7, section 6.
31. The occasion is the feast at which the prince 'was giving his [elder] daughter in marriage' (p. 286).
32. For a discussion of this, see Chapters 2, section 3.3, and Chapter 3, section 1.4. Princess Mary is similarly unprotected by a paternal presence.
33. *Kukla* in Russian can also mean 'puppet', a perhaps not accidental double meaning.
34. For a similar proprietary use of this pronoun, see Chapter 3, note 21.
35. See Turner, *Pechorin*, pp. 39–40 for a serious discussion as to whether Pechorin really does love Mary.
36. For a discussion of Vera's role in the plot, see ibid., p. 41.
37. Such metaphors are common in the novel of seduction: 'In a series of cruel assaults, the aggressor wreaks destruction upon his female adversary by deploying a weapon of propulsion. The feminine response, symmetrically, is coded as a military topography: the vulnerable territory under attack gives way to the invader.' See N. K. Miller, *The Heroine's Text*, p. 57.
38. The hypocrisy of this particular piece of male self-justification is obvious if we consider that the action of *Bela* occurs after that of *Princess Mary*.
39. We should remember that Pechorin's bloodthirsty quest is almost always for young women and not enemies in general.
40. See Chapter 3, section 3.4.
41. For a discussion of Werner's role, see Turner, *Pechorin*, pp. 36–8.
42. Ibid., pp. 34–6.
43. Vera's husband, according to Pechorin, 'is glad that he has no daughters . . .' (p. 435); one might add in the space left by the three dots 'to protect''.
44. For a discussion of these terms, see Tanner, *Adultery in the Novel*, especially pp. 36 and 51, and Gallop, *Feminism and Psychoanalysis*.
45. Pechorin repeats this simile a little later: 'she's as timid as a chamois' (p. 299).

46.   Implicitly, the travelling narrator also shares this point of view in his hoped-for tragic denouement, the heroine's death.

47.   For a discussion of the 'coquette' in Pushkin, see Chapter 3, section 3.5.

48.   For discussions of the various traditional stereotypes of women in Western fiction and thought, see the work of Ellmann, Gornick and Moran, Hays, Okin, and K. M. Rogers.

49.   See Chapter 3, note 49.

50.   Even poor, suffering, timid Bela is categorised in such terms by Pechorin: 'A devil, not a woman' (p. 301).

51.   For a discussion of these stereotypes, see Ellmann, *Thinking About Women*.

52.   The lack of originality of this simile is apparent when we remember Pechorin's description of Vera as he embraces her on their first meeting in the story: 'her hands were as cold as ice, her head was on fire' (p. 380).

53.   Rather later Pechorin himself receives this same accolade. Towards the end of the tale Vera informs him: 'do you know, she's in love with you to distraction . . . poor girl! . . .' (p. 430). The Russian phrase confirms the apparently irrational nature of women; *do bezumiya* literally means 'to insanity'.

54.   For an outline of this paradigm, see N. K. Miller, *The Heroine's Text*, p. 59.

55.   See *Yevgeny Onegin*, 3: X, lines 5 and 14.

5 NIKOLAY GOGOL: THE RUSSIAN 'MALLEUS MALEFICARUM'

1.   Quoted in Daly, *Gyn/Ecology*, p. 180. The quotation is from *Malleus Maleficarum*, by the Dominican priests Kramer and Sprenger, first published in 1486.

2.   Ibid., p. 181, from H. R. Trevor-Roper, *The European Witch-Craze of the Sixteenth and Seventeenth Centuries and Other Essays* (New York, 1969), p. 127.

3.   For a discussion of Gogol's life and works from this perspective, see especially S. Karlinsky, *The Sexual Labyrinth of Nikolai Gogol* (Cambridge, Mass. and London, 1976).

4.   For general discussions of Gogol's various reputations, see Andrew, *Writers and Society During the Rise of Russian Realism*, pp. 76–113, and R. Peace, *The Enigma of Gogol* (Cambridge, 1981).

5.   See Karlinsky for an extended discussion of Gogol's sexuality, and D. Rancour-Laferriere, *Out from under Gogol's Overcoat: A Psychoanalytical Study* (Ann Arbor, 1982).

6.   Reference to this work is to the following edition, N. V. Gogol, *Sobraniye Sochineny v Semi Tomakh* (Moscow, 1967), Vol. VI, pp. 7–11.

7.   See Karlinsky, *The Sexual Labyrinth of Nikolai Gogol*, pp. 26–30.

8. See J. B. Woodward, *The Symbolic Art of Gogol: Essays on his Short Fiction* (Ohio, 1982), pp. 10–12.

9. See Chapter 3, section 3.5, and Chapter 4, section 2.7.

10. See Chapter 2, section 1.3.1.

11. For 'mutism' in Gogol's male characters, see Woodward, *The Symbolic Art of Gogol*.

12. For references to this work, see N. V. Gogol, *Sobraniye Sochineny v Shesti Tomakh* (Moscow, 1952), Vol. I, pp. 187–213.

13. See Woodward, *The Symbolic Art of Gogol*, p. 17.

14. For a discussion of the demure heroine in the period, see Chapter 2, section 1.4, Chapter 3, sections 1.6 and 3.5, and Chapter 4, section 2.7.

15. For a discussion of this phenomenon elsewhere in Russian literature, see my analysis of the characters of Starodum (Chapter 2, section 1.5) and the Old Gipsy (Chapter 3, section 2.4). For more general accounts of the problem, see Gallop, *Femininism and Psychoanalysis*, and Tanner, *Adultery in the Novel*.

16. For a rather different interpretation of this detail, see Woodward, *The Symbolic Art of Gogol*, pp. 33–8.

17. See Karlinsky, *The Sexual Labyrinth of Nikolai Gogol*, p. 44.

18. For this, see Chapter 2, section 1.1.

19. For a discussion of 'masculinised' females and 'feminised' males in this story, see Woodward, *The Symbolic Art of Gogol*, pp. 17–43.

20. Given the 'feminised' aspect of Shponka, it is significant that the latter activity is a favourite of Tatyana in *Yevgeny Onegin*: see Chapter 3, section 3.3.

21. For references to this work, see N. V. Gogol, *Sobraniye Khudozhest-vennykh Proizvedenyy v Pyati Tomakh* (Moscow, 1960), Vol. I, pp. 5–331.

22. For the background to these changes, see C. Proffer, *The Simile and Gogol's 'Dead Souls'* (The Hague, 1967), pp. 183–200.

23. For discussions of these themes in Gogol's works, see R. Poggioli, 'Gogol's *Old-Fashioned Landowners*: An Inverted Eclogue', in *Indiana Slavic Studies*, Vol. III (1963), pp. 54–75, and R. Sobel, 'Gogol's *Rome*: A Final Draft for a Utopia', in *Essays in Poetics*, 5.1, (1980), pp. 48–70.

24. For discussions of this work and its sexual relations, see Karlinsky, *The Sexual Labyrinth of Nikolai Gogol*, pp. 62–7; Woodward, *The Symbolic Art of Gogol*, pp. 44–62; Poggioli, '*Gogol's Old-Fashioned Landowners*' and H. Maclean, 'Gogol's Retreat from Love: Towards an Interpretation of *Mirgorod*', in *American Contributions to the Fourth International Congress of Slavists* (The Hague, 1958), pp. 225–45.

25. A point also made by Karlinsky, *The Sexual Labyrinth of Nikolai Gogol*, p. 84.

26. For other representatives of this type in Russian literature of the period, see Girey in *The Fountain of Bakhchisaray* (Chapter 3, section 1.1 and Tamara's father in *The Demon* (Chapter 4, section 1.4).

27. See Karlinsky, *The Sexual Labyrinth of Nikolai Gogol*, pp. 80–6.

28. It should be noted that the Russian word for courage is *muzhestvo*, a literal translation of which would be 'manliness'.

29. Because women are unnamed they are necessarily marginal to the fiction. As a recent writer on the problem has put it: 'And because women, inaccurately and unproblematically identified with feminine subjects, are marginal to the symbolic order, they come to represent the boundary between symbolic order and imaginary chaos.' As Toril Moi observes: 'It is this position which has enabled male culture sometimes to vilify women as representing darkness and chaos – the chaos of the *chora* or of the imaginary, one might add – and sometimes to elevate them as the representatives of a higher and purer nature than men.' See Cameron, *Feminism and Linguistic Theory*, pp. 126–7. For further discussion of this term, see Moi, *Sexual/Textual Politics*, pp. 161–2 and 164–5. The term *chora*, derived from the Greek word for enclosed space, womb, is originally that of Kristeva.

30. For discussions of 'suffering femininity', see Chapter 2, section 3.4, Chapter 3, section 3.5 and Chapter 4, section 2.7. It should be noted that these stock clichés may be applied to old and young alike.

31. Ibid.

32. It should be noted that the majority of women in the stories, although not identified by name, are nevertheless identified by their relationship to a male, usually as a wife or daughter.

33. For a general discussion of this theme in Gogol, see A. de Jonge, 'Gogol', in Fennell, *Nineteenth-Century Russian Literature*, pp. 69–129.

34. Tatyana in *Yevgeny Onegin*, Princess Mary in *A Hero of Our Time*, are viewed by male narrators seated at windows: see Chapter 3, section 3.5 and Chapter 4, section 2.4.

35. In Gogol this paradigm, as so much else, is inverted: the male gaze leads not to power over the woman but to destruction by her.

36. See Chapter 4, section 2.4.

37. See Chapter 4, sections 1.4 and 2.7.

38. Maksim Maksimych makes a very similar remark about Bela in *A Hero of Our Time*: see Chapter 4, section 2.6.

39. See Karlinsky, *The Sexual Labyrinth of Nikolai Gogol*, pp. 73–4.

40. For a discussion of this, see Proffer, *The Simile and Gogol's 'Dead Souls'*, pp. 166–82.

41. Karlinsky, *The Sexual Labyrinth of Nikolai Gogol*, (p. 93) offers a rather different interpretation of this incident, seeing it as a suture into the repressed homosexuality of Gogol's world.

42. See Tanner, *Adultery in the Novel*, p. 37.

43. A similar, though less directly fatal encounter is that between Khoma and the father of the dead *pannochka*: see Gogol, p. 256.

44. For a discussion of women in this tale, see Karlinsky, *The Sexual Labyrinth of Nikolay Gogol*, pp. 69–77.

45. For references to these tales, see Gogol, Vol. III, pp. 7–264.

46. For a discussion of these themes, see Andrew, *Writers and Society During the Rise of Russian Realism*, pp. 76–113, and D. Fanger, *Dostoevsky and Romantic Realism. A Study of Dostoevsky in Relation to Balzac, Dickens and Gogol* (Cambridge, 1965).

47. For a discussion of this, see O'Toole, *Structure, Style and Interpretation in the Russian Short Story*, pp. 26–7.
48. See Karlinsky, *The Sexual Labyrinth of Nikolai Gogol*, p. 112.
49. See N. K. Miller, *The Heroine's Text*, p. xi.
50. See Ellmann, *Thinking About Women*.
51. It would appear that 'little feet' were a *conditio sine qua non* of all 'feminine' heroines of the period: see Chapter 3, note 49.
52. See de Beauvoir, *The Second Sex*, and Cameron, *Feminism and Linguistic Theory*, pp. 126–7; see also note 29 above.
53. For a discussion of Gogol's Slavophilism, see Andrew, *Writers and Society During the Rise of Russian Realism*, pp. 77–8 and 94–7.
54. For a rather different account of her significance, see Woodward, *The Symbolic Art of Gogol*, pp. 95–7.
55. For a discussion of the equally pejorative connotations of another loan-word (*koketka*) in the literature of the period, see Chapter 3, section 3.5 and Chapter 4 section 2.7.
56. Piskaryov's ideal (and obviously sexual) woman is also a *brunetka*.
57. Repeated lexis, which emphasises the interchangeability of women, is also a feature of *A Hero of Our Time*: see Chapter 4, section 2.7.
58. See ibid., and Chapter 3, sections 1.6, 2.3 and 3.5.
59. For this predatory use of the possessive pronoun, see Chapter 3, sections 1.6, 2.3 and 3.5.
60. See Karlinsky, *The Sexual Labyrinth of Nikolai Gogol*, p. 112.
61. See Daly, *Gyn/Ecology*, pp. 180 ff.
62. See note 34.
63. For a similar use of *syatynya* ('holy thing') in Lermontov, see Chapter 4, section 1.3.

6 IVAN TURGENEV AND THE 'NEW EVE'

1. See R. Freeborn, *The Russian Revolutionary Novel* (Cambridge, 1982), p. 11.
2. See de Maegd-Soep, *The Emancipation of Women in Russian Literature and Society*, p. 236.
3. See V. Ripp, *Turgenev's Russia* (Ithaca and London, 1980), p. 173. See pp. 159–86 of this work for an excellent discussion of love in *On the Eve* and *First Love*.
4. See P. Lavrov in V. V. Grigorenko *et al.* (eds), *Turgenev v vospominaniyakh sovremennikov* (Moscow, 1969), pp. 374–5.
5. All references to works by Turgenev are to I. S. Turgenev, *Polnoye Sobraniye Sochineny i Pisem v 28 Tomakh* (Moscow and Leningrad, 1960–68). *Asya* is in Vol. VII, pp. 77–121.
6. See O'Toole, *Structure, Style and Interpretation in the Russian Short Story*, p. 150. His chapter on *Asya*, pp. 142–79, offers many illuminating comments on the setting of this story.
7. See ibid., p. 150.

8. A different, if equally portentous, use is made of this same locus in *On the Eve*.

9. This plot is particularly in evidence in the 'rake's economy' organised by Pechorin in *A Hero of Our Time*: see Chapter 4, section 2.4.

10. Tatyana in *Yevgeny Onegin* and Princess Mary in *A Hero of Our Time* behave in an homologous way: see Chapter 3, section 3.5 and Chapter 4, section 2.7.

11. For a discussion of the way in which male/male relationships, from which women are excluded, are presented as the norm, see Chapter 3, section 3.4, Chapter 4, section 2.5, and, especially, Chapter 5, section 3.5.

12. It is also a recurrent tendency in Turgenev's work: see the later discussion of *On the Eve*. In reality, women's relationships with other women was a central feature of nineteenth-century life in Russia as elsewhere: see Showalter, *A Literature of Their Own*.

13. See, for example, the 'display' of Bela in the story of that name: see Chapter 4, section 2.4.

14. See O'Toole, *Structure, Style and Interpretation in the Russian Short Story,*. 150.

15. This is also done in *A Hero of Our Time*: see Chapter 4, section 2.6.

16. See O'Toole, *Structure, Style and Interpretation in the Russian Short Story*, p. 150, although a slightly different point is made there.

17. Here reference is to two women, both Pushkin's heroine and her own mother.

18. This text is in Vol. IX pp. 7–76.

19. See Ripp, *Turgenev's Russia*, p. 181.

20. See Freeborn, *Turgenev. The Novelist's Novelist*, p. 133: 'Alongside *Fathers and Children* one must place that most enchanting and brilliant of his stories, *First Love*.'

21. See Turgenev, p. 460. The words are conveyed by A. V. Polovtsev in his memoirs.

22. See Ripp, *Turgenev's Russia*, pp. 182–3 for a rather different view of this scene.

23. For a discussion of this see Andrew, *The Structural Analaysis of Russian Narrative Fiction*, pp. ix–xi.

24. See Ripp, *Turgenev's Russia*, pp. 182–3 for his interpretation of this scene.

25. For a feminist-cum-Freudian interpretation of this implement, see Gallop, *Feminism and Psychoanalysis*, pp. 16–19.

26. See J. Miller, *Women Writing About Men*, p. 203, for how much is 'left out' of men's novels.

27. The word used at this point is the foreign *passiia* (p. 74) which, as Ripp observes (*Turgenev's Russia*, p. 185), 'suggests how little he now feels for Zinaida'.

28. See O'Toole in Andrew, *The Structural Analysis of Russian Narrative Fiction*, p. 12.

29. See Chapter 3, section 3.3 for Onegin's behaviour at the theatre and Chapter 4, section 2.3 for Pechorin's at the wedding party where he encounters Bela.

30. For the repetitious use of this iconic locus, see Chapter 3, section 3.5, Chapter 4, section 2.4 and Chapter 5, section 3.3.

31. See O'Toole, *Structure, Style and Interpretation in the Russian Short Story*, p. 150.

32. See, for example, Showalter, *A Literature of Their Own, passim.*

33. For a discussion of the significance of the word *starukha* ('old woman') in the works of Gogol, see Chapter 5, section 3.3.

34. For a discussion of the significance of this word in Pushkin, see Chapter 3, section 3.5.

35. See note 12.

36. For a discussion of male rivalry for women see Chapter 4, section 2.5.

37. See Ripp, *Turgenev's Russia*, pp. 182–3 for a rather different interpretation of these relationships.

38. See especially Freeborn, *Turgenev*, pp. 108–26 for a discussion of this theme in Turgenev's work. The theme is not, of course, peculiar to this writer, but has very ancient antecedents. Marina Warner (p. 51) traces it back to Genesis: 'When they [Adam and Eve] sinned, death and sex as we know them entered the world. The association of sex, sin, and death is ancient.'

39. See Chapter 5 for a discussion of the debilitating effect sensual women have on men in the work of Gogol.

40. See Chapter 5, section 3.3 for the particular significance of this word.

41. This text is in Vol. VII, pp. 123–294. The title of this work in Russian might be literally translated as 'The Nobles' Nest'. *Home of the Gentry* is the one most favoured currently in this country; Ripp, for example, uses another title, *Nest of the Nobility*.

42. For a discussion of this, see Andrew, *Russian Writers and Society in the Second Half of the Nineteenth Century*, pp. 19–20 and p. 30.

43. See Ripp, pp. 152–5.

44. This, it must be noted, is a rather more flattering use of an arboreal simile than that of Dr Werner: see Chapter 4, section 2.6.

45. See Ripp, *Turgenev's Russia*, p. 153.

46. See Andrew, *Russian Writers and Society in the Second Half of the Nineteenth Century*, p. 15.

47. For a discussion of this point, see Freeborn, *Turgenev*, pp. 88–92 and 108–26.

48. The only textual interruption between the night of love and the morning of disastrous revelation is Liza's brief biography. This portrait of the young woman in all her serious virtue may, if anything, make the cheap trick of the coincidence even more heavy-handed.

49. It should be noted that we do learn something of Liza's inner life, especially from the biographical sketch.

50. See note 38.

51. For a discussion of this point, see Ripp, *Turgenev's Russia*, pp. 169–71.

52. This alienation from the Russian context and society was also a phenomenon of actuality, as in the case of Alexander Herzen. For a discussion of his unconventional origins, see M. Malia, *Alexander*

Herzen and the Birth of Russian Socialism (New York, 1965), pp. 9–37.

53. This detail, like so many others, forges a clear link between Liza and Pushkin's Tatyana.

54. For discussions of this in the characters of Tatyana, Bela and Princess Mary, see Chapter 3, section 3.5 and Chapter 4, section 2.7.

55. The collocation of 'virgin' and 'child' is also to be found in Tatyana: see Chapter 3, section 3.5.

56. See Chapter 2, section 2.3 and Chapter 3, section 3.3.

57. See C. McCabe, *Godard: Images, Sounds and Politics*, p. 99. As this remark was made with reference to a French film made in 1975 (Godard's *Numéro Deux*), one can only note the longevity of such patriarchal strategies and add, 'plus ça change'!

58. Freeborn is clearly one reader who is beguiled into sharing this view of Liza. He notes: 'Liza's is a unique and remarkable portrait in Turgenev's gallery of heroines. Her mixture of candour and deep feeling, of lucidity and superstition, of lyrical youthfulness and earnest religious devotion is the novel's poetry, so carefully blended that her image calls to mind not a face or a voice but the nostalgic residue of a love song or the compact and exactly phrased lines of an immaculate sonnet' (*Turgenev*, p. 113).

59. This is the title of a sketch of 1874 included in Turgenev's *A Sportsman's Sketches* and which details the serene quietude of the paralysed Pulkheriya. See also Andrew, *Russian Writers and Society in the Second Half of the Nineteenth Century*, p. 17.

60. For the equally pejorative use of this word in Gogol's work, see Chapter 5, section 4.1.

61. This text is in Vol. VIII, pp. 5–167.

62. This is the phrase of de Maegd-Soep: see notes 1, 2 and 3.

63. See Chapter 3, note 1.

64. See Ripp, *Turgenev's Russia*, p. 172.

65. See Freeborn, *Turgenev*, pp. 88–92 for a discussion of this scene and its themes.

66. See Ripp, *Turgenev's Russia*, p. 178 for a discussion of this point.

67. See note 28 for this term.

68. There had been at least three instances prior to this in Russian literature where a male author had employed first person narrative with a woman as the narrator, namely Dostoevsky's *Netochka Nezvanova* (1848), Tolstoy's *Family Happiness* (1859) and Chulkov's *Prigzhaya Povarikha* (1774). I am indebted to Professor Malcolm Jones for drawing my attention to the first and last instances.

69. See Ripp, *Turgenev's Russia*, p. 173.

70. The radical critic Dobrolyubov objected to this last detail, amongst others, See Andrew, *Russian Writers and Society in the Second Half of the Nineteenth Century*, pp. 32–3.

71. See Ripp, *Turgenev's Russia*, pp. 179–80 for an excellent discussion of the significance of Venice in the novel.

72. See note 66.

73. See Ripp, *Turgenev's Russia*, p. 177 for an interesting account of this problem.

74. See Chapter 2, section 1.3.1.
75. See Ripp, *Turgenev's Russia*, pp. 169–70.
76. This is George Gibian's phrase: see Chapter 3, note 31.
77. Because no dates are included in Yelena's diary, it is difficult to say at precisely what point she dreamed of Insarov in this way.
78. See Ripp, *Turgenev's Russia*, pp. 174–80, especially p. 175.
79. This also offended the radicals Dobrolyubov and Chernyshevsky. See Andrew, *Russian Writers and Society in the Second Half of the Nineteenth Century*, p. 36.
80. For a discussion of this, see Ripp, *Turgenev's Russia*, p. 177. Ripp also has interesting things to say about the seedy circumstances of Insarov's mission and the lurid details of his ensuing dream.
81. For a discussion of this, see Freeborn, *Turgenev*, p. 118.
82. See note 12.
83. See note 2.
84. See, for example, the description offered by the narrator to introduce her (p. 21): '[she] was a sweet, a tiny bit squinting Russian German, with a little dimpled nose and tiny red little lips, blonde, plumpish.' This deliberately inelegant translation still fails to convey the flavour of the Russian, in which there are eight patronising diminutives in less than three lines.

7 NIKOLAY CHERNYSHEVSKY AND THE REAL DAY

1. I will return to this question at the end of the present chapter.
2. All references to the text are to N. G. Chernyshevsky, *Chto Delat?* (Izdatelstvo 'Khudozhestvennaya Literatura', Moscow, 1969), pp. 27–426.
3. See Stites, *The Women's Liberation Movement in Russia*, p. 89. This book, especially pp. 89–114, is an excellent background source for the present chapter.
4. See Freeborn, *The Russian Revolutionary Novel*, p. 244.
5. Quoted in ibid., p. 24. Lenin's enthusiasm for the novel did not seem to extend to later adherents of Chernyshevsky's views on the 'woman question'. For a discussion of this, with particular reference to this work and Kollantai, see Stites, *The Women's Liberation Movement in Russia*, p. 92.
6. See ibid., pp. 89–114.
7. See ibid., as well as Freeborn, *This Rise of the Russian Novel*, p. 133, and C. Moser, *Antinihilism in the Russian Novel of the 1860s* (The Hague, 1964). For a more general discussion of Dostoevsky's response, see Andrew, *Russian Writers and Society in the Second Half of the Nineteenth Century*, pp. 58–9, 68–9, 75–9, 89, 91–3, and D. Offord, 'The Causes of Crime and the Meaning of Law: *Crime and Punishment* and Contemporary Radical Thought', in M. V. Jones and G. M. Terry (eds), *New Essays on Dostoevsky* (Cambridge, 1983), pp. 41–66. I am indebted to Christopher R. Pike for drawing my attention to the last work.
8. For a discussion of the somewhat fraught relations between the two

men, see Andrew, *Russian Writers and Society in the Second Half of the Nineteenth Century*, especially pp. 9–10, 33 and 36–9.

9. The title of this work is *Chto delat?*: Yelena asks her parents the slightly different question, *chto delat v Rossii?* The phrase has two differing meanings: 'What is there to do?' (Yelena's meaning) and 'What is to be done?' (Chernyshevsky's meaning). In Russian, however, the basic phrase is the same.

10. For a discussion of the end of what Dostoevsky called 'landowners' literature', see Andrew, *Russian Writers and Society in the Second Half of the Nineteenth Century*, pp. 44–5, 47 and 54–60. For a more general discussion of the role of the city in Dostoevsky, see Fanger, *Dostoevsky and Romantic Realism*. For an account of St Petersburg in literature more generally, see M. Berman, *All That Is Solid Melts Into Air: The Experience of Modernity* (London, 1983), pp. 173–286. For the particular relationship of Dostoevsky's *Notes from the Underground* with Chernyshevsky's novel, see K. Mochulsky, *Dostoevsky: His Life and Works* (Princeton, 1967), especially pp. 250–1.

11. For a discussion of this, see E. Lampert, *Sons Against Fathers: Studies in Russian Radicalism and Revolution* (Oxford, 1965). Paradoxically the newest of the 'new people', Rakhmetov, is an aristocrat.

12. This last mentioned social group clearly links Chernyshevsky's world once more with that of Dostoevsky, especially *Crime and Punishment*.

13. This is the title of a celebrated essay on Ostrovsky's works by Dobrolyubov, first published in *The Contemporary* in 1859.

14. Onegin was fond of directing his 'double lorgnette at the boxes of unknown ladies', while Lavretsky first espied the perfidious Varvara Pavlovna at the opera. Later famous operatic scenes were to be in Tolstoy's *War and Peace* and *Anna Karenina*.

15. The 'fictitious marriage' was already a real occurrence in Russian radical groups: see Stites, *The Women's Liberation Movement in Russia*, p. 91.

16. The metaphor used for Yelena's imprisonment in *On the Eve* is a 'cage': it is arguable that a 'damp, dark cellar' is the worse!

17. Boris Eykhenbaum notes the novelty of Tolstoy's treatment of marriage as a beginning and not the end of the real plot in *Family Happiness* (1859). See B. M. Eykhenbaum, 'On Tolstoy's Crises', in R. E. Matlaw (ed.), *Tolstoy. A Collection of Critical Essays* (New Jersey, 1947), p. 53.

18. The conservative reaction, particularly that by Professor P. Tsitovich, to such goings-on is discussed by Stites, *The Women's Liberation Movement in Russia*, p. 97.

19. For the role of women in Russian medicine, see Stites, *The Women's Liberation Movement in Russia*, especially pp. 83–6 and p. 93. There was considerable opposition to women becoming doctors through-out Europe, as the following extract from *The Lancet* in 1862 indicates: 'whether they are to be physicians is secondary to whether they are to cease to be women and to forsake the sphere which *nature*, reason and religion alike have imposed on them.' Quoted in S. Delamont and S. Duffin (eds), *The Nineteenth-Century Woman: Her Cultural and*

Physical World, p. 47 (Duffin's italics).

20. The phrase of Henry James utilised by R. Freeborn as the title of his monograph on Turgenev.

21. See Chapter 2, section 1 *passim*, of the present work, and Dobrolyubov's essay, *The Kingdom of Darkness*. Again, Chernyshevsky anticipates the social world of Dostoevsky, especially in *Crime and Punishment*.

22. For a discussion of the domestic education of Turgenev's heroines, see Ripp, *Turgenev's Russia*, pp. 169–70.

23. Dobrolyubov followed his earlier essay on Ostrovsky by *A Ray of Light in the Kingdom of Darkness*, a study of *The Thunderstorm*, first published in 1860. The 'ray of light' in Ostrovsky's play is primarily the character of the heroine Katya. By marked contrast not only with Vera Pavlovna, but even Turgenev's Yelena, this 'positive' heroine follows a highly traditional female path by committing suicide.

24. For discussions of the representation of women as images in Lermontov and Turgenev, see Chapter 4, section 2.7 and Chapter 6, sections 1.6 and 2.3.

25. Chernyshevsky would seem to be polemicising once more, as Frenchness has negative associations in Turgenev's *Home of the Gentry* (in the characters of Panshin and Varvara Pavlovna) and *a fortiori* in Gogol and Fonvizin: see Chapters 6, 5 and 2 respectively. For Gogol's negative use of the word *dama* ('lady'), see Chapter 5, section 4.1.

26. See Chapter 4, section 2.4 and Chapter 6, section 1.5. For a more general discussion of this theme, see N. K. Miller, *The Heroine's Text*, *passim*.

27. For a discussion of the use of this adjective in female characterisation, see Chapter 4, section 2.7 and Chapter 6, section 3.4.

28. For a discussion of this, see Chapter 6, section 2.3.

29. In *The Minor*, Prostakova's language is similarly marked by violence: see Chapter 2, section 1.5.

30. For a famous treatment of the saintly prostitute, one need look no further, of course, than Sonya in *Crime and Punishment*.

31. For an example of this tendency in Russian literature (Radishchev), see Chapter 2, section 2.2.

32. For more general discussion of the novel, see the works of Stites, de Maegd-Soep, and Lampert.

33. It should be noted, however, that the fetishising of a part of the female anatomy in the original is not that far from pornography: see Chapter 3, section 3.5.

34. See Chapter 4, section 3.5.

35. See N. K. Miller, *The Heroine's Text*.

36. See Chapter 4. Pechorin comments: 'But there is a boundless pleasure in the possession of a young, scarcely burgeoned soul' (p. 401).

37. This may be a covert reference to *Asya*, where the heroine's half-brother acts as an intermediary between his sister and the narrator. Chernyshevsky, of course, was familiar with this text, having written a famous review of it.

38.   See Chapter 4, section 2.4 and Chapter 6, sections 1.6 and 2.2 for discussion of this phenomenon in *A Hero of Our Time*, *Asya* and *First Love*.

39.   This is the word used as a metaphor for love in *First Love* and, by implication at least, in *On the Eve*: see Chapter 6, sections 2.6 and 4.2.

40.   Turgenev had also used this gesture as a sign of female emancipation and self-confidence in the relationships between Liza asnd Lavretsky, and Yelena and Insarov.

41.   In the original the verb is an indeterminate third-person plural, *dumayut*. Yet again, this would appear to have Turgenev in mind.

42.   *Strast* ('passion') is a key-word in *First Love*, where the linguistic link with its cognate *stradanye* ('suffering') is not accidental: see Chapter 6, sections 2.6.

43.   See Lampert, *Sons Against Fathers*, p. 224.

44.   This, again, has Turgenevan associations: it is the word used, with some feeling, by Lavretsky to describe his wife's homecoming. See Chapter 6, section 3.1.

45.   A similar view is expressed by Stites, *The Women's Liberation Movement in Russia*, p. 89.

46.   Stites also addresses the question of sexual love in the novel: see ibid., p. 95.

47.   The equation made by Volodya's father in *First Love*: see Chapter 6, section 2.6.

48.   For a discussion of hegemony in literature, see Chapter 1, and Femia, *Gramsci's Political Thought*.

49.   See Stites, *The Women's Liberation Movement in Russia*, p. 94. The use of the word 'flattering', which lends a certain amount of equivocation to Stites's remark, seems unfortunate and unnecessary.

50.   See Freeborn, *The Rise of the Russian Novel*, p. 133.

51.   For a discussion of such devices in the formative period of the Russian novel, see Eykhenbaum.

52.   Freeborn refers to this device as 'Chernyshevsky's own ineptly funny "perspicacious reader"', a remark which seems to miss Chernyshevsky's parodic and polemic purpose. See Freeborn, *The Russian Revolutionary Novel*, pp. 25–6.

53.   The term of R. Barthes. For an excellent introductory discussion (and bibliography) of this *penseur* and the particular term used, see N. Cornwell, 'Roland Barthes: A Man for All *Ecritures*', in *Essays in Poetics*, 10.1 (1985), pp. 50–65.

54.   See Chapter 4, section 2.7 and Chapter 6, sections 1.6 and 2.2.

55.   See Ripp, *Turgenev's Russia*, p. 209.

56.   See Offord, 'The Causes of Crime and the Meaning of Law', p. 64, n. 40.

57.   Quoted in Lampert, *Sons Against Fathers*, pp. 104–5.

Bibliography

Adburgham, A., *Women in Print* (London, 1972).
Althusser, L., *Lenin and Philosophy and Other Essays* (London, 1977).
Andrew, J., *Writers and Society During the Rise of Russian Realism* (London, 1980).
——————, *Russian Writers and Society in the Second Half of the Nineteenth Century* (London, 1982).
——————, (ed.), *The Structural Analysis of Russian Narrative Fiction* (Keele, 1984).
Ardener, S. (ed.), *Perceiving Women* (London, 1975).
——————, *Defining Females* (London, 1978).
Atkinson, D., Dollin, A., and Warshovsky, G. (eds), *Women in Russia* (Brighton, 1978).
Auerbach, N., *Communities of Women: An Idea in Fiction* (Cambridge, Mass. and London, 1978).
de Beauvoir, S., *The Second Sex* (London, 1972).
Berger, J., *Ways of Seeing* (Harmondsworth, 1972).
Brownstein, R. M., *Becoming a Heroine: Reading About Women in Novels* (Harmondsworth, 1984).
Cameron, D. C., *Feminism and Linguistic Theory* (London, 1985).
Carter, A., *The Sadeian Woman* (London, 1979).
Charvet, J., *Feminism* (London, 1982).
Colby, V., *The Singular Anomaly: Women Novelists of the Nineteenth Century* (New York, 1970).
——————, *Yesterday's Woman: Domestic Realism in the English Novel* (Princeton, 1974).
Coote, A. and Campbell, B., *Sweet Freedom. The Struggle for Women's Liberation* (London, 1982).
Cornillon, S. K. (ed.), *Images of Women in Fiction: Feminist Perspectives* (Ohio, 1972).
Cott, N. F., *Root of Bitterness* (New York, 1972).
Cunningham, G., *The New Woman and the Victorian Novel* (London, 1978).
Daly, M., *Gyn/Ecology* (London, 1979).
Delamont, S. and Duffin, L. (eds), *The Nineteenth Century Woman: Her Cultural and Physical World* (New York, 1978).
Diamond, A. and Edwards, L. R. (eds), *The Authority of Experience: Essays in Feminist Criticism* (Amherst, 1977).
Donovan, J. (ed.), *Feminist Literary Criticism: Explorations in Theory* (Lexington, 1975).
Dworkin, A., *Pornography: Men Possessing Women* (London, 1981).
——————, *Our Blood* (The Women's Press, 1982).
Eagleton, T., *The Rape of Clarissa* (Oxford, 1982).

Eisenstein, H., *Contemporary Feminist Thought* (London, 1984).

Ellmann, M., *Thinking About Women* (New York, 1968).

Engels, F., *The Origin of the Family, Private Property and the State* (London, 1972).

Evans, M. (ed.), *The Woman Question: Readings on the Subordination of Women* (London, 1982).

Femia, J. V., *Gramsci's Political Thought: Hegemony, Consciousness and the Revolutionary Process* (Oxford, 1981).

Fetterley, J., *The Resisting Reader. A Feminist Approach to American Fiction* (Bloomington and London, 1978).

Fiedler, L. A., *Love and Death in the American Novel* (New York, 1960).

Figes, E., *Patriarchal Attitudes* (London, 1981).

————, *Sex and Subterfuge: Women Writers to 1850* (London, 1982).

Firestone, S., *The Dialectic of Sex: The Case for Feminist Revolution* (London, 1980).

Foucault, M., *Madness and Civilization: A History of Insanity in the Age of Reason* (London, 1967).

————, *The Birth of the Clinic* (New York, 1973).

————, *Discipline and Punish: The Birth of the Prison* (New York, 1977).

————, *The History of Sexuality. Vol. I. An Introduction* (London, 1979).

Freud, S., *Totem and Taboo* (London, 1950).

————, *Civilization and Its Discontents* (London, 1957).

Gallop, J., *Feminism and Psychoanalysis. The Daughter's Seduction* (London, 1982).

Golitsyn, N. N., *A Bibliographical Dictionary of Russian Women Writers* (St Petersburg, 1889).

Gornick, V. and Moran, B. K. (eds), *Women in Sexist Society* (New York, 1971).

Greene, G. and Kahn, C. (eds), *Making a Difference: Feminist Literary Criticism* (London and New York, 1985).

Greer, G., *The Female Eunuch* (London, 1970).

Griffin, S., *Pornography and Silence: Culture's Revenge Against Nature* (London, 1981).

————, *Woman and Nature: The Roaring Inside Her* (London, 1984).

Hardwick, E., *Seduction and Betrayal: Women and Literature* (New York, 1970).

Hartman, M. S. and Banner, L. (eds), *Clio's Consciousness Raised: New Perspectives on the History of Women* (New York, 1974).

Hays, H. R., *The Dangerous Sex: The Myth of Feminine Evil* (London, 1966).

Heilbrunn, C. G., *Towards a Recognition of Androgyny: Aspects of Male and Female in Literature* (New York, 1973).

————, *Reinventing Womanhood* (London, 1979).

Heldt Monter, B., 'Rassvet (1859–1862) and the Woman Question', *Slavic Review* (March 1977), pp. 76–85.

————, 'Tolstoy's Path Towards Feminism', in V. Terras (ed.), *American Contributions to the Eighth International Congress of Slavists. Vol. II. Literature* (Ohio, 1978). pp. 523–35.

Jacobus, M., *Women Writing and Writing about Women* (London, 1979).

Joll, J., *Gramsci* (London, 1977).

Kaplan, E. A. (ed.), *Women in Film Noir* (London, 1980).
——————, *Women and Film: Both Sides of the Camera* (New York and London, 1983).
Kaplan, S. J., *Feminine Consciousness in the Modern British Novel* (Urbana, 1974).
Lukacs, G., *The Theory of the Novel* (London, 1970).
McCabe, C., *Godard: Images, Sounds, Politics* (London, 1980).
McMillan, J. F., *Housewife or Harlot: The Place of Women in French Society 1870–1940* (Brighton, 1981).
de Maegd-Soep, C., *The Emancipation of Women in Russian Literature and Society* (Ghent, 1978).
Marcuse, H., *Eros and Civilization* (London, 1972).
May, K. M., *Characters of Women in Narrative Fiction* (London, 1981).
Mead, M., *Male and Female* (Harmondsworth, 1950).
Mellen, J., *Women and their Sexuality in the New Film* (London, 1974).
Mill, J. S., *On the Subjugation of Women* (London, 1861).
Miller, C. and Swift, K., *The Handbook of Non-Sexist Writing* (London, 1981).
Miller, J., *Women Writing about Men* (London, 1986).
Miller, N. K., *The Heroine's Text: Readings in the French and English Novel 1722–1782* (New York, 1980).
Millett, K., *Sexual Politics* (London, 1971).
Mitchell, J., *Woman's Estate* (Harmondsworth, 1971).
——————, *Psychoanalysis and Feminism* (Harmondsworth, 1975).
——————, *Women: The Longest Revolution. Essays in Feminism, Literature and Psychoanalysis* (London, 1984).
—————— and Rose, J. (eds), *Feminine Sexuality. Jacques Lacan and the 'école freudienne'* (London, 1982).
Moi, T., *Sexual/Textual Politics. Feminist Literary Theory* (London, 1985).
Neale, S., *Genre* (London, 1980).
Newton, J. L., *Women, Power and Subversion. Social Strategies in British Fiction 1778–1860* (London, 1981).
Oakley, A., *Subject Women* (London, 1982).
Okin, S. M., *Women in Western Political Thought* (London, 1980).
O'Toole, L. M., *Structure, Style and Interpretation in the Russian Short Story* (New Haven and London, 1982).
Ponomareva, S. I., *Our Women Writers* (St Petersburg, 1891).
Porter, C., *Fathers and Daughters* (London, 1976).
Pratt, A., *Archetypal Patterns of Women's Fiction* (Brighton, 1982).
Praz, M., *The Romantic Agony* (Oxford, 1970).
Procek, E. M., 'The Role of Psychiatry in the Social Control of Women', PhD Dissertation, University of Keele, 1980.
Rich, A., *Of Woman Born. Motherhood as Experience and Institution* (London, 1977).
Richards, J. R., *The Sceptical Feminist. A Philosophical Enquiry* (Harmondsworth, 1982).
Rogers, K. M., *The Troublesome Helpmate. A History of Misogyny in Literature* (Seattle and London, 1966).
Rowbotham, S., *Hidden from History* (London, 1973).
——————, *Woman's Consciousness, Man's World* (Harmondsworth, 1973).

Russian Literature Triquarterly, 9 (Spring 1974), 'Women in Russian Literature'.

Ruthven, K. K., *Feminist Literary Studies. An Introduction* (Cambridge, 1984).

Sargent, L. (ed.), *Women and Revolution. The Unhappy Marriage of Marxism and Feminism. A Debate on Class and Patriarchy* (London, 1981).

Satina, S., *Education of Women in Pre-Revolutionary Russia* (New York, 1966).

Sayers, J., *Sexual Contradictions. Psychology, Psychoanalysis and Feminism* (London, 1986).

Shorter, E., *A History of Women's Bodies* (Harmondsworth, 1984).

Showalter, E., *A Literature of their Own. British Women Novelists from Brontë to Lessing* (London, 1979).

Spacks, P. M., *The Female Imagination* (New York, 1975).

Spender, D., *Invisible Women: The Schooling Scandal* (London, 1982).

Spender, L., *Intruders on the Rights of Men. Women's Unpublished Heritage* (London, 1983).

Stites, R., *The Women's Liberation Movement in Russia: Feminism, Nihilism and Bolshevism (1860–1930)* (Princeton, 1978).

Stone, L., *The Family, Sex and Marriage in England 1500–1800* (London, 1977).

Stubbs, P., *Women and Fiction: Feminism and the Novel 1880–1920* (Brighton, 1979).

Tanner, T., *Adultery in the Novel: Contract and Transgression* (Baltimore and London, 1979).

Taylor, B., *Eve and the New Jerusalem: Socialism and Feminism in the Nineteenth Century* (London, 1983).

Thomson, P., *The Victorian Heroine: A Changing Ideal* (London, 1956).

Vicinus, M. (ed.), *Suffer and Be Still: Women in the Victorian Age* (Bloomington, 1972).

Warner, M., *Alone of All Her Sex: The Myth and Cult of the Virgin Mary* (London, 1976).

Watt, I., *The Rise of the Novel* (Harmondsworth, 1968).

Williams, M., *Women in the English Novel 1800–1900* (London, 1984).

Wilson. E., *Adorned in Dreams. Fashion and Modernity* (London, 1985).

Woolf, V., *Three Guineas* (Harmondsworth, 1977).

Index